BESTSELLING
BOOK SERIES

Aquariums For Dummies

Cheat Sheet

What to Look for When Buying Fish

You can look at several physical characteristics to determine whether a fish is in good health.

- Body color is rich, not faded or dull. The color should be complete and not missing in any areas.
- No open sores, visible ulcers, boils, or obvious skin problems, such as peeling scales or blemishes.
- Fins are long and flowing, or short and erect. The fish should not have any ragged, torn, or missing fins.
- Scales are flat and smooth, not protruding away from the body.
- The stomach is well rounded, not sunken or concave.
- Girth of the entire body is of normal size, not bloated or emaciated.
- Visible excreta (fish waste) should be dark in color, not pale.
- All the fins on the fish's body should not be collapsed or completely clamped shut.
- Eyes are clear, not cloudy or popping out of the sockets.
- No visible parasites, such as ich or velvet.

Common Medications

The following is a list common medications for fish:

- **Salt:** Common table sale or marine salt is generally used to treat ich and other parasitic diseases in freshwater fish.
- **Methylene blue:** You often use this liquid to treat diseases such as ich, fungus, and velvet.
- **Copper:** This liquid treatment cures diseases such as flukes, velvet, and parasites that are characteristic of salt water ich.
- **Malachite green:** Use this wonderful medication to treat velvet, fungus, and ich.
- **Formalin:** This is a bath type treatment only, and should not be used in the main display tank. This is a great remedy for parasites, but it doesn't work well on internal infections and can be very toxic.
- **Penicillin:** Penicillin treats bacterial infections and is non-toxic.
- **Tetracycline:** This antibiotic is great for bacterial infections and is non-toxic.
- **Acriflavine:** Acriflavine treats ich and fungus, but may turn the water green.

For much more information on using medications and treating sick fish, see Chapter 16.

For Dummies: Bestselling Book Series for Beginners

Aquariums For Dummies®

Space Requirements for Tanks

Tank Volume	Space Requirements in Inches
10 Gallon	Regular: 20 × 10 × 12
	Long: 24 × 8 × 12
	Hex: 14 × 12 × 18
15 Gallon	Regular: 24 × 12 × 12
	Long: 20 × 10 × 18
	Show: 24 × 8 × 16
20 Gallon	High: 24 × 12 × 16
	Long: 30 × 12 × 12
	Hex: 18 × 16 × 20
25 Gallon	Regular: 24 × 12 × 20
29 Gallon	Regular: 30 × 12 × 18
30 Gallon	Regular: 36 × 12 × 16
	Breeding: 36 × 18 × 12
40 Gallon	Long: 48 × 13 × 16
	Breeding: 36 × 18 × 16
45 Gallon	Regular: 36 × 12 × 24
	Hex: 22 × 22 × 24
50 Gallon	Regular: 36 × 18 × 18
55 Gallon	Regular: 48 × 13 × 20
75 Gallon	Regular: 48 × 18 × 20
100 Gallon	Regular: 72 × 18 × 18
125 Gallon	Regular: 72 × 18 × 22
200 Gallon	Regular: 84 × 24 × 25

Characteristics of Good Fish Dealers

- Friendly, helpful, knowledgeable staff members who answer your questions willingly, go out of their way to help, and who are familiar with aquarium equipment, the different types of aquarium systems, and individual species of fish.

- A large selection of aquarium equipment, food, medication, and fish on hand.

- Free services, such as water testing.

- Some type of guarantee on the fish they sell and the commitment to stand behind the equipment that they sell.

- A willingness to tell you where you can get a certain species or piece of equipment if they cannot get it themselves.

- Autopsies of dead fish to help determine the cause of the disease and medication advice to help prevent the need for an autopsy.

- A genuine interest in you and your aquariums.

- Clean tanks and shops.

Copyright © 1999 Wiley Publishing, Inc. All rights reserved.

Item 5156-6.

For more information about Wiley Publishing, call 1-800-762-2974.

For Dummies: Bestselling Book Series for Beginners

Aquariums

FOR

DUMMIES®

Aquariums
FOR
DUMMIES®

by Maddy Hargrove
and
Mic Hargrove

WILEY

Wiley Publishing, Inc.

Aquariums For Dummies®

Published by
Wiley Publishing, Inc.
111 River St.
Hoboken, NJ 07030
www.wiley.com

Copyright © 1999 by Wiley Publishing, Inc., Indianapolis, Indiana

Published simultaneously in Canada

For general information on our other products and services or to obtain technical support, please contact our Customer Care Department within the U.S. at 800-762-2974, outside the U.S. at 317-572-3993, or fax 317-572-4002.

Wiley also publishes its books in a variety of electronic formats. Some content that appears in print may not be available in electronic books.

Library of Congress Control Number: 99-64202

ISBN: 0-7645-5156-6

Manufactured in the United States of America

20 19 18 17 16 15 14 13 12

1O/QY/QT/QU/IN

About the Authors

Maddy Hargrove is a contributing writer and columnist for *Tropical Fish Hobbyist* and *Marine Fish Monthly*. She is currently working on her master's degree in marine biology.

Mic Hargrove is a contributing writer for several tropical fish magazines. He is an expert advisor in the areas of aquarium equipment and water chemistry.

Dedication

This book is dedicated to my husband and best friend Mic, who is the wind beneath many wings, especially mine. I must also thank our three children for putting up with leaking aquarium tanks, noisy air pumps, and fish swimming merrily in the oddest household places over the years.

This book project was a joy to complete thanks to the crew at Wiley who treated us like family. Stacy Collins, Tim Gallan, and Kathleen Dobie went out of their way to make sure that we were happy while doing this project, and we greatly appreciate it. The people at Wiley really are a wonderful group of people, who strive to produce only the best. We could never ask for a better set of literary team members.

Special thanks to David Boruchowitz at *Tropical Fish Hobbyist* for his kind support, friendship, and encouragement. David's wisdom is a gift that we will always cherish.

We must thank Dr. Eric Olsen, his wife Terry, Richard Lee, Lillian and Dottie Hargrove, and Richard and Lee Bell for being there. Sometimes silent support is the best medicine. A special thanks to Bart whose training provided internal strength when it was needed the most.

And finally, our hats go off to all the "wet pets" that constantly inhabit (and sometimes take over) our household, and our two dogs who reminded us that we needed to drop our pencils once in a while so that we could all go for a relaxing and much needed walk.

Publisher's Acknowledgments

We're proud of this book; please send us your comments through our online registration form located at www.dummies.com/register.

Some of the people who helped bring this book to market include the following:

Acquisitions, Editorial, and Media Development

Senior Project Editor: Tim Gallan

Acquisitions Editor: Stacy Collins

Copy Editors: Kathleen Dobie, Donna Love

Technical Editor: David Boruchowitz

Editorial Coordinator: Maureen Kelly

Editorial Manager: Seta K. Franz

Editorial Assistant: Alison Walthall

Cover photo: © J. C. Carton / Bruce Coleman, Inc. / PictureQuest

Production

Project Coordinator: Regina Snyder

Layout and Graphics: Angela F. Hunckler, Brian Massey, Dave McKelvey, Barry Offringa, Brent Savage, Mary Jo Weis, Dan Whetstine

Proofreaders: Kathleen Sparrow, Marianne Santy, Rebecca Senninger, Toni Settles

Indexer: Liz Cunningham

Publishing and Editorial for Consumer Dummies

Diane Graves Steele, Vice President and Publisher, Consumer Dummies
Joyce Pepple, Acquisitions Director, Consumer Dummies
Kristin A. Cocks, Product Development Director, Consumer Dummies
Michael Spring, Vice President and Publisher, Travel
Brice Gosnell, Associate Publisher, Travel
Suzanne Jannetta, Editorial Director, Travel

Publishing for Technology Dummies

Richard Swadley, Vice President and Executive Group Publisher
Andy Cummings, Vice President and Publisher

Composition Services

Gerry Fahey, Vice President of Production Services
Debbie Stailey, Director of Composition Services

Contents at a Glance

Cartoons at a Glance

By Rich Tennant

page 101

"It's that weird Ahab friend of yours. He probably wants to come in and stare at the Albino tigers again for about 9 hours."

page 267

"Of course being clownfish, we supplement their feed with a little cotton candy, ice cream and a corn dog now and then."

page 173

"Honey! I think the angelfish have outgrown the neon tetras!"

page 127

Kyle spent many happy hours admiring his handcrafted fish/reef/flooded basement aquarium

page 239

What exactly did you say you were breeding your cichlids with?

WOOF!

page 211

"Naturally we need to adjust the chemicals, but it seems to be the only thing that relaxes him after work."

page 5

Cartoon Information:
Fax: 978-546-7747
E-Mail: richtennant@the5thwave.com
World Wide Web: www.the5thwave.com

Table of Contents

· ·

Introduction

*W*elcome to the wonderful world of tropical fishkeeping! *Aquariums For Dummies* is a handy reference guide for those of you who want the basics involved in setting up and maintaining an aquarium system. (Sorry, swimming lessons are beyond the scope of this book.) Everything you need to know to get started on your very own freshwater, brackish, or marine system can be found right here in this book.

In *Aquariums For Dummies*, I tell you about tank styles and equipment, disease prevention and cures, aquarium decoration, maintenance routines, species of fish and their habits, test kits for your water, and tips on working with plants and invertebrates. You're likely to encounter all sorts equipment and different fish species in pet shops, but all you need is the information contained in this book to get you started on the road to successful fishkeeping. After you master the basics, you will be able to venture into new areas of aquarium keeping with confidence.

So sit back and journey into the fascinating world of the aquariums, and enjoy the basics of keeping your fish healthy and happy the easy way. Your new aquatic pets will love you for it.

Why a Book for Dummies?

You may have heard horror stories about your neighbor's aquarium. Or maybe your best friend told you that his new aquarium that used to be located in his second floor apartment is now decorating the downstairs tenant's apartment. Okay, problems happen, but these rare aquarium misadventures can be avoided with a proper knowledge of the basics.

About 99 percent of all potential aquarium problems will never occur if hobbyists take the time to learn a few simple fish-keeping basics. But wet floors can be mopped and tanks can be repaired. Aquarium keeping will still move forward, despite the occasional setbacks encountered from time to time.

It's really very easy to become a successful fishkeeper. All you require is a little bit of help to get you going. Hey, that's why you bought this book right? *Aquariums For Dummies* provides you with good, basic information, and it gives you the ammo you need to battle any problems that may occur as you live with your aquarium.

What I Assume about You

If you're an absolute beginner — you've never owned an aquarium before and never even fed a goldfish — this book has all the information you need to get started. I assume that you have no prior knowledge of how to set up an aquarium or take care of fish.

However, if you do know a little something about fishkeeping, you'll find this book to be a great resource as well. You'll discover how to keep your aquarium cleaner and how to make your fish healthier. What can I say: This book is for just about anyone who's the least bit interested in aquariums.

How to Use This Book

You need to be aware that there are several types of aquarium systems to choose from, including tropical, coldwater, brackish, and marine. Many systems use similar equipment, and often, the only difference between systems is the water temperature or salt content. It really is as simple as that. No hidden doors, and no mysteries to solve. So most of the information in this book applies to just about every aquarium setup (unless otherwise stated).

This book is a reference, not a tutorial. You don't have to read it from Chapter 1 to Chapter 26 if you don't want to. Just use the Table of Contents or Index to find the topics that interest you and go from there.

How This Book Is Organized

Even though this book is a nonlinear reference, we did go to the trouble of organizing the chapters in a logical fashion. Here's how things break down:

Part I: Aquarium Setup

The chapters in this part present all the information required to get an aquarium started. From choosing a tank and equipment to adding plants and substrate, you'll find everything you need to create a safe home for your fish.

Part II: Plants and Invertebrates

No aquarium is complete without plant life (for freshwater tanks) or invertebrates (for marine tanks). The two chapters in this part give you the
lowdown on what plant and invertebrate species can make your aquarium
more beautiful and also more hospitable for your fish.

Part III: The Fish

In addition to telling you what makes fish tick, we run through all kinds of fish
species, detailing their behavior patterns, eating habits, and much more. On
top of all that, we offer some helpful tips on finding the right dealer from
whom to purchase your fish.

Part IV: Caring for Your Aquatic Friends

Taking care of your fish involves more than just sprinkling flakes into the tank
every morning on your way out the door. I explain what food options are
available, and tell you how to identify, treat, and prevent many common
illnesses.

Part V: Breeding Your Fish for Fun and Profit

What do the birds and the bees have to do with fish? The chapters in this
part tell the story. If you're interested in getting your fish to mate, I have all
the information you need.

Part VI: Fun Stuff

This part explains how to keep a log book, how to take pictures of your fish,
and how to show them off at fish shows, if that's something you desire.

Part VII: The Part of Tens

This part consists of several fun lists. It's sort of a way for us to squeeze a bunch of extra information at the back of the book in as succinct a way as possible.

Where to Go from Here

If you don't already own fish and don't know how to set up an aquarium, start with Part I. If you have a little more background in fishkeeping, maybe you want to check out the species guide in Part III. Or maybe the chapter on plants has caught your fancy. Go ahead and skip around. That's what this book is for.

Icons Used in This Book

If you've flipped through this book at all, you've probably noticed little pictures, called *icons*, in the margins. Here's what they mean:

This icon indicates some good advice — information that will help you keep your fish healthy and safe.

When I discuss a task or procedure that might be problematic, I use this icon. I also use it to point out things that might be dangerous to you or your fish.

This icon flags information that's, well, technical, and you can go ahead and skip that paragraph if you want to.

When I make a point or offer some information that I feel you should keep with you forever, I toss in this icon.

Part I
Aquarium Setup

The 5th Wave   By Rich Tennant

"Naturally we need to adjust the chemicals, but it seems to be the only thing that relaxes him after work."

In this part . . .

The first nine chapters are the meat and potatoes of this book. Here, you find out everything you need to know to set up a basic aquarium that your fish will love to reside in.

Chapter 1

The Practice of Aquarium Keeping

*L*et me be the first to welcome you to the world's greatest hobby! I have always loved fishkeeping, and hope that you do, too. This book can help you achieve your goal of setting up and maintaining a successful aquarium.

Imagine it: It's eight o'clock and you're just getting home from the office where you spent the last half hour listening to your irate boss rant and rave about problems beyond your control. Your ears are still ringing, your head is pounding, and your mood is ugly. You walk in the front door of your home, plop down in your best easy chair, and let the healing therapy begin.

Directly in front of you is your beautiful 55-gallon aquarium. In your private underwater world, you see bright green hairgrass plants waving softly in the gentle current. The aqua blue water soothes your tired eyes as it swirls endlessly through a cheerful airstone. A frolicking school of brightly colored neons dart merrily though a small hole in a towering rock wall. The smooth pebbles on the aquarium floor reflect the dazzling array of colors around them. The soothing bubbling from the filter reminds you that there is always a place you can go to relax and get away from it all. (Hey, your aquarium sounds fantastic! Can I come over?)

At first, any hobby can be as complicated as an IRS long form, but rest assured that this book dispels the "mystery" surrounding keeping a healthy aquarium.

The Benefits of an Aquarium

Okay, it's time to snag a comfortable chair and travel with me through the marvelous world of aquarium-keeping. There are a lot of great reasons for having tropical fish. Fishkeeping is a hobby that the whole family can participate in and enjoy together. A fish tank is a great way to teach children the responsibility of animal care as well as the biological principles that go hand in hand with our own species' daily survival. The older generation can also benefit — scientific research shows that aquariums can help lower stress and prolong life (be it freshwater, marine, or brackish).

Another advantage of keeping an aquarium, is that the tanks don't require a lot of space, and are perfect for apartment dwellers who may be prohibited from owning larger, roaming pets, such as dogs and cats. You can match an aquarium to almost any space that you have. You can get a tank that takes up an entire wall in your home, or one small enough to fit on your desk — and every size in between. And speaking of desktops, an aquarium in your office is a great way to spend a little bit of time goofing off each day without your boss finding out. Besides, your coworkers will think you're cool if you have a tank that they can come look at.

Other advantages to keeping aquariums are that fish don't bark at the neighbors, caterwaul at the moon, chase the letter carrier, make unsightly messes on the floor, or whimper all night. You probably will never have to bail a renegade goldfish out of the local pound, either.

An aquarium encourages your artistic side to run wild when it comes to aquatic decorating, and you won't find another hobby quite as soothing — nothing compares to dipping your tired arms into nice cool water to do a little underwater planting or rearranging.

Getting Started

Daily care and maintenance of a home aquarium is simple, and really doesn't require a great deal of time or money. You can set up a complete aquarium system with a relatively small amount of money as long as you don't go overboard at the beginning, and are content to add to your system as you go along. But if you're like me, you may find yourself paying off several charge accounts at your local pet shops. (Honest, I put a check in the mail yesterday!)

Doing Your Homework

Setting up an aquarium is simply a matter of following a few basic rules. Knowledge is the key to success, and you're making a good start by buying this book. But, you can find out about fishkeeping from many other sources also. Chapter 26 lists Web sites and other resources that can provide you with more information about your hobby. A little research can go a long way and make all the difference between complete success and unnecessary failure. Do your homework well, and you'll be prepared to handle any aquatic situation.

Aquariums of old

The ancient Egyptians are generally believed to be the first "true" aquarium keepers. Historical evidence suggests that Egyptians kept fish in ponds as a source of food, and smaller species in their homes to impress their friends. (I don't know if they had pyramid-shaped aquariums back then, but I kind of doubt it.)

High-ranking Roman officials are rumored to have kept ponds full of hungry eels. If an eel-keeping official happened to have a politically uncooperative neighbor . . . well the neighbor may have gotten a fish-eye view of their good buddy's aquatic pets.

From Rome, fishkeeping began spreading in the Far East. Oriental aquarists became so fascinated with the common goldfish that they went into aquatic hyperdrive and started selectively breeding them at a rate of about 10 gazillion per minute. Needless to say, they came up with a bunch of cool-looking goldfish!

Public aquariums began to show up in Europe in the late 1800s. Those first aquariums were quite a bit different that the ones we have today, and displayed only a few different species. Later on, expensive glass aquariums were manufactured for the elegant homes of the rich and famous (darn, that leaves me out). Unfortunately, because they were heated by open flames or oil lamps, these primitive tanks were unsafe. Often, members of high society with aquariums ended up with a very large pile of ashes where their mansions once stood, and a fish fry dinner.

During these early and dark days of aquarium-keeping, hobbyists had to make do with makeshift equipment and scary potions. The situation finally began to improve in the 1900s when fish shows and *aquarium societies* (a bunch of fish nerds gathered together in one place) emerged to help the increasing number of hobbyists maintain their tanks.

What Kind of Aquarium Do You Want?

Immediately after you decide to set up an aquarium, you need to decide which type of system you want.

You can choose from three general types of systems: saltwater, freshwater, and brackish. Individual types of fish, tank size, equipment, and plants vary dramatically from system to system, so this chapter contains a brief overview of each type of setup to give you a better idea how space considerations, initial financial outlay, difficulty level (do you have a lot of time to work with a reef system?), and availability of species many effect your decision.

Freshwater systems

The most popular type of aquarium is a *freshwater* system. It's probably the most practical system for a beginning aquarist for several reasons:

✔ A freshwater system is not quite as expensive to set up as a saltwater system. (Saltwater systems require larger tanks and extra equipment; see the "Marine systems" section later in this chapter.)

✔ Freshwater fish are generally less expensive than marine fish. It's much better to work with less expensive fish when you're just starting out, and still learning the ins and outs of the hobby.

✔ Freshwater fish are readily available at most aquarium shops and offer a wide variety of colorful species to choose from. Many hardy species, such as guppies, platys, and swordtails, are very forgiving of beginners' mistakes. Marine fish are much more sensitive to water conditions and don't tolerate mistakes as easily.

✔ Many varieties of freshwater fish breed quite easily and may provide you with opportunities to sell your overstock (don't quit your day job, though), and a chance to experiment with new breeds.

✔ You can keep significantly more freshwater than marine fish in the same amount of space.

You can set up either tropical or coldwater freshwater systems. Each system has slightly different equipment requirements and houses different types of fish.

Freshwater tropical aquariums

Freshwater tropical aquariums house the largest majority of retail freshwater fish. If you choose this system, you can set up a *community aquarium* with a variety of species that can coexist peacefully, or you may decide to try a *species tank* for a few of the more aggressive species, such as cichlids. A freshwater tropical aquarium offers the greatest number of choices in livestock and plants out of all the systems I discuss in this chapter.

Most tropical freshwater fish are inexpensive and pretty easy to keep, which is why this is the best system for a beginning hobbyist. You can purchase a system at many superstores in kit form. A kit generally includes a tank, hood, filter, net, food, instruction book, and heater necessary for a tropical tank, but often doesn't include gravel, plants, or livestock.

Popular species of tropical freshwater fish include platys, guppies, mollies, neons, swordtails, catfish, angelfish, algae eaters, bettas, tetras, and barbs.

Freshwater coldwater aquariums

A *coldwater aquarium* usually houses species such as goldfish, sunfish, shiners, and bitterlings than normally live in lower temperatures in their native habitat. Large koi are often kept in coldwater ponds. The equipment you need for a coldwater aquarium is similar to that for a tropical aquarium, except that coldwater tanks don't require a heating system. Larger tanks are better for this type of system because coldwater species are generally larger than most tropicals and they consume more oxygen. Take care in choosing plants for this system because many plants can't survive the lower temperatures.

Aside from goldfish, most coldwater fish are difficult to obtain in many areas of the country. Setting up a coldwater system drastically reduces your choices of fish and live plants.

Marine systems

Marine, or *saltwater, systems* require saltwater. You see marine fish on most scuba and underwater programs. The most popular of these fish includes the coral reef species often found living in close proximity to various *invertebrates* (animals without backbones), and are often very colorful and quite beautiful. But don't fool yourself, beauty has its price. Saltwater fish can be very expensive.

You would be wise to gain a little experience with freshwater fish before attempting a complete coral reef system. Although many people say that new hobbyists shouldn't begin with a marine system, I disagree. It's the type of fish that matters, and though I can think of many specialty freshwater fish (discus and pencilfish, for example) that can be disastrous for newcomers, other species can be very rewarding.

The saltwater used in a marine system is usually obtained by mixing fresh water with a manufactured salt mix. A good filtration system is important in marine tanks to keep the oxygen levels high and the ammonia levels low. Marine fish have a lower tolerance to ammonia (a fish waste product) than freshwater species do, and an inadequate filter soon leads to disaster in a saltwater tank.

Like freshwater, marine aquariums can be broken down into a few subcategories.

- **Coldwater marine.** Many tanks of this type house animals such as lobsters and rockfish that are native to colder Pacific areas.
- **Tropical marine.** These tanks generally contain fish native to coral reef areas, such as tangs, clownfish, and damsels.
- **Reef tank.** Some reef tanks contain only invertebrates, such as anemones, scallops, organisms growing on live rock, and clams. Other tanks may have both invertebrates and fish.

You can set up a saltwater system in a variety of ways. Invertebrates are a little more difficult to care for, so if you do set up a saltwater system you may want to start with a fish-only tank, or choose your invertebrates carefully.

Gaining a little experience with a freshwater system is a great way to prepare yourself to enter the marine side of the hobby. Don't get me wrong. A beginner can maintain a successful marine tank, but the lessons you learn can be very expensive. I see many new hobbyists become disheartened with fish-keeping because they start out with a marine setup that's just too much for them to handle. If you have a close friend who is experienced in marine systems, ask her for advice — she may be able to help you get started successfully.

Many marine fish are social time bombs waiting to explode all over the other fish in your tank. In fact, saltwater fish can be down right rude. Most community freshwater fish have reached a state of enlightenment or something like that, and are pretty cool with each other.

Brackish systems (reading between the lines)

The *brackish aquarium* is the least popular of all the three systems, simply because the fish are generally unavailable from local pet stores, and are usually more expensive than freshwater tropical fish. The water in a brackish aquarium lies somewhere between fresh and marine in salt content. Popular species for this type of system include monos, archers, puffers, and scats. The equipment for a brackish system is similar to that for a freshwater setup, but only specific plants can tolerate a brackish system.

Organization Is the Key to Success

One of the keys to success in almost any project you do is organizing your goals and ideas. If you're like me, you probably own one of those all-purpose planners that weigh about as much as the family car. If you don't have a planner, and your earliest memory goes back to yesterday's breakfast, then you should probably begin your aquarium project by making a simple list. If you have a good memory, make a list anyway.

A good list provides you with a set of short- and long-term goals to help you set up and maintain your new aquarium system. For example, your short-term goals may include purchasing your tank and equipment, and picking out a few starter fish. Long-term goals may be breeding your fish and trying different types of systems. By setting a few goals, you give yourself a plan to follow. You can begin your own list of goals as you read through this book.

A little knowledge can spell the difference between success and ultimate failure. I realize that research brings up frightening memories of the old town librarian (you know, the one who looks like preserved cheese and is somewhere between 50 and 200 years old), but there are other practical ways to gain knowledge. With the advent of the Internet, aquarists can access current information on the aquarium hobby.

It is important to keep researching the type of system you're interested in, even after you have it set up. By researching a fish's natural environment, and finding out how and where it lives in the wild, you arm yourself to provide your fish with the best aquarium conditions and environment you can. A natural, stress-free environment promotes long and healthy lives for your wet pets.

Final Choices

If you're wondering what type of system to start with, let me make a suggestion: Read this book through first, then go window shopping at your local pet store to get a good idea of the costs of each type of system and the availability of the livestock. After you gather all the information necessary, then make your final decision.

Chapter 2

Finding a Good Location

● ●

In This Chapter

▶ Understanding room temperature and your fish

▶ Running your fish ragged

▶ Finding a water source

▶ Considering space, electricity, and cleaning

● ●

*W*hen you look for a good place to put your aquarium, keep in mind that many of the physical aspects of your home can have a major effect on the success or failure of your aquarium system. Carefully inspect the place where you plan to set up your aquarium to check for a few easily avoided hazards. A little good judgment goes a long way.

To start you off, I examine a few common physical problems that can occur when aquariums are put in the wrong spot. (Check out Chapter 3 for some of the psychological aspects of tank placement.) I know, you're probably like me, and are bound and determined to put an aquarium on your breakfast bar no matter what the cost. Well, after a few days of poached eggs floating around in your tank and greasy fingerprints all over the aquarium glass, not to mention the fact that the breakfast bar is sagging under the aquarium's weight, you probably will be forced to change your mind. So start your aquarium in the right place and save yourself a bunch of migraines.

Starting Out Right

Nothing is more frustrating than having to move an aquarium because you put it in a place that just isn't working out for one reason or another. Aquariums are very heavy when fully loaded, and must be drained when moved. Don't spend a lot of time setting up a tank if you're not sure about its location. It's better to take a day or two and look over your options instead of just putting up the aquarium randomly. Start out on the right foot if you want to be successful.

Room Temperature and Its Effects

Most aquariums need a stable water temperature. Coldwater aquariums do not require constant heating. But tropical setups are different. Constant fluctuations in temperature can cause your fish to get sick or die in a tropical tank. Heaters can keep your water temperature high enough to prevent your fish from becoming floating fishcicles. But, if you place your aquarium in a room where the temperature is 20 below zero, your heater is going to go south for the winter, and your aquarium may end up looking like an ice sculpture. The point is, your heater can only handle so much.

Too high a water temperature can also cause various types of disease. Poor water conditions such as fluctuating temperature can lower your pets' immune systems and increase their risk of contracting disease. There is another problem that can occur when water temperature is not stable. As water temperature rises, the water loses oxygen. After a short period of time in a too-hot tank, your fish start gasping at the surface and eventually die of asphyxiation. The only piece of equipment designed to keep water temperature down is a chiller, which is very expensive.

So now you know not to put your aquarium in an area that is too cold or too hot. You may be thinking, "But, my house is well insulated." And you're probably right, but two items in even the most well-insulated home can cause temperature fluctuations: Windows and doors.

Windows

Windows may seem innocent enough, but an aquarium placed near one is going to have several problems. When normal, direct sunlight shines on an aquarium tank, the water temperature can reach lethal levels in a period of just a few hours — even if the windows have curtains or blinds. Heavy drapes are about the only material that blocks out enough light to prevent this problem.

Placing your aquarium near a window may also promote a tremendous overgrowth of algae. I'm not talking about a little algae — I'm talking about your aquarium looking like a golf course. Once algae begins to overrun your aquarium, it can be really difficult to get rid of.

Keep an eye on your window for a day during normal sunlight hours to get a good idea of just how far the sun's rays reach inside your window. Place your aquarium beyond the outermost limits of the sun's potentially lethal grasp.

Deadly doors

There are two types of doors in most homes: Interior doors that connect rooms and exterior doors that lead outside. Both types can wreak havoc on your aquarium in different ways.

- ✔ **Exterior doors** can be very drafty. Every time someone opens a door in wintertime, cold air seeps in. It doesn't take long for an aquarium to chill under these conditions. Place your tank well away from any outside doors to avoid drafts.

- ✔ **Interior doors** may be safe from cold drafts, but they can be deadly if they hit your aquarium. It seems that most doorknobs are at a perfect level to hit the glass on your tank. I have seen many expensive aquariums broken by a door hastily flung open. If you must place an aquarium near a door, open the door a few times to make sure that it has plenty of room to safely clear your tank.

High Traffic Areas and Children (Spell D I S A S T E R)

High traffic areas are those places in your house where the carpet is really dirty. (I have two teenagers, so unfortunately that's about 90 percent of my house.) Anyway, high traffic spots such as hallways, entranceways, kitchens, and so on are not good places for your aquarium. Constant movement along the tank's glass keeps most fish continually spooked. Fear leads to stress. Stress leads to disease. Disease leads to death. A very simple but all too frequent pattern.

To avoid freaking your fish out all day, place them in a nice quite spot such as a corner in the living room or den. These types of rooms give your fish an opportunity to get used to people moving around them, without overloading them with traffic 24 hours a day.

Children are another major problem for aquariums. Children can tend to get a little wild sometimes. If you have children, I haven't told you anything you already don't know firsthand. Even if you don't have children living in the house, you may have neighbor kids or nieces and nephews who come over once in a while. Aquariums can be great learning tools for children, but youngsters need to be reminded that the fish have needs and wants that have to be considered in the overall scheme of things.

When you have young children in your home, you childproof rooms by locking up chemicals, putting away sharp objects, and hiding anything that can harm your child. You need to do the same thing with your aquarium. If you have young children, place the aquarium where the kids have a hard time getting at it, such as on top of a large cabinet-style stand in an area you're in frequently. If your family spends most of its time in the family room, that's a great place to have the aquarium so that you can keep a close eye on it when your children are near.

A few examples of childhood play that can be devastating to your aquatic friends:

- A couple of kids tossing a Nerf ball back and forth in front of the tank (guaranteed to give your fish whiplash)
- Children floating toy boats on top of the aquarium water
- A child practicing finger painting on the tank's glass.

Now, if you were a fish, what would you think of all these situations? You may likely think that it's about time to check out and visit that great fishbowl in the sky. Give your fish a break by teaching your children to respect their privacy.

Water Sources

One important thing to remember when placing your aquarium is the availability of a water faucet. Nobody wants to spend hours of backbreaking work hauling water around. You have to have water to fill up your tank when you first set it up, and you also need to top off your tank from time to time as the water evaporates. And don't forget those weekly water changes. All of that water lugging gets old quickly.

It's best to use a faucet that other family members don't use very often so you don't inconvenience them by using the tap all the time. A faucet in a spare bathroom is an excellent place to work from.

Checking the source

If you do end up using a bucket to change water, try to place your aquarium close to a sink or bathtub. This really saves you a lot of time in the long run. It may also save you from your spouse, if you end up turning your home or apartment into a family water park during your frequent water changes. Make sure your aquarium isn't in a place that requires you to carry water through every room in the house to top off your tank.

Using a python

Don't panic — I'm not talking about a snake here. The python I'm talking about is actually an amazing aquarium vacuum. A *python* is a long, clear, water hose with one end that connects to your sink faucet. (Sometimes, depending on your fixture, you may have to purchase an adapter.) The other end of the python has a large plastic tube that suctions up water and gathers debris from around the substrate (gravel or other aquarium floor covering). The faucet end has a little gadget that you can push up or down which directs the water either to go from the faucet to the end of the hose or to suck water from the other end so that water spills into the sink.

Pythons are usually available in 25- or 50-foot lengths at pet shops. All you really have to do is hook one end up to the sink and suck the water out of the aquarium with the other. To replace the water, reverse the python's plastic switch, put the other end in a bucket by your aquarium, and fill it up. After adding dechlorinator, pick up the bucket and slowly pour the water into your aquarium. This method is much easier than hauling water back and forth across your home.

Space Considerations (How Much Furniture Can I Sell?)

Make sure you have enough space in your home to fit your aquarium without having to sell any furniture. If you do find the need for more space, casually suggest to your spouse that the loveseat and couch are looking kind of shabby and need to be replaced. While your spouse is hauling the furniture away, set up your tank. Rant and rave about how great the new aquarium looks and hope your mate doesn't have the heart to make you move it after you've gone through all the trouble of setting it up.

An easier method is to just make sure that you have room for the tank you buy. Measure the intended spot carefully so that you know exactly what size tank you can purchase.

Electrical Considerations

I remind you several times throughout this book to check for an electrical outlet near the place you want to set your tank. Nothing is more frustrating than setting up a tank, only to find out that you have nowhere to plug in your equipment. Make sure that electrical outlets (you probably need more than one) are in good working condition and up to code. If necessary, install an extra outlet or use a multi-outlet strip, like the one shown in Figure 2-1.

Figure 2-1:
You're going
to need one
of these
for your
aquarium.

Cleaning Considerations

Once in while, you have to do a little cleaning and maintenance on your aquarium. Leave enough room around the tank so that you can easily reach all sides of it without pushing against the tank itself. Trying to squeeze in behind a tank that is too close to the wall is flirting with disaster.

Marine tanks often suffer from salt creep. *Salt creep* is when the marine salt in your aquarium is pushed out of the tank along with a little dribble of water and begins to run down the glass. Salt also forms along the rim of the tank when it's pushed up through aeration and is left as a deposit after the water around it evaporates. Once in a while (usually once a week), you have to go all around the tank and clean this excess salt off of the glass and the rim. You want to make sure that you have plenty of room to do that.

Even aquariums with tight-fitting hoods tend to have drips and dribbles every so often. So one way or another, you have to get behind your aquarium at some point. Make sure when you are setting up your tank that you have plenty of space to take care of any problems that may occur.

Chapter 3

The Tank and Stand

• •

• •

Two of the largest items that you will purchase for your aquarium system are the tank and the stand. There are many different styles, shapes, and sizes of aquariums on today's market, and the construction involved in these modern acrylic and glass tanks is of much better quality today than the old steel-framed aquariums that were around when the hobby began.

Aquarium stands have also come a long way over the years. The old heavy iron stands have now been replaced with beautiful cabinets and fancier wrought-iron varieties. Now aquarium keeping is truly an art form in itself.

What to Consider Before Buying a Tank

The first step in setting up your new aquarium system is purchasing a tank. But before you go out and actually buy one, look at a few of the variables that may affect your purchase: Your aquarium has to fit into your individual situation, plus, you have to match your tank to its surrounding environment and to any of your special needs. (Dang, there's a drawback to everything!)

Stop for a moment and think about the purpose for your tank. Are you setting it up so that everyone in your family can enjoy it? Or do you want to have the aquarium in your own private office or bedroom? A freshwater community or hardy marine tank may be more suitable for family viewing than a species tank would be.

Decide where to put the tank. Take a measurement of the intended space so that you don't end up with an aquarium blocking the refrigerator or being used as a doorstop. Don't forget that you need to add a few inches on to the back measurement so that you have plenty of room for aquarium equipment such as filters, pumps, and protein skimmers.

Hitting the ATM machine

Before you go shopping, check to see how much mad money you have available for this particular fish-keeping project, taking into consideration that even though your aquarium is probably the largest piece of fish-keeping equipment you'll ever own (and the one with the largest price tag), the cost of all the other hardware — filters, pumps, gravel, chemicals, and heaters — adds up quickly. Without proper planning, you may find yourself making a whole bunch of trips to the ATM machine.

A larger tank requires more expensive equipment, so you may not want to purchase a 125-gallon aquarium if that leaves you five bucks left to spend on equipment. In this situation, it's better to purchase a small tank, so you have more than enough money left over for substrate, plants, filters, and other essentials.

The type of system you set up really makes a difference as far as cost is concerned. For example, a saltwater or brackish tank costs quite a bit more in the long run than a freshwater tank, because of the extra equipment needed for marine setups and the higher cost of livestock for both systems. Make a few pricing trips to the fish shop to get a firsthand idea of how much each set up costs.

Don't be nickled-and-dimed to death

If you're not careful, you can get nickled-and-dimed purchasing the extras for your tank. Skip the fancy decorations when you first set up your tank, so you have enough money to purchase the equipment you need. Make sure you figure in the price of filters, lights, gravel, chemicals, hoods, plants, air hose, nets, test kits, heaters, marine salt (if needed), medications, decorations, and, of course, your fish. Take a calculator with you when you go to purchase your equipment so that you don't end up digging for a hundred dollars' worth of change in your pockets when you get up to the register.

Aquariums are really a good value, and generally cost quite a bit less than many other hobbies such as skydiving and bungee-jumping. The money you spend in the beginning will pay you and your family back with years and years of unending pleasure.

Checking out a starter kit

If you don't want to get nickled-and-dimed to death when you buy your aquarium equipment, you can always purchase a *starter kit*. A starter kit is a system-in-a-box that usually contains:

- ✔ Tank
- ✔ Filter
- ✔ Food
- ✔ Hood
- ✔ Heater
- ✔ Net
- ✔ Thermometer
- ✔ Water conditioner
- ✔ A beginning aquarium book

Unfortunately, many starter kits don't have gravel, decorations, stands, or light bulbs, so they're not really complete. These kits are usually for freshwater systems only, so if you want a brackish or marine system, you have to purchase salt and other pieces of equipment separately.

Finding free space

Okay, you finally decided where you want to put your aquarium, but now you want to know what size tank won't require a two-foot shoehorn in order to squeeze it in. For example, you live in a small apartment or house and want to purchase an aquarium that you can enjoy without cramping your living space. If you find yourself sleeping on the sofa the following week, then you probably miscalculated your available free space for a bedroom tank.

In order to avoid space hassles (and your spouse's fury), use Table 3-1 to see quickly the *minimum space requirements* (length by width by height) you need for various sizes of several standard aquarium tanks. Remember, these are the *minimum* requirements — the space that extra equipment takes up is not figured in.

Table 3-1	Space Requirements for Tanks
Tank Volume	*Space Requirements in Inches*
10 Gallon	Regular: 20 x 10 x 12
	Long: 24 x 8 x 12
	Hex: 14 x 12 x 18
15 Gallon	Regular: 24 x 12 x 12
	Long: 20 x 10 x 18
	Show: 24 x 8 x 16
20 Gallon	High: 24 x 12 x 16
	Long: 30 x 12 x 12
	Hex: 18 x 16 x 20
25 Gallon	Regular: 24 x 12 x 20
29 Gallon	Regular: 30 x 12 x 18
30 Gallon	Regular: 36 x 12 x 16
	Breeding: 36 x 18 x 12
40 Gallon	Long: 48 x 13 x 16
	Breeding: 36 x 18 x 16
45 Gallon	Regular: 36 x 12 x 24
	Hex: 22 x 22 x 24
50 Gallon	Regular: 36 x 18 x 18
55 Gallon	Regular: 48 x 13 x 20
75 Gallon	Regular: 48 x 18 x 20
100 Gallon	Regular: 72 x 18 x 18
125 Gallon	Regular: 72 x 18 x 22
200 Gallon	Regular: 84 x 24 x 25

People considerations

An important part of your placement decision are the people living with you. Face it, your aquarium is going to make some noise, even if it is outfitted with the most up-to-date equipment on the market. Sure, it won't bark, meow, chirp, croak, hiss, or growl, but it probably will do a little bit of bubbling, rattling, and/or humming once in a while.

If your friends or family are like me, they enjoy all the neat little sounds that an aquarium is bound to make. They may even find them relaxing. But other people may think that your little aquatic setup is downright annoying. I usually get rid of the people before the tank, but if that's not practical for you, your placement options may be limited quite a bit.

Children are another important factor in considering the type of system you purchase. If you have small tots in the house, a tank full of piranhas will probably go over with your spouse like a lead balloon. A community tank (filled with friendly fish such as guppies and platys) may be more appropriate for younger children.

Purchasing a Tank

You have a few choices when it comes to where to purchase an aquarium.

- ✔ **Your local pet shop** or fish shop is an obvious choice. The advantages of buying from a dealer are numerous. Dealer tanks usually have a warranty of some kind (depending on the store's policy) and are in good condition. If you have any problems with your aquarium, you can often return it for a replacement. A dealer can also give you advice and help you pick out your equipment and livestock. The drawback of purchasing from a pet shop is that the prices are usually higher.

Pet superstores usually carry a small line of aquarium equipment, but you don't generally find a whole lot of specialty items (like protein skimmers necessary for most saltwater setups). The employees are usually trained in the basics of aquariums at best, so you may end up with bad advice on more complicated systems. Also, I find that the quality of livestock in this type of store is not the greatest. (In fact, it's downright scary!)

- ✔ **Garage sales** are a really fun and practical place to purchase used equipment at a really outstanding price. But keep in mind that the aquarium equipment is used and may have some problems.

- ✔ **Newspaper ads** can lead you to a nice set-up at a nice price, although reservations about buying used equipment apply. Buying through an ad, however, may give you a chance to see the tank up and running before you purchase it.

Before you purchase a used tank, carefully inspect it for possible leaks, glass cracks, and worn silicone. Check to see that the *silicone seal* (the goopy-looking stuff in the corners and seams) is not cracked, peeling away, or missing in some areas. A small break in the silicone can cause the aquarium to leak. Look at each individual piece of glass in the tank to ensure that it does not have any cracks or broken glass. If the aquarium has any of these problems, you're probably better off buying a new tank.

If you're a first-time buyer, avoid buying used equipment such as pumps. An old pump could have frayed or worn wires that might pose an electrical hazard. Once you get a comfortable with how your aquarium equipment works, then it might be okay for you to try out used equipment.

Ask the person selling the equipment if you can try the stuff out. If he or she is uncooperative, simply look at your watch with a worried expression, and then burn rubber to the nearest pet shop.

Types of Aquariums

The high-quality aquarium products now offered by manufacturers is quite mind-boggling compared to the old glass aquariums of the '60s and '70s that I was stuck with when I was young. The original metal frame tanks were not properly suited for saltwater setups because they contained metal. Salt could eventually corrode the metal frame and become toxic to the inhabitants of the tank. Fortunately, nonmetallic materials were developed and eventually replaced heavy-metal frames and inadequate seam adhesive. This breakthrough in aquarium construction was a direct result of complaints filed by tropical fish–keeping enthusiasts who demanded a better product — one they could use for all types of systems.

Figuring water volume without getting a Ph.D.

If you happen to run across an older tank at a local garage sale or auction, the seller may not know how many gallons the aquarium holds. Although aquarium tank sizes made today are standardized, many older tanks are not. A good formula for obtaining an on-the-spot total for the gallon capacity of any rectangular or square-shaped aquarium is as follows:

Length (inches) x width (inches) x height (inches) = capacity (in gallons)

Glass aquariums

The all-glass aquariums (one is shown in Figure 3-1) on today's market are still the most popular of all available tanks. These new tanks are constructed of plate glass and sealed with a non-toxic silicone. The glass in these aquariums is either *tempered* (stronger, lighter in weight, shatters when it breaks) or *plate* (heavier and thicker but only cracks when it breaks).

Figure 3-1:
An all-glass
aquarium.

Testing and repairing a leaker

One way to test an aquarium for leaks is to fill it with water and let it stand on a piece of newspaper for 24 hours. If the newspaper gets wet, the tank leaks (make sure you aren't fooled by condensation drips). To repair a leak, drain and dry the tank, remove the old silicone with a safety razor (please be careful!), and then replace it with new aquarium sealer. Let the sealer dry for 48 hours before you add any water to the tank.

The *frames* (usually plastic and come in a wide variety of colors) are glued onto the rim. Glass tanks do not scratch easily and provide a good viewing area because all of the walls are flat. Some glass tanks can be purchased *reef ready,* which means that they have holes drilled in them for equipment and hoses, allowing you to hide equipment inside of a cabinet. However, these reef-ready tanks can be quite expensive and are intended more for experienced hobbyists.

One of the disadvantages of glass aquariums is that they can be formed into only a limited number of shapes — basically, rectangles or squares. If you really want a tank with an unusual shape, you won't find much to please you in the glass department.

Glass aquariums are also heavy because the glass used in construction gets thicker as the tank gets larger. This can be a real problem if you want a big tank and have weak floors in your home, or if you attempt to move the aquarium. Glass aquariums can break or shatter and leave you with a lot of dead fish and a huge mess to clean up.

Cool-looking acrylic aquariums

Acrylic tanks have made a big splash (no pun intended) in the aquarium marketplace in the last few years. These lightweight tanks are available in a number of amazing shapes and sizes such as bubble, half spheres, L-shaped, tubular, triangular, and convex. A neat one is shown in Figure 3-2. With acrylic, the shape possibilities end only with the designer's creativity. There is an acrylic tank somewhere out there to please almost everyone's personal tastes and desires.

Can I build my own tank?

Building your own glass tank can be very dangerous unless you really know what you're doing. This is not recommended for inexperienced hobbyists and craftsmen. It really is safer to purchase a tank at a dealer rather than risk building an inferior product that leaks water like a typhoon blowing through a sieve and turns your room into a permanent water display that could put Seaworld to shame.

Figure 3-2:
An acrylic
aquarium.

The advantages of acrylic over glass tanks are numerous:

- Acrylic is much lighter than glass. Acrylic tanks are easier to move and produce fewer hernias. If your aquarium is upstairs, acrylic may give you the option of having a larger tank.

- Many acrylic tanks come with colored backgrounds, which can be quite stunning with the proper tank decoration.

- You can use common household tools to drill holes in an acrylic tank to make it reef-ready.

- Acrylic is also much stronger than glass and it takes an exceptional blow with a blunt instrument to shatter it.

Distortion problems

Unfortunately, acrylic tanks have small amounts of visual distortion because of the way the material is bent during construction. These tanks are generally made out of one large piece of acrylic that is heated and bent to shape; this method produces a seamless look that is really outstanding. These transparent corners allow you to view your fish from almost any angle with ease.

The beauty (and expense) of acrylic

The modern look of acrylic tanks you just cannot find in a standard glass aquarium. You also get more choices in colors and styles to match the interior of your home or office. An acrylic tank gives any room an upscale appearance and generally looks more expensive than glass tanks. Speaking of which, acrylic aquariums are *a lot* more expensive than their glass counterparts. These babies can cost some serious bucks, but they are well worth the investment.

Scratches

The big disadvantage that you run into with acrylic aquariums is that they are quite easily scratched. Be careful when using rough algae pads to avoid leaving scratches or smears. Moving gravel around can also damage the surface, so pay close attention when you are moving, cleaning, or adding decorations to the aquarium. There are good scratch remover kits (which can be found through your local pet shop or on the Internet) on the market that easily cover most simple blemishes caused by carelessness.

Plastic aquariums

Plastic tanks can still be found collecting dust on superstore shelves. These types of aquariums are very inexpensive. The problem is that plastic tanks have more serious drawbacks than any other type of aquarium and really are not worth purchasing. Plastic tanks are now almost obsolete (kind of like the computer I purchased last year) and for several good reasons:

- ✔ They scratch easily, and there is really no way to repair the scratches.

- ✔ They often take on a yellowish cast as they age.

- ✔ They're available only in small sizes (usually between 2 and 5 gallons) which don't provide enough water volume and surface area to insure a biologically stable environment.

- ✔ They suffer major distortion problems due to their odd shapes.

- ✔ They can buckle when they come in contact with any heat source, including their own hood and light! Whoever designed these tanks needs to have his or her little (and I do mean *little*) gray cells examined.

Choosing the Right Tank

There are many issues you need to address when you're preparing to actually purchase your tank. A tank's size, water volume, and shape have a lot to do with the type of aquatic creatures you can actually put in it. If you start off with a tank that meets the needs of your individual project or system, you have one foot in the right door toward success.

Tank size

If you plan on setting up a freshwater system, you should purchase at least a 10-gallon tank to make sure that your new fish have an adequate surface area to provide stable water conditions. A smaller tank is harder to work with, can turn your fish into instant sardines, and will bring you disappointment and heartache. Smaller aquariums are more prone to foul water conditions, which can damage your fish's health. A small tank also does not leave much room for adding larger decorations and extra fish.

Always buy the largest tank that your budget and space limitations allow, because increased surface area means better overall biological stability. A large surface area provides good oxygen absorption and carbon dioxide exchange.

Small tanks can be a real problem if you have a power or equipment failure. Due to the small amount of water the tank holds, the temperature can drop very quickly. An extended period of lost filtration (usually after several hours depending on your aquarium size) can also foul the water to lethal proportions.

Tank shape

Although it is cool to have an oddly shaped aquarium, be aware that a few drawbacks go along with these tanks. The shape of an aquarium helps determine the amount of oxygen its water contains. Vital _gas exchange_ (carbon dioxide for oxygen) occurs at the water surface. A tall, thin tank with a small water-surface area has less gas exchange going on than a shorter tank with a longer, and therefore larger, surface area. Another factor to take into consideration is that odd-sized tanks (especially if they are really tall and narrow) can be hard to clean or decorate without professional scuba gear. There may be several specific areas near the bottom that are totally unreachable. You may also find yourself having a hard time locating equipment, such as filters and hoods, to fit a tank that isn't a standard size. Even if you do find a good match, it probably costs twice as much as the same piece does for a standard-sized tank.

Carrying capacity

The _carrying capacity_ is simply the total number of fish you can keep in your aquarium safely without them going belly up. If you choose to buy a tank that is very tall and narrow, you can't keep as many fish in it as you can in a tank with a larger surface area. It's as simple as that. I'll say it one more time: If you get a fancy tank that has a small surface area, don't count on having a whole bunch of fish.

Choosing the Right Stand

Choosing a good stand can be just as important as picking the right aquarium. A stand needs to be sturdy and strong, and look cool at the same time. The one thing that you don't want to do is use granny's antique table as an aquarium stand, because any unforeseen water leaks will ruin the finish quickly. (Unless her eyesight has failed, in which case you can cover up the marks with a couple of her doilies.) A heavy tank can warp the wood on your regular household furniture too. So it is always best to use a manufactured aquarium stand built to support a tank's weight and designed to be perfectly level.

Make sure your aquarium fits its stand correctly. If the tank hangs over the stand, the stand is too small and can cause the aquarium to warp or break.

Manufactured stands are generally made out of iron, steel or wood. All three materials make great stands, so it is just a matter of individual preference as to which one you decide to buy. (Okay, okay, I'll give you a few hints: Just read on.)

Wooden cabinet stands

Stands that include a built-in wooden cabinet are enclosed on the bottom so that you can hide equipment and hoses that generally spoil the overall look of your aquarium system. Chemicals, test kits, nets, and other paraphernalia can be conveniently stored behind closed doors (see Figure 3-3). Such a cabinet also allows you to buy a bunch of expensive aquarium junk and hide it from your spouse. The only problem with wooden stands is that they can warp under extreme weight and tend to cost a little more than standard iron stands (make sure that the aquarium you choose matches the stand that you buy to avoid these problems). Despite the aforementioned drawbacks, these are the best stands that you can buy because they look good, will not tip over easily, and often contain shelves for storing items.

Angle and wrought iron stands

Iron stands are made of either angle iron or wrought iron. Angle iron stands are welded together and have a bulky look to them. They look great if you happen to be living in a medieval castle. These stands can also leave nasty marks on your floor or carpet. Wrought iron stands are made of thinner metal than angle iron and are a little bit more fancy.

Figure 3-3:
A wooden
tank stand
with storage
space.

Do-it-yourself stands

There are a few stands that you can purchase and build yourself. You can
assemble them easily with a few household tools. The pieces are usually
made of pressboard and include at least one shelf. These stands are not as
strong as manufactured ones and may warp or buckle if they get wet.

Another option is to head down to the hardware store, buy some lumber, and
build one yourself. You may find out that a homemade stand costs as much
or more than a manufactured stand. But if you have the know-how, an interesting idea, cool tools, and the energy to turn off the TV and head out to the
garage, go for it.

Placing the Stand Correctly

The first step in setting up your aquarium system is finding a permanent
place to put your stand. Set the stand in an area away from drafts and direct
sunlight to keep the water in your tank from overheating or chilling. Don't put
your tank in a garage or basement unless the room is insulated or heated.
Placement near doors, windows, and other drafty areas where the temperature can change unexpectedly is a no-no.

Checking the floors

Make sure that the stand is on a solid surface. Check the floor carefully so that your new aquarium doesn't end up decorating the downstairs neighbor's apartment. Remember that a 100-gallon tank weighs somewhere in the neighborhood of 1,000 pounds! To determine completed aquarium weight, simply multiply the total number of gallons in your aquarium by 10 pounds. This provides you with a good rough estimate of total weight.

Make sure that you do not place the stand directly against a wall. You need room back there for hanging equipment.

Looking for power

When determining where you want to place your aquarium keep in mind that your system requires a few electrical outlets in order to run. A friend of mine once set up a complete aquarium system — water and all — and then realized that there was no electrical plug anywhere near the tank! (He was a couple sandwiches short of a mental picnic anyway.) Try to locate and use an electrical plug that is not connected to a wall switch. You don't want anyone to hit the switch and unknowingly shut off your aquarium equipment.

Moving an Aquarium (What Are Friends For?)

It is important to remember that you should never try to move an aquarium all by yourself, no matter how small it is. Any aquarium should always be lifted by a minimum of two people. You can really cause yourself unnecessary physical injury if you attempt to haul your tank around by yourself.

The best way to get help moving an aquarium is to put on a dirty apron, throw some flour on yourself, call your couch potato neighbors, and tell them you want them to try out an exciting new recipe of yours. When they arrive, simply tell them that your aquarium is blocking the way to the food supply. Works every time.

When you're ready to move your tank, make sure to unplug all equipment and then remove it from the aquarium after a period of 15 minutes. Fill a plastic bucket with water from the aquarium and place the fish in the bucket. Drain the rest of the water. Before you lift the aquarium, remove any large rocks or other heavy decorations, which can shift positions and break the glass.

Never lift your tank by grabbing the top of the frame. Lifting an aquarium by its frame can damage and break the sealer or glass, eventually causing water leaks. The proper way to lift an aquarium is to place your hands (and your hungry neighbors' hands) beneath the bottom corners of the tank, as shown in Figure 3-4.

Figure 3-4:
The right way to lift an aquarium.

When you have placed the tank in its new position, put the gravel, decorations, equipment, and water back into the tank. Make sure that the water that you put back into the tank has been dechlorinated by aging or through use of a dechlorination chemical. Add the fish back to the tank when the system is running properly.

Chapter 4

Substrates and Decorations

. . . .

. . . .

*A*quascaping (a fancy word that means decorating a glass or acrylic box with water in it) your aquarium with different types of rock, wood, and substrate (gravel, sand, coral, and other aquarium floor coverings) can be a lot of fun and gives you a good chance to show off your personal creative talents in front of your friends and family. I can think of no greater joy than creating a pleasing arrangement of rocks, plants, and substrate for my fish to enjoy.

But while aquascaping can be a real blast, you need to remember that certain types of substrates, rocks, and wood are suitable only for specific aquarium setups. You really need to know what to purchase before you begin randomly throwing things into your aquarium. This chapter can help.

Planning Ahead

The first thing to do when aquascaping any aquarium is to take a close look at the *native environment* of the fish you're planning to keep in your tank. For example, marine fish are much happier in an aquarium full of coral and live rock than in one with green plants and driftwood — which you generally use in a freshwater or brackish setup.

A quick trip to the local library or a spin through the Internet can give you much information and many ideas on how to aquascape your aquarium properly.

If you use your imagination and follow a few simple aquascaping rules I present in this chapter, you'll quickly realize that the possibilities are endless.

I find that it often helps to sit down and draw out a placement plan on a piece of paper before adding any substrate or decorations to a tank. This way, you can get a better overall "feel" for the layout you want, and can trick your friends into thinking that you're a real artist at the same time.

A few common decorations are used in specific aquarium setups. But, the final decisions and placement ultimately rests with the individual aquarist. It's kind of like cheating at solitaire: If it works, do it. No one is really going to know but you and your fish, and we know they won't spill the beans. And if by chance someone finds out that you're using the wrong type of substrate or decorations and calls you on it, you simply tell him or her that you created a new type of aquatic system. Just be vague on the details, and change the subject as quickly as possible.

Be aware, though, that you should never use common objects such as marbles and glass as substrates in your aquarium because they're not safe for your fish and can be very detrimental to the aquarium's natural biological cycle. Marbles leave large gaps between them where food can fall unnoticed. This uneaten food can rot and foul the water. Glass objects pose the threat of physically injuring your fish. Make sure that all decoration surfaces are smooth. Marbles and glass objects really look unnatural, too.

Just in case you want to be perfectly safe and play by the universally accepted aquarium rules, the following list gives you a few good ideas about which substrates and decorations are most often used in individual types of systems.

- ✔ **Freshwater Tank:** Pebbles, igneous and shale rocks, live plants, artificial plants, driftwood, with sand and standard fish shop gravel for substrate.

- ✔ **Brackish Water Tank:** Pebbles, shale, stratified rocks, plants, driftwood, pea gravel, and small amounts of coral sand for substrate.

- ✔ **Marine Tank:** Live rock (rock that has invertebrates attached), tufa rock, and dolomite with coral sand and live sand (pre-cultured sand that contains biological organisms for filtration) for substrate. Selected algae, such as grape plant, for decoration. Invertebrates such as anemones and tubeworms are common in many marine tanks.

Types of Substrate

Substrates come in many different shapes and sizes to suit the needs of each type of aquarium. You can find substrates in grades from fine to course and in different shapes such as smooth or chipped.

Choosing the proper substrate gives you a good start on maintaining a healthy aquatic system for your fish. So you're probably wondering how to find your way though this substrate mess. Right? Well, read on.

Gravel

Manufactured gravel is usually the best bet for a freshwater or brackish tank. It is easily cleaned and is widely available in pet stores and super centers by the bag (see Figure 4-1), or in many instances, by the pound.

Most manufactured gravel is lime-free (this type of substrate can be used in freshwater and brackish tanks that do not need alkaline pH values) and is very inexpensive, which makes it one of the most popular substrates. This gravel comes in a wide variety of cool colors and is easy to work with and measure.

One disadvantage of gravel is that it is a completely inanimate substance and does not provide any type of nutrition for living aquarium plants. Hey, there are drawbacks to everything. So, if you decide to use live plants in your freshwater or brackish setup, then you have to supply extra nutrition for them by using plant plugs or liquid food. Say what? (Chapter 8 explains all that, I promise.)

Figure 4-1:
All kinds of gravel for sale.

Dolomite

Although gravel works well as a substrate base in a freshwater or brackish tank, it doesn't cut the mustard in a saltwater setup. Instead of using regular gravel for a marine tank, get commercial dolomite or crushed coral. You can also use coral sand, which is often added in small amounts to aquariums that house cichlids which normally inhabit alkaline lakes and rivers in Africa.

Dolomite is generally white (it looks kind of like gravel but is smaller and much more expensive) and available in large bags (see Figure 4-2). It's a shame that few stores sell this material by the pound, so you may have to purchase much more dolomite than you really need. At least you can use the extra dolomite as an excuse to get another tank!

Substrates and pH

Putting the right substrate in an aquarium setup is just as important as providing the correct water conditions. One important point to remember is that substrates can affect the pH of your aquarium water so make sure that you purchase the correct type for the species that you own.

Figure 4-2:
Bags of
dolomite.

For example, marine dolomite raises the pH of aquarium water to an alkaline level, and therefore is unsuitable for most freshwater tanks. If you put dolomite in your freshwater tank, your fish will do the backstroke permanently. Standard aquarium gravel doesn't affect the water's pH, and therefore isn't suitable for a marine setup which requires a consistently higher pH level.

If you're not sure how much calcareous material a substrate contains, perform this simple test: Add a few tablespoons of vinegar to the substrate and if it has calcareous (that is, containing calcium) material, it will fizz. If it fizzes, don't put it in your freshwater tank.

Crushed coral (pieces of dead coral gathered from coral beaches) and shells have the same effect on your water's pH values as dolomite does and should not be used in a freshwater setup. Besides, a guppy swimming around a large seashell just doesn't look right at all.

Keeping it safe

Get all substrate materials from a reputable fish dealer so that you know that it's pure.

No matter which substrate you choose for your aquarium, make sure that it's safe for all the fish in your tank. Sharp edges on gravel, coral, and shell pieces can damage your fish's body. Jagged surfaces can be especially injurious to bottom-dwelling species that continually dig in the substrate. If your bottom dwellers look like dartboards, check your substrate carefully.

In addition, the substrate or gravel that you put into your aquarium plays a very important role in its overall biological cycle. In time, beneficial bacteria starts growing on top of the substrate bed and helps break down waste in the aquarium water. Substrate is also quite useful for anchoring live plants and for holding down various types of artificial decorations.

No marbles

Several types of familiar items sometimes found in a beginner's freshwater aquarium are not really suitable for a fish's natural environment. Never use marbles, glass flakes, or other such materials to cover the bottom of any aquarium. Marbles are quite large and allow debris to become trapped between their surfaces, which can eventually lead to water fouling and diseased fish.

Stay away from disco gravel

Brightly-colored or *neon gravels* take away from the natural beauty of your fish and from their environment. They should be avoided if it all possible. Neon gravel tends to make your fish look like they have the starring role in a made-for-TV movie about a bad night on a disco floor.

Keep an aquarium's colors simple and natural looking for the best results. You can get away with a few plastic decorations such as treasure chests and scuba divers once in a while, but shocking-pink gravel is too much of an eye-strain for both you and your fish. If you wake up one morning to find your fish sporting sunglasses, you know you need to tone down your gravel a little bit. Neon gravels may also keep your fish from spawning, and make them shy away and hide in corners.

Substrate size

Choose the size of your gravel carefully to avoid water fouling. Avoid large-grained materials because they allow food to fall between the granules, and these particles can cause serious water problems in a short period of time. If you use an undergravel filter, choose a medium-size substrate so that the plastic plates don't get clogged.

Larger granules also have a smaller surface area because of their shape, and don't allow space for the growth of the proper bacteria for biological filtration. Let me put it this way — if you think you can break a window at 10 feet with a piece of your aquarium gravel, then it is too large for your tank, and probably should be used to pave your driveway instead. Gravel with a particle size of one-eighth of an inch works best for most setups.

Small-grained substrates such as sand quickly clog the water flow in your aquarium if they slip down into the undergravel filter plate and can subsequently cause a rise in unwanted *anaerobic bacteria* (bacteria that thrive without oxygen). So if you decide to use sand in a freshwater or saltwater aquarium, it should only be laid down in a very thin layer (or have a mesh plate beneath it to stop it from falling through into the filter).

If you can't find the right size at your local pet store, either order some on the Internet or wait until it becomes available from your dealer. A little bit of patience can definitely save you many headaches in the future.

Adding substrate to your system

Before adding gravel to a freshwater system, clean it thoroughly by rinsing it under fresh water. As you clean, carefully check for and remove defects such as extremely large clumps, foreign matter, and sharp pieces in the gravel.

How much substrate do I really need?

The amount of substrate required for a freshwater tank varies not only with the size of the aquarium, but with the type of filtration used as well.

If you have an undergravel filter, you need a two- to three-inch layer of substrate in order to create a proper bacterial bed. If you're not using an undergravel filter, use only an inch of substrate to cover the bottom of the tank.

On the average, a standard-size, rectangular aquarium needs about a pound and a half of substrate per gallon of water. It should be obvious that this rule doesn't work for a tank two inches wide and eighteen feet tall. You'd end up with a column of gravel that would look great as a pillar on your front porch.

Adding dolomite for the saltwater setup

Calcareous substances such as dolomite and other types of crushed coral are used in marine tanks for their buffering ability (keeping the pH at a high level), and are not suitable for freshwater aquariums. Other appropriate substrates for a saltwater tank include oyster shells, coral sand, and limestone.

Rinse dolomite thoroughly several times before adding it to your aquarium tank; otherwise, its fine, chalky-white powder can make your water look like cream of mushroom soup. Rinse the dolomite in a plastic bucket until the milky colored water that is running though it changes to a faint white color. The bucket that you use should be made of plastic because metal containers can taint the water quality. Never use any type of soap during the cleaning process. A fresh water rinse is all that is needed.

Rocks and Wood

Rocks and wood are a great way to add a natural looking effect to your aquarium. You can use rocks in freshwater, brackish, and marine tanks. Normal, everyday rocks that you can find at a quarry are generally used for freshwater and brackish setups. Rocks and wood also provide hiding and spawning areas for your fish. I discuss the live rock used in marine tanks later in this chapter.

- ✔ In a **brackish** setup, use driftwood.
- ✔ In a **freshwater** tank, use hardwoods.
- ✔ In a **saltwater** aquarium, don't use wood. (How many trees have you seen growing in the ocean?)

Rocks for freshwater and brackish tanks

Rocks can help break up the total bottom space into individual territories. Establishing territories often prevents fighting among fish. Squabbles often break out during spawning or feeding times. Some individual fish may also be more aggressive than others, so it never hurts to have a few rocks in your aquarium that can provide shelter if needed.

You can purchase several varieties of rock at your local aquarium store that are safe to put into any tank (see Figure 4-3). These rocks are pre-cleaned and won't crumble. You can also pick up a little slate while you're at the store. Slate and other inert rocks don't change the water conditions in your aquarium and promote a pleasing and natural layout.

Figure 4-3:
A variety of rocks for sale at the aquarium store

Wood for a freshwater or brackish tank

You can easily attach gnarled, oddly shaped, or long, slender branches of wood to a large piece of slate using any brand of aquarium silicon, which can be purchased, at your local pet store. Then bury the slate in the substrate to anchor the wood arrangement in place. Use gnarled branches whenever possible, because they look cool and provide nifty little mazes for your fish to swim around in (see Figure 4-4).

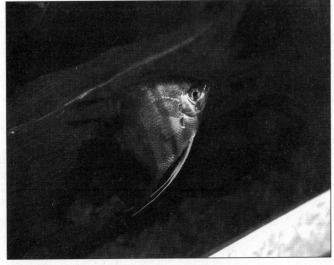

Figure 4-4:
A cool-looking
piece of
wood is in the
background.

Saturating your wood

If your driftwood tends to float, pre-soak it in water until it's saturated. Saturated wood usually stays down on the bottom of the tank. If wood still floats after being submerged for a very long period of time, forget it and find another piece. Nothing is more aggravating or unsightly than a big chunk of wood floating all over your aquarium. Plus, floating chunks of wood may cause dents in your fish, and they will hate you for it.

Expense

Although driftwood is very beautiful and helps create interesting scenes in your aquarium, it can be very expensive. I've found woodworker's shops often carry small pieces of driftwood at a much more reasonable price. A few hobbyists may look down on others for buying materials at stores that are not in the pet shop industry, but the way I figure, it's much better to be a cheapskate and have a really cool-looking aquarium than to be a snob and have a tank that looks like the surface of the moon.

Attachment procedures

You can use plastic suction cups to attach rocks and driftwood to the glass of your freshwater or brackish aquarium. Simply add the cups to the wood using hard plastic screws or aquarium-safe silicone. Anchoring the wood keeps it from floating or being knocked around by the fish in your tank. You can buy suction cups at most hardware and aquarium stores.

Now playing in your marine aquarium: Live rock

For marine tanks, you can use live rock, which you purchase dry at your local aquarium shop, in place of standard rock. *Live rock* is exactly what the name indicates; it is rock with living organisms attached to it, or inhabiting the holes that invertebrates have bored in the rock. Strategically place your live rocks in the tank after you add all your other substrates such as dolomite and live sand.

Good quality live rock can have many interesting types of living organisms on its surface such as tubeworms, anemones, algae, brittle starfish, bacteria, small clams and other types of invertebrates. It is important that you never let your live rock dry out, or many of the beneficial organisms living on it may die.

Reef rock consists of pieces of rock collected from outer reef areas: It can be quite stunning in appearance. This type of live rock is also known as *show rock*. Reef rock contains a lot of coral. Rock collected closer to shore usually contains a lot of clams, crabs, shrimp, and other larger invertebrates. These animals can be quite beautiful and interesting to observe.

Why buy live rock?

The main reason to purchase live rock is so that other serious marine hobbyists will think you're cool for having it. You can purchase several types of live rock for your saltwater setup. Show rock is generally the best quality and is visibly coated with numerous invertebrates. This is the best type of rock to purchase in order to impress people. Reef rock also provides the highest quality of filtration for your aquarium. (Beginners should not rely on live rock as their main filtration system.) If you have live rock in your tank, you can eventually grow organisms even on base rock, which has few organisms and looks quite bare.

Algae, which grows on the surface of live rock, assimilates phosphates, ammonia, and nitrates and then converts them to less harmful substances.

Always buy the best rock available so that your marine tank has a good foundation of organisms to promote the healthy biological cycle of your tank. Live rock acts as its own filtration system because it has a large surface area to support the growth of beneficial bacteria.

Keep in mind that live rock tends to be quite expensive, depending on the area you live in. You can always start with a few pieces and then add more as you go along.

It is not a good idea to collect live rock yourself for several reasons. Live rock obtained from a polluted area can contain harmful parasites and viruses. It is also illegal to collect live rock in many areas and permits are often required in other areas. In the long run, it's much better to buy live rock from a reputable shop so that you don't end up wearing striped pajamas with a ten-digit number at the jailbird hotel for the next few years.

In an overstocked tank, or one with an excess of food, live rock becomes overrun with nitrates and other substances, which it cannot clean efficiently — It's like asking your teenager to keep her room clean for a whole week. You may as well forget that bad idea.

Figuring how much you need

Okay, you're interested in purchasing live rock for your marine aquarium and need a few guidelines on how much to add. Generally, one pound of live rock per gallon of water is sufficient to start with. You can add more or less according to your individual taste. An aquarium can look great with one or two interesting pieces of rock, or can have an entire reef built near the back of the glass. The choice is really yours.

Make sure that your live rock is not packed so tightly together in the tank that it completely cuts off all water circulation along its surface area. Keep in mind that the many living organisms on the rock depend on the water current in the tank to bring nutrients and remove debris. Many of your invertebrates depend on water flow for survival.

Don't lean live rock against the back glass, as this can cause "dead areas" on the rear surface. These tightly enclosed areas do not allow for proper water circulation in the tank and will contribute to uneven heating and water fouling.

Cycling and cleaning live rock

Live rock needs to go through its own conditioning cycle just like the water in your tank. During this time period, organisms on the rock die and are replaced with bacteria and other invertebrates. The dead organisms produce a small amount of waste product, so it is best to have back up filtration during this cycling period.

A better method of cleaning live rock is known as *seeding*. In order to seed live rock, simply place it in an unlit aquarium for a period of about three weeks. (Remove any sponges before placing rock in the holding tank — Sponges die quickly and pollute the water.) This holding tank should have plenty of filtration and be as dark as possible. Using a holding tank prevents organisms that die off from fouling your main aquarium. In some shops, you can purchase live rock that has already been seeded. This rock may be a little bit more expensive, but is well worth it.

Another method of cleaning live rock involves placing the individual pieces on a sheet. Fill a spray bottle with salt water and use it to keep the rock from drying out. As you spray the rock, search for sponges or dead invertebrates and remove them — much more easily accomplished when the rock is sitting in front of you on a plastic sheet than when it's in the main aquarium.

After removing unwanted organisms, rinse the rock gently in plastic buckets of salt water until you feel that most of the dead animals have been successfully removed. After this process is complete, you can add the live rock to your main display tank.

Other Aquarium Decorations (From Your Neighbor's Yard)

Okay, I have to admit that I have been tempted once or twice to sneak over and snag a few rocks and other decorations out of my neighbor's yard — He really has some cool stuff out on his lawn! My first attempt at piracy (I mean borrowing) failed when his large ceramic gnome got stuck halfway into my tank. I beat a hasty retreat and quickly replaced it before he noticed that it was gone.

The neighbor's decorations may look cool, but they can contain all sorts of parasites and other nasty things that can cause disease in your tank and foul the water. It is not safe to use these types of decorations (rocks, wood, plastic sunflowers) for standard aquarium use. Despite the fact that the wagon wheel holding up Mr. Earp's mailbox would make a great centerpiece in your 250-gallon cichlid tank, it's not worth the trouble.

Unsafe decorations that can cause problems

Your best bet for safe decorations to purchase pieces from a reputable aquarium dealer or other retail store. I can't emphasize this important point enough. Unsafe decorations can kill your fish, ruin your aquarium conditions, and cost you a lot of money and heartache.

Statutes and toys that you find around the house may contain internal parts made out of metal, which can cause destruction in a marine tank. Dyes and other surface materials can produce ill affects on freshwater fish and other species.

Safely sealing your decorations

Because several types of wood (bogwood, for example) contain *tannins* which produce acidic conditions, not all woods are suitable for every type of system. Bogwood (which produces a golden-colored water) lends itself best to systems that contain species that prefer soft conditions that are slightly acidic.

If you're not sure how a particular piece or type of wood will affect your aquarium conditions, the safest thing to do is to seal it with *polyurethane varnish*. Use at least three coats of this sealer, allowing each coat to dry before applying the next. The varnish keeps wood from releasing any products that can affect your water conditions.

You can seal an interesting piece of wood from the wild with polyurethane varnish as well.

Coral, Live Sand, and Shells

Saltwater tanks take coral, sand, and shells as substrate. These materials are found in native marine habitats and they provide *pH boosters* to keep the alkaline content of the water from dropping too low. You can use crushed coral and live sand individually, or combine them as a substrate. When combining these two substances, layer the live sand on top of the crushed coral.

Shells

Take great care when you use shells gathered from a beach. There may be living or decaying organisms still inside the shell. Make sure you thoroughly rinse any shells with clean water before you put them into your marine aquarium.

Cleaning natural coral

Wash natural coral before placing it in your aquarium, even if you purchase it from a dealer. You need to remove the dust and organic material these coral skeletons contain before using the coral. The cleaning process is lengthy but not complicated, as the following steps show.

1. **Place the coral in a bucket of fresh, room-temperature water.**

2. **Let the coral sit for a week.**

3. **Put the coral pieces in a plastic bucket with water containing 5 ounces of bleach per gallon.**

4. **Soak the coral pieces in this solution for another week.**

5. **Soak the coral in a bucket of declorinated water (which can be obtained using aged water, or a liquid declorinator) for five days.**

   Change the water frequently and leave the coral in the bucket until you can no longer smell any chlorine.

6. **Place the coral pieces on a plastic sheet in the sun until dry.**

   By the time you collect Social Security, your coral should be ready for use.

Crushed coral

Only substances composed of calcareous material, such as coral, should be used as substrate for a saltwater aquarium. Live sand is an obvious exception to this rule. Calcareous substances act as a buffer to help maintain the proper pH, which should be in an *alkaline range* (usually 8.1–8.4) in a salt-water tank.

Basically, crushed coral serves the same purpose as dolomite and crushed shells in the buffering department. All these substances raise the pH in your marine tank and help keep it where it should be.

Live sand considerations

Live sand is a neat and functional substrate for marine aquariums because it already contains beneficial bacterial colonies which can help keep your water clean. Live sand contains many different kinds of organic matter. The most important material found in live sand is bacteria, which helps break down wastes in the saltwater aquarium. So, live sand acts as an extra filtration system in many ways.

Getting the right stuff

You can use live sand (purchased from a reputable dealer) in combination with live rock and a small amount of dolomite as a substrate for your marine aquarium. Avoid gathering live sand from a coastal beach because it may contain harmful pesticides or waste. Whether you use live sand as the main filtration system or not (using live sand without additional standard filtration systems is not recommended for beginners), make sure that the sand contains a good growth of organisms. These "mini" animals constantly aerate the sand and so distributes oxygen to all the substrate layers.

Your live sand may not be wholly living by the time you get it home from your dealer — many of the organisms in the sand may die. This decomposing material can cause ammonia levels to rise. High ammonia levels can be lethal to your fish. There really is no foolproof method of cleaning live sand without destroying the beneficial organisms as well.

You need to let your live sand go though a natural cycling process in your tank. This cycle usually lasts anywhere from a few days to a couple of weeks. The beneficial bacteria in the sand remove dead and dying debris during this time. It is best to hold off on adding a bunch of new fish to your aquarium after you have purchased live sand. Instead, monitor your water conditions until the ammonia level rises and fall, followed by a rise and fall in the nitrite level. When the nitrite level falls off after peaking, your tank is conditioned, and you can add new fish.

How much should I add?

It is best to add live sand in small increments. You can start with one pound per gallon, and then add more each week until the total layer of sand is about 2 inches. This method keeps the lower layers from becoming oxygen-starved and producing hydrogen sulfide, which can be lethal to your fish. The good news is that live sand is fairly inexpensive.

When live sand is added directly to the glass on the bottom, you need to use a little bit less sand than if you were using an undergravel filtration and dolomite substrate beneath (an inch to an inch and a half of live sand should be used). Too much sand will clog easily and prevent water flow.

Adding other critters

One good way to increase the filtration effectiveness of live sand after its cycling is complete is to add other invertebrates such as worms, snails, sea stars, and other burrowing invertebrates that keep the oxygen flowing throughout the surface area. These animals can be added periodically (every few weeks as your aquarium space allows) as your system matures. Small invertebrates are readily available at fish shops and other types of pet stores.

Putting in Plastic Divers and Other Oddities

Plastic divers, treasure chests, mermaids, sunken ships that bubble, castles, and mutant oysters may be fine and dandy in the safety department, but you need to exercise a little control when buying these items or your aquarium may end up looking like a scene from *Toy Story*.

Manufactured decorations sold in aquarium shops are quite safe for freshwater tanks (you never want to put these in a marine tank or you may get hassled by your saltwater buddies) but they tend to become a little unsightly, and will turn your naturally behaving fish into Toys R Us kids in a heartbeat.

One exception to this rule is the use of new synthetic corals, which are difficult to tell apart from the real thing these days. Synthetic coral weighs less than its natural counterpart and is completely safe. Use of synthetic coral is also helpful in conserving the environment. Purchasing this product means one less item taken from its rightful place in the wild.

Artificial items like plastic scuba divers do not help much when you are trying to get your fish into the spawning mood either. Be honest, would you feel romantic with a larger-than-life man with a knife standing over your favorite make-out spot? I didn't think so.

The natural tank

When aquascaping, keep your fish's natural habitat in mind. A natural tank shows the beauty of your fish in a better light, and allows them the freedom to act more naturally. Many native decorations such as plants, rocks, and wood have a lot to do with the successful spawning of many freshwater and brackish species.

By providing natural conditions in your aquarium, you can enjoy the environmental interactions that make aquarium keeping so fascinating. For example, a guppy weaving its way in and out of dense plant leaves is much more exciting to watch than an oscar trying to make lunch out of a plastic diver's helmet.

Providing a balanced aquatic system for your fish shows your children basic biological principals that they can apply to other scientific areas in the future. The delicate balance between plant and animal life in a marine, freshwater, or brackish tank is easily illustrated in an aquarium ecosystem.

Chapter 5

The Equipment (And Other Technical Stuff)

In the wild, a fish's environment functions without equipment for one basic reason: Mother Nature takes care of everything. You know the old saying: don't upset Mother Nature. Well, unfortunately we have done just that by placing our wet pets in an enclosed environment. So at home, we need to provide the natural systems that we have taken away in captivity. Now that you have your aquarium tank and stand, you need some equipment to keep it running smoothly. An aquarium's equipment is the life-blood of the whole system.

Ocean, river, and pond water is heated and regulated by the sun and seasons. In your home aquarium, you duplicate these effects by using a heater, thermometer, and artificial lighting.

In the wild, currents remove fish waste and rain replenishes the water. Natural bacteria help eliminate waste, plant debris, and other undesirable materials. At home, you accomplish these necessary tasks with filters, water changes, protein skimmers, and other specialty equipment.

As you can see, aquarium equipment is vital to the health of your fish. It also helps keep your water crystal clear, so that you can enjoy the view.

Taking the Mystery out of Filters

Filters play an essential role in performing mechanical, biological, and chemical functions in your aquarium. Some filters cover only one function; others may do two or three.

The two main functions of a filtration system are to promote the *nitrogen cycle* (which removes unwanted ammonia and nitrites from your system) by providing a medium for bacteria growth, and to remove debris and waste from the water. Filtration also helps aerate the aquarium's water by producing water flow and bubbles.

When you check out the astounding number of filters at a pet shop, you'll probably want to reach for the aspirin by the time you get to the second or third shelf. But don't worry, filters really aren't as complicated as they may first seem.

Your system needs all three types of filtration (mechanical, biological, and chemical) to perform correctly! You accomplish this balance by combining several filters, or by using one that performs all functions.

Mechanical filtration

Mechanical filtration removes solid wastes and debris suspended in the water by passing it over materials, such as synthetic foam or nylon fiber floss, which captures small particles. In time, this same filter can perform biological functions when the surface area of the filter *medium* (the foam or floss) becomes covered with beneficial bacteria. The medium is usually contained in a small cartridge that slips inside of a power filter unit, or is added in bulk form from a bag or box as with a corner filter.

Popular mechanical filter types include canisters, power filters, and corner filters. Mechanical filters come in many different sizes to accommodate the many different tank sizes. A good filter cycles your tank's water volume at least eight times per hour. Mechanical filters are rated on the number of gallons of water that flow through them every hour. If you look carefully at a filter box, you can usually find a *GPH* (gallons per hour) rating. Manufacturers generally indicate on the label which size tank the filter is designed for.

Biological filtration

The main purpose of biological filtration is to provide a home for the bacteria that produces the necessary nitrates and nitrites your aquarium needs. (All filter units eventually work in the biological realm in one form or another.) The function of nitrifying bacteria is to convert deadly *ammonia* (produced by fish waste) and food debris into less harmful nitrites and nitrates. This amazing biological purification process is also known as *detoxification* or the *nitrogen cycle*.

Large filters don't necessarily mean better biological filtration. What counts is the amount of *surface area* on the medium. The larger the total surface area of the medium, the more bacteria your system and fish have to use.

Filters you can rinse and reuse are better than the disposable type where you lose the whole bacteria colony when you throw the filter medium away. The filter box or instructions indicate what parts of the filter you need to replace and when to do it.

Undergravel filters are unique biological filters — they allow a bacteria colony to live and grow in an airspace between the filter plate and the bottom glass of the tank. Countless numbers of bacteria live in this little micro-motel on the bottom of the tank. Nitrifying bacteria is also gathered in small amounts on the carbon filter cartridges that sit on top of the plastic uplift tubes (which allow air to rise up from beneath the undergravel filter plate).

Chemical filtration

Chemical filtration takes place through mediums such as *activated zeolite* and *activated charcoal*, which absorb chemicals and dissolved minerals as water passes over them. Proper chemical filtration helps keep your aquarium water clean and sparkling.

You generally find activated charcoal in corner, undergravel, and power filters. Replace the filter medium according to the manufacturer's instructions — once a month in most cases.

Sifting through Filtration Systems

After you understand the importance of filtration systems and what they do (check out the preceding section for this information), you need to know what types of filters are out there and how they work. The many types of filters on the market fall into several categories as far as function and purpose are concerned. Technology is advancing rapidly, and a few new systems combine the best aspects of several different filters.

Undergravel filters

An undergravel filter is one of the best systems for almost any type of aquarium setup. I recommend starting with an undergravel filter, and building up from there. You can combine a good mechanical filter (such as a power filter) with an undergravel unit, and have a complete setup. You can use this type of filter with any type of system, and it's an excellent tool for creating good biological filtration.

Undergravel filters have one or more perforated plastic plates that sit on the bottom of the aquarium with a gap between the bottom of the plate and the bottom of the tank. The base plates have holes for the insertion of plastic *uplift tubes* (which allow air to flow up from beneath the filter plate) containing an airstone which connects to an air pump.

An undergravel filter pulls water down through the gravel and the slots in the plates, and returns it to the tank via the airlift tubes. During this process ammonia is broken down as the water passes over a colony of beneficial bacteria living on the substrate's surface and in the space beneath the plates. Debris is trapped along the substrate bed, making it easy to vacuum away. Periodic vacuuming is a must with this type of system to keep the bed from becoming clogged. (If you don't vacuum, eventually your substrate bed looks as if a mudslide hit it.)

Undergravel filters are great for systems that do not have big rocks or decorations to block large sections of the gravel bed. (Blocked plates create dead spots on the filter.) A medium-size substrate is best for this system — no smaller particles to fall through; or larger ones to hide big chunks of debris (your lost golf balls; you child's hidden leftovers). Set the undergravel filter in place before adding the substrate.

Sponge filters

A *sponge filter* provides biological filtration. This type of filter is simple in design and, when attached to an air pump, draws aquarium water though a large sponge that acts as a medium for bacteria to gather on. Sponge filters are good to use in quarantine and hospital tanks because they have no chemical filtration that can ruin the effectiveness of medications you may be using. Sponge filters are also useful in fry tanks, because they eliminate the danger of youngsters getting sucked up into standard filtration units. However, sponge filters only take care of biological filtration and are inadequate for use in large tanks. One other problem with a sponge filter is that it makes your aquarium look kind of like the junk shelf underneath your kitchen sink.

Corner filters

Corner filters function primarily as mechanical filters but also provide biological and chemical filtration. This is the oldest filtration system known to the aquarium hobby. Corner filters were originally designed for the small aquariums that were the staple of aquarium-keeping years and years ago. Generally, this clear plastic filter is shaped like a small square box and contains an airstone that pushes water through a layer of charcoal and floss with the help of an air pump. A corner filter is supposed to rest on the gravel bed inside the tank (if you can manage to keep it from floating all over creation and back by weighting it down with small pebbles or gravel).

Corner filters are good only for cleaning small aquariums and can be quite noisy. This type of filter is almost obsolete due to the emergence of better pump-driven systems and electronically powered units. You can still buy corner filters at superstores, but don't waste your money. There are much better filter products out there to choose from. If you do happen to get stuck with one, remember that corner filters are usually used only on freshwater tanks.

Power filters

Power filters are cool because you can use them for mechanical, chemical, and biological filtration. A power filter runs on electricity (with an internal motor so a pump isn't needed) and usually hangs on the outside of the aquarium. Power filters are box-shaped and come in a variety of sizes to meet the needs of different-sized tanks. These units usually have one or two slots on the inside of the unit that hold removable fiber-coated _filter pads_. The inside of these cartridges usually contain charcoal.

A power filter sucks up tank water through an intake tube, which hangs inside the aquarium. The water passes over the filter pads (which house biological colonies which provide biological filtration) and then returns to the water surface. The charcoal in the pads work as chemical filters, and the fibers pick up debris.

Clean the pads on these filters with dechlorinated water or replace them every month. Unfortunately, replacing the pads destroys the biological colony.

Some power filters contain a _bio-wheel,_ which rotates so that it comes into contact with both the water and beneficial oxygen in the air. This wheel keeps the bacteria colony alive even if you change the internal pad. Biowheels are the best type of power filters to buy.

You can use power filters in any type of system.

Powerheads

A *powerhead* is a cool piece of equipment that isn't really classified as a filter, but it can help increase an undergravel filter's output and efficiency by drawing water up through the tubes at a faster rate than most air pumps can. A powerhead is nothing more than an electric motor-driven pump sealed in hard plastic which you can insert into the top of the uplift tubes of an undergravel filter system.

The really neat thing about powerheads is that they have adjustable valves to regulate the speed of the airflow (thus increasing or decreasing the speed and force of the water flow). This little valve is convenient (not to mention fun to play with) in smaller tanks when you want to cut down the flow to keep the tank's inhabitants from being blown all over the aquarium or permanently embedded in the glass walls. Powerheads also have a rotating outflow that you can turn to direct the water flow to a specific area in your aquarium. (Or turn the outflow straight up and have your whole family shower at the same time.)

Canister filters

A canister filter provides biological, chemical, and mechanical filtration. This type of unit is very popular with hobbyists and is often used on larger aquarium systems. A canister filter contains several media compartments that usually contain sponges, carbon, and some type of ceramic or aqua-charged medium. The aquarium water is drawn through the filter via hoses attached to a high-pressure pump.

Canister filters are capable of turning over several hundred gallons of aquarium water per hour and have an internal motor to accomplish this task. Most canister filters sit on the floor beneath the aquarium, but some models attach to the back of the aquarium glass (hang on tank, also know as H.O.T). You can adjust the filter's output to any part of the tank that meets your personal desires. A canister filter can be very large, bulky, and unsightly, so make sure you have a place to hide it so that your house doesn't look like a water-processing plant.

Fluidized bed filters

A fluidized bed filter is one of the best biological filters on the market. The only drawback is that they can be very expensive. But if you happen to make a few extra bucks selling some fry, it's well worth the investment to purchase one of these units.

Fluidized bed filters are extremely compact and use sand as a filter medium. The sand is continuously kept wet by water flowing through it and has a huge surface area where a large colony of beneficial bacteria can grow and multiply. This type of filter improves oxygenation because the sand is constantly tumbled in a stream of water that creates what is known as a *fluidized bed*. Sand grains move with the water flow to create a high-quality transfer between the water and the bacteria present.

Another important feature of fluidized bed filters is that they respond quickly to any rise in the aquarium water's ammonia levels. This filter does biological filtration only, so you must also have mechanical and chemical filters working in conjunction with it in order to balance your overall cleaning system.

Pond filters

Most pond filters are just glorified canister filters in box form. One is shown in Figure 5-1. Some pond filters are even disguised as flowerpots. Some models go directly in the pond, whereas others rest on dry land. These filters turn over massive amounts of water, which is essential for a healthy, well-planned pond system. The only problem with a pond filter is that you have to have a pond to put it in. (Putting a good pond in your backyard will probably be on the same wish list as the swimming pool you always wanted.)

Figure 5-1:
A pond
filter kit.

Natural filtration

Long before artificial filters appeared on the market, nature had its own special way of taking care of everyday cleaning. Plants in freshwater and brackish systems, and live rock and live sand in marine systems, act as natural filters and complement the manufactured units in your home aquarium.

Plants

Freshwater and brackish plants (including algae) help biological and chemical filtration in the home aquarium. These aquatic marvels remove ammonia, nitrates, and carbon dioxide from the water with relative ease. In marine aquariums, algae serves the same purpose.

In aquatic systems, plants take in inorganic molecules and carbon dioxide from the aquarium water and return oxygen and organic molecules for your fish's benefit as long as the plants have enough light to carry out the process of photosynthesis.

Live rock and live sand

Live rock and live sand contain many natural micro-organisms which help the filtration process. If you have a marine system, look into purchasing a little bit of high-quality rock and live sand.

Gauging Heaters and Thermometers

If you plan to set up any type of tropical freshwater or marine system, you need to have at least one *heater*.

The two types of heaters you can purchase at a fish shop are:

- **Submersible heaters,** which as their name suggests, you completely submerse in the aquarium water. Ideally, you should place them in a diagonal line across the rear piece of glass, so that heat flows evenly throughout the tank.

  This type of heater has a watertight glass tube containing an electrical element wound around a ceramic core. A small light red or orange light lets you know whether the heater is on or off. At the top of the heater is a temperature adjustment valve you use to change the range of your heater. Submersible heaters usually have an internal thermometer that you can see through the glass tube. You simply rotate the adjustment valve so that the temperature line moves to the temperature you want to set. The heater automatically maintains the temperature you choose.

Make absolutely sure that the heater is a submersible model before you put it completely under water!

✔ **Nonsubmersible heaters** hang on the aquarium frame, with the glass tube hanging in the water. The adjustment valve sits above the water line. This type of heater generally does not have an internal thermometer. You make adjustments in small increments by turning the valve and repeatedly checking the temperature.

The safest arrangement is to keep two heaters operating at the same time just in case one unit happens to fail. In this unfortunate situation, disaster can be adverted by the second heater, which can keep the water temperature from dropping while you replace the failed unit.

The rule for determining which size heater your aquarium needs is to allow 5 watts of heater per gallon. For example, a 50-gallon aquarium needs at least a 250-watt heater.

Never remove a heater from the aquarium without letting it sit for at least 20 minutes AFTER unplugging it! Never turn a heater on for the first time in an aquarium until AFTER you let it sit in the water for at least 20 minutes!

If your heater does not have a built-in thermometer, you can purchase one separately. Extreme fluctuations in water temperature can cause disease or death to your fish, so it is important to closely monitor the thermometer readings. Thermometers are very inexpensive and come in three main varieties.

✔ **A hanging thermometer** hangs from the aquarium from on the inside of the aquarium glass. This style of thermometer is composed of a capillary tube containing mercury that moves up and to display the temperature.

✔ **A stick-on thermometer** is flat and adheres to the outside of the aquarium glass. Degree panels light up as the temperature changes, displaying the current water temperature. The two disadvantages of stick-on thermometers are that they're permanent and they can be hard to read in rooms with low lighting.

✔ **A floating thermometer** slowly cruises around the top of your aquarium, and displays the current temperature where the water level meets the glass. (Unless you watch a bunch of tennis, you may get whiplash trying to read it.)

Making Little Swirls (And Other Cool Bubble Projects)

One of the big advantages of having an aquarium is that it makes a bunch of cool sounds. Air bubbles produce the best tone and can be very soothing. After you get your filter system all figured out, it's time to have a little fun and create a few cheerful bubbles.

You can do this in a couple of cool ways.

- ✔ **An air pump** (used to run filters and decorations) usually has some kind of bubble or current outflow that is fun to watch.
- ✔ **Airstones** can create mega-bubbles, which will impress your friends and neighbors.

Air pumps

An *air pump* is kind of a "jack of all trades." Pumps can power filters, airstones, and several types of plastic decorations. Air pumps are available in both vibrator and piston models. When added to an undergravel filter, a pump drives air though the uplift tubes. The air is then broken up into small bubbles as it passes through an airstone.

An air pump should always sit above the midpoint level of the aquarium to avoid water backflow if electrical power is lost.

Air pumps come in a variety of different sizes to suit almost any filter. (All filters are driven either by an air pump or an electric motor.)

- ✔ **Vibrator pumps** are great for the home aquarium because they are not as expensive as piston pumps, and don't require a whole lot of mechanical maintenance. Vibrator pumps do have one big drawback: They can be very noisy, especially if you purchase a poor-quality model.
- ✔ **Piston pumps** are much more powerful than vibrator pumps and are often used on very large or multiple systems. The disadvantage to piston pumps is that they are hard to find, need to be oiled, and require traps to keep oil from getting into the aquarium system.

Airstones and circulation

An *airstone* is a neat little tube-shaped artificial stone used to split the air supplied by the pump into small bubbles. These bubbles help increase water oxygenation. Airstones are generally made of ceramic or perforated wood-based materials. Airstones can be short and round or tall and thin. The tall stones tend to emit a finer stream of bubbles than the shorter ones do. Airstones are very inexpensive, and should be replaced when they become clogged.

You attach airstones to one side of standard air-line tubing, and attach the other end of the tubing to the air pump. You can use airstones in undergravel filter tubes, corner filters, and animated decorations.

To create a big bubble stream in your aquarium, you can always purchase a bubble disk. A *bubble disk* is a larger version of an airstone that looks like a plastic flying disc. You simply connect the disk to an air pump with tubing and then slip it into the tank. The disk makes a large stream of bubbles, which can aid in water circulation. Bubble disks may become clogged with algae (usually this takes quite some time), but you can clean them by rinsing them gently under clear water.

Try to stay away from *bubble wands*. These delicate little stones are shaped like rods and usually have suction cups attached to the back of them so that they can be mounted on glass. The problem with bubble wands is that they can become clogged and stop functioning quite quickly. Bubble wands break easily, so you may end up trashing half the decorations in your tank trying to remove one for cleaning.

Connecting Tubing, Valves, and Tees

Air-line tubing functions like the veins and arteries in the human body. Without your veins and arteries, your internal organs would just kind of lie there, lifeless, because they have nothing connecting them — nothing keeping the life-blood flowing. So it is with air-line tubing and your aquarium equipment; therefore, a supply of good air-line tubing is an absolute must.

I need to mention some of the other important elements of your aquarium system. At first, you may think that some of this equipment is unnecessary, but everything has its place. Even if you don't use everything, some of these extra gadgets are nice to have lying around just in case of an emergency. Besides, the more fish junk you have, the better you look in the eyes of other hobbyists.

Air-line tubing

Air-line tubing connects equipment, such as airstones and bubble disks, to an air pump. Some tubing is shown in Figure 5-2. Tubing is really a necessity — not an option. Older tubing (the standard clear stuff you purchase at your local pet store) is semi-rigid. Standard tubing has a few drawbacks: It tends to crack as it ages, turns yellow, and bends out of shape (even when it is still new, right out of the package) when you set it over equipment connections. Because it is rigid, older tubing also tends to pinch and kink easily, which can diminish or completely cut off the airflow to your equipment. Working with old air-line tubing can be as frustrating as untangling a cheap garden hose.

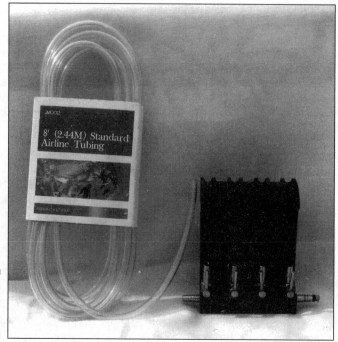

Figure 5-2:
Some
tubing.

Fortunately, a new type of tubing manufactured out of a silicone/rubber-based material provides greater flexibility and makes this superior tubing much easier to work with. Rubber tubing is blue-green in color and blends in nicely with the natural tint of the aquarium water. Rubber tubing is easy to bend, simple to maneuver around decorations, and does not crack easily when it begins to age.

Valves and tees

Valves and tees help you split the air from an air pump in several directions. You use *valves* to run several pieces of equipment or decorations off of one air pump. A valve usually hangs on the back of the tank, and is made out of plastic or brass. The air-line tubing from the pump hooks into one side, and the tubing directed toward decorations and equipment is connected to one of the multiple outlets on the valve. You can adjust the strength of the airflow coming out of the valve for each piece of equipment simply by turning the individual shut-off nozzles.

Tees are usually made of plastic or copper, and are shaped like the letter "T." A tee splits a single air source in two directions.

Creating the Best Lighting

Unless you can see in the dark like Catwoman, you need a little bit of lighting for your aquarium. Your fish probably were not born in a black hole either, and will be much happier if you provide them with a little daylight. Without light, your fish can't see their food or each other, and may miss the mark by a fraction of an inch when they spawn. Lighting kits of all types are available, including the ones shown in Figure 5-3.

Figure 5-3:
Lighting
options.

Live plants in an aquarium require light in order to *photosynthesize* and manufacture their own food and expel oxygen beneficial to your fish. If you have a marine system with invertebrates, many of them may also require light to survive and grow.

Setting Up the Hood

Some hoods have a built-in light (full hoods); others don't. If you purchase a unit that has a light built in to it, you can change the bulb when it burns out or put in a bulb that better suits your needs. Check the manufacturers' instructions so that you don't end up with a meltdown due to excessive heat build-up. Also make sure that the hood fits the tank correctly to prevent water loss from evaporation and the escape of any high-jumping fish.

If your light is not connected to the hood *(strip light),* and sits on top of a glass cover *(canopy),* you can experiment a little bit by moving the light around to see which position illuminates the tank best. The main advantage of strip lights is that they provide you with the freedom to add more lighting later on; full hoods do not.

Make sure the lighting system is unplugged when you put it on top of your tank. Do not plug the unit in until you're sure it's stable!

Looking at bulb types

You have several bulb options to consider:

- **Tungsten (incandescent)** lighting is used in household lamps. Tungsten lighting is not good for aquariums because it is too hot, burns out quickly, produces excess algae, has a limited spectrum, and distributes light unevenly. You may see colored tungsten lights in your pet store, but they don't show your fish's colors very well, so just avoid them.

- **Actinic blue** bulbs produce long-wave ultraviolet radiation. This type of lighting is great for plant growth but also produces an abundance of algae if you have it on a lot.

- **Metal halide** lights produce a very pleasing effect in your aquarium because they have a high red and yellow spectrum. Unfortunately, they are very expensive. But if you plan on setting up a reef tank, metal halides are great for marine invertebrates. You can also use them in heavily planted freshwater tanks.

- High-powered **mercury vapor lights** can hang over aquariums and are often used to light very deep tanks. Mercury vapor lights are a little short in the green and blue wavelength department, and may need supplemental lighting to complete a full spectrum. The cool thing about mercury vapor lights is that they usually retain 90 percent of their original capacity over a period of several years.

- **Fluorescent lighting** is great for aquariums with live plants. They last a long time, do not emit excessive heat, and have an even spectrum of light. There's a fluorescent light to match almost any system you plan to set up. Even though they continue to burn, fluorescent lights often begin to dim when they lose a portion of their power after about six or seven months.

Whichever lighting you choose, make sure to purchase it from a pet store. Even though a hardware store can sell you a replacement bulb that fits your hood, these bulbs were not intended for that purpose and will not provide good lighting.

Making a lighting choice

The best lighting system for you depends a lot on your personal taste, the depth of your aquarium, and whether you have live plants or invertebrates in your tank. Some hobbyists swear by one certain type or brand of lighting, while others swear by another. But, here are a few general rules you can follow.

Actinic blue lighting is important to many types of invertebrates in a marine system. Combine it with a fluorescent tube to produce lighting that provides a pleasing look and helps promote invertebrate growth. For most brackish and freshwater systems, a good fluorescent tube can do the job.

Really Expensive Toys

Hey, just because I'm a fish nerd, doesn't mean I can't have a few play toys. Car nerds get to buy expensive hubcaps and awesome paint jobs, so I get my own little wish list, too. Let me be the first to wish that I had more of the equipment on the following list!

Protein skimmers (essential for a good marine system)

Protein skimmers are a piece of equipment that remove unwanted chemical substances from your tank by producing a fine stream of foam (see Figure 5-4). You can then easily remove the debris from a collection cup. Protein skimmers are most efficient in marine systems. Be aware that skimming often removes trace elements, which you can replace by adding bottled trace mixes.

Ozone (not essential)

You can use an *ozone unit* together with a protein skimmer. This machine produces ozone, which is a powerful tool for killing bacteria, parasites, and viruses, by generating electricity. An ozone unit also helps increase the effectiveness of water purification by oxidizing food and waste compounds.

UV units (not essential)

Ultraviolet sterilizers kill parasites and bacteria in your aquarium water. These units contain an ultraviolet lamp, which you need to change two or three times per year.

Looking at an UV light can damage your eyes! Be careful when installing this unit!

Reverse osmosis units (not essential)

A *reverse osmosis* (RO) unit removes minerals from the aquarium water. RO filters remove particles, such as chlorine and chloramine, with a small filter, which, in turn, produces very soft water.

Catching the New Wave: Reef Tanks

Aquarium systems have changed dramatically over the years, and a couple of systems have recently become very popular. Although detailing all these new systems is beyond the scope of this book, I can give you a quick look at some of them.

A *reef tank* is a marine system that tries to mimic a natural coral reef. One is shown in Figure 5-5. A reef tank may have invertebrates, fish, or a combination of the two. Full reef tanks can be expensive, and describing how to set them up is really beyond the scope of this book.

Figure 5-5:
A reef tank.

Berlin system

A *Berlin system* is basically a reef tank that utilizes filtration through the presence of live rock and a protein skimmer. This system is still in the controversial and experimental stage and should be left to experienced marine hobbyists.

Jaubert method (plenum)

The *Jaubert method* is similar to the Berlin system, except that it contains a 2- or 3-inch dead space (called the plenum) on the bottom of the tank where anerobic bacteria live. These bacteria help eliminate nitrates. This is also a system that should be left to more experienced fishkeepers. I've depicted one in Figure 5-6.

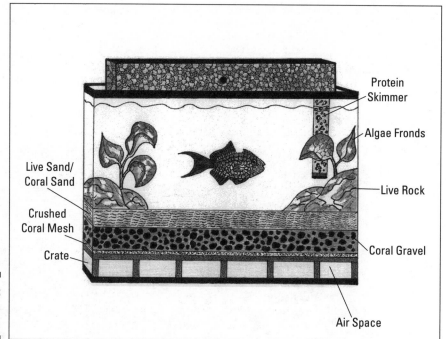

Protein Skimmer

Algae Fronds

Live Rock

Live Sand/ Coral Sand

Crushed Coral Mesh

Crate

Coral Gravel

Air Space

Figure 5-6: A plenum system.

Short on cash (Now what?)

Okay, if you're like me and never have any money, you can still set up a halfway decent aquarium system. Probably the least expensive way to get a small system going is to go to a superstore and buy a freshwater aquarium kit. Make sure to check the contents on the box to insure that you have a heater, thermometer, airline tubing, a filter, light, hood, and pump. Grab a few bags of gravel on the way out the door, and you're ready to go.

If you want to set up a marine or brackish system, but are short on cash, I recommend holding off until your financial situation improves.

Chapter 6

Water Sources (All Water Is Not Created Equal)

In This Chapter

▶ Considering the pros and cons of tap water, rainwater, bottled water, and well water

▶ Looking at saltwater and synthetic saltwater

▶ Adding water to your aquarium

Adding the correct type of water to your aquarium is very important to the long-term health of your fish. Water can be obtained from many sources, but only a few provide the correct requirements for your aquatic pets. Understanding the correct water perimeters for your tank and choosing reliable sources for your water can help you to become a successful hobbyist right off the bat.

My college biology professor made the entire class look at pond water through a microscope. I could barely believe my eyes. There must have been 800 billion creatures floating or crawling in it. Remember that almost any natural source of water has some type of living organism in it.

Water Types

You can obtain water from a variety of sources. The following sections cover the pros and cons of tap water, rainwater, bottled water, and well water.

Tap water

In order to protect the human population from being killed off by drinking water, water companies add chemicals such as *chlorine* to wipe out organisms with the potential to make us all sick. This treated *tap water* may be safe for humans, but it can be deadly to your aquatic pets.

You have to get rid of the chlorine from water, whether you use it in a freshwater, saltwater, or brackish tank. Chlorine kills all types of fish and invertebrates.

Getting rid of the nasties

You have a few options for removing chlorine and chloramines from tap water to make it perfectly safe to use in your aquarium. One option you can choose (if you're like me, you'll opt for this method because it's the easiest), is to go down to your local fish store and purchase a bottle of *dechlorinator,* a product which instantly removes chlorine and chloramines from your water. After adding dechlorinator, you can safely put your new fish in the aquarium water.

The best time to add dechlorinator is after your tank is filled and all equipment is up and running.

You need to dechlorinate all the water you add to your aquarium — even the water you put in to replenish water lost to evaporation.

I ran out of dechlorinator, now what do I do?

Company is on the way, your tanks are low, and you're out of dechlorinator. No problem, except that your company happens to be fellow hobbyists who want to go over your aquariums with a fine-toothed comb. Nothing is worse than looking uncool in front of your friends, so you're frantically trying to figure out a way to *top off* your aquariums (fill them up completely) before your guests arrive.

If you want to be a practical hobbyist, you can simply dechlorinate water the old-fashioned way. (Don't panic; this method doesn't involve a lot of work.) Take a few plastic jugs (gallon milk containers work great) and rinse them thoroughly with clear water. Glass jars work fine, but they can break, so plastic is really your best bet for safety.

Never use soap or other chemicals to clean out containers for aquarium water! The soap leaves a residue that can be deadly to your fish.

After rinsing, fill the plastic containers with tap water, allow them to sit with the lids off for 48 hours, and, voilá, chlorine-free water! You can add an *airstone* (a small stone that splits an air supply from your pump into smaller bubbles) to each jug to cut your waiting time in half (24 hours). If you keep three or four jugs sitting around, you always have a supply of safe water. When company is on the way, simply grab a jug, and start filling your tanks.

Guarding against metals

Let the water from your tap run down the sink for a minute before you start filling containers with water for your aquariums. This precaution allows water that's been in constant contact with metal sink pipes (and as a result is slightly contaminated) to flow through.

Depending on the area in which you live, your tap water may have *metal deposits,* such as copper, in it. Large amounts of metal can be deadly for your fish. Marine invertebrates are especially vulnerable to copper. To be safe, you can buy water treatments from your pet dealer that safely remove the metals from water.

Rainwater

A few hobbyists collect *rainwater* for use in their aquariums. This process is really more trouble than it's worth, unless you have a lot of spare time and energy on your hands or live in a region of the country that receives a tremendous amount of annual rainfall. If you live in the desert southwest, your fish will probably die from old age before you collect enough water to top off your tank.

Another problem with rainwater is that it may contain contaminants from factories, smog, and other pollutants. To be honest, you may end up spending twice as much for chemicals to treat your rainwater than if you had just used your trusty old kitchen faucet.

If you decide to gather rainwater to help condition your fish for breeding (see Chapters 17 and 18 for more information), make sure that you use nonmetallic containers for collection. Also keep in mind that rainwater tends to be very soft (low in dissolved minerals) and may not be suitable for hard-water fish. Hard-water fish (whose water has a high mineral content in the wild) that are forced to live in soft water conditions can not spawn properly or maintain good health.

You should always check the *water perimeters* (specific water requirements) for your particular aquatic species before using rainwater.

The advantages of bottled water (not Perrier)

Okay, when I mention *bottled water,* I'm talking about the kind you can get in a machine outside of your local grocery store or the gallon jugs that you can purchase inside. Let me put it this way: If the water is really expensive, it's the wrong kind; if it's inexpensive, it's the right kind.

You can use bottled water in your aquarium without adding any chemicals to it. But to be safe, I always add dechlorinator to my water no matter where it came from. Spending a few pennies on dechlorinator is a much better route to take than losing a bunch of expensive fish.

Well water (don't count on it)

At one time, I lived on a farm. A deep well, located somewhere out on the back 40, furnished the farm's entire water supply. The water from this well was truly one of life's great mysteries — all the filters and chemicals in the world couldn't change the composition of this amazing liquid.

The water was guaranteed to turn to every color of the rainbow within a period of five minutes when I took a shower, and my body took on those glorious colors when I stepped out. Instead of buying an expensive Halloween costume, trick-or-treaters saved money by coming over to my house for a shower.

The point of my reminiscence is that well water is generally not a good source to use for filling your aquariums because too many bad things can get into it, including sulfur, lead, and mud. If you insist on using it anyway, take a small sample down to your local water company and ask them to test it for you. After you get a dirty look from the water department clerk because your sample destroyed her expensive equipment, you can forget that bad idea altogether and use some real water.

Collecting Water (Why You Want to Forget This Bad Idea)

If you're planning to set up a freshwater aquarium, someone has probably suggested that you can be a real naturalist and go down to your local river or pond to snag the water for it. You may be thinking that this isn't a half-bad idea — you can keep your fish closer to their natural environment. After your dream of a cameo on *National Geographic* fades a bit, you can forget this idea entirely.

To begin with, most of the freshwater fish you purchase from the pet shop are raised in a hatchery and have never been near any river or pond. These fish are raised in standard aquarium water conditions. When you collect water from a pond or river, you take a great risk of introducing disease into your tank.

If you live near the coast and are planning to set up a saltwater tank, you probably thought about collecting *natural seawater* for your marine aquarium. To start with, you would have to collect water that is well away from the beach area where it can be polluted by sewage, boat fuel leaks, and so on. Next, you would have to lug gallon after gallon of water back to your home, and the living organisms in the seawater would start dying during the process (usually within an hour). This job can turn into a real nightmare, real fast. You never know what dangerous organisms and pollutants lurk in sea water, so save yourself a lot of heartache and go buy a synthetic salt mix.

Using Synthetic Marine Mixes for Your Saltwater Tank

Why bother with the back-breaking work of carting water from the ocean when you can buy *synthetic saltwater mixes* that are easy to use, formulated to mimic natural seawater, and provide all the trace elements that your fish need?

Marine salt mixes come in many different sizes. You usually find it in a bag or a small box in sizes to treat 20-, 50-, and 100- gallon tanks. If you have a 55-gallon tank, a bag rated to treat 50 gallons should work. Remember that the substrate, decorations, and equipment take up quite a bit of the water volume in your tank, so you won't need as much salt as you think you do.

Mixing up marine water

You can mix up your synthetic marine water in a couple of different ways. The first method is to set up your tank completely and just dump the salt into the water. However, this is not the best option because most people add too much salt right at the start, forgetting to take into consideration the water volume that the decorations and substrate displace. If, when you test your water with a *hydrometer* (a gauge that measures the amount of *salinity*, or salt, in water), you find out that your salt level is too high, what can you do? Well, the only way to fix things is to remove salt water and add fresh water until you reach the proper level. That job can be a real chore: Remove water, add water, check levels, remove water, add water, check levels, remove water, take aspirin, check levels . . . . I think you get the idea.

Take heart; there is a better way. The easiest method is to take a bunch of plastic buckets (the 5-gallon size is best, because they won't be too heavy) and mix the water and salt in them before you add it to your tank. That way, when you add a bucketful of water to your tank, the correct salinity level is already established. When you figure out the correct amount of the salt mixture to add to one bucket, you use that same amount for the rest of the buckets.

Checking the salinity

You can choose from a couple of different types of hydrometers to check the salinity of the water you're mixing.

✔ One type is shaped like a box and has a floating needle, as shown in Figure 6-1. You simply fill the box with water from your mixing bucket, and the needle magically rises and points to the salinity level. The only problem with this type of hydrometer is that the needle sometimes sticks or falls out of the box.

✔ Another type of hydrometer floats in the water and resembles a thin fishing bobber. Readings are taken along a shaded area. Unfortunately, this type of hydrometer can be very difficult to read in a bucket.

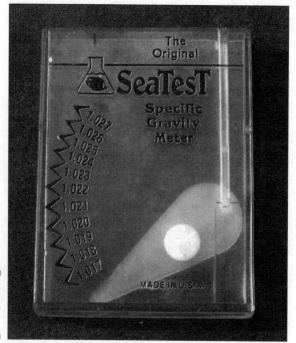

Figure 6-1:
A
hydrometer.

After checking your salinity readings, add more fresh water or salt to adjust the level to where you want it. (The hydrometer reading should be about 1.022–1.023 for most marine fish.) If the hydrometer is shaped like a box, the needle will point to the correct reading; if it is shaped like a thermometer, a mercury line will display the water's salinity. Make sure to keep track of how much salt mix you add to the bucket so that you can quickly duplicate your newfound aquatic recipe in the other buckets.

When mixing synthetic sea salt, it is important that the water temperature is the same in each bucket. Water temperature can affect salinity levels.

Adding Water to Your Aquarium

When you're ready to add your carefully treated water to your aquarium, do it slowly so that you don't disturb the substrate or any of the decorations already in the tank. One trick is to place a small dinner plate or saucer on the substrate and pour the water directly onto the plate, which acts as a barrier to keep your substrate from being spread all over the tank into tiny mounds that look like anthills.

Chapter 7

Those Crazy Chemicals

*H*ave you ever been at the aquarium store and noticed shelf after shelf of mysterious-looking *chemicals*? Ever wonder whether you need a wizard's license or some type of magical scroll to decipher and use them properly?

In this chapter, I take a closer look at a few of the chemical products made for specific use in home aquariums. There are a multitude of aquarium chemicals out there, believe me. It is virtually impossible to cover them all in this chapter. (I doubt that I could cover them all in this entire book!) But by the time you finish reading this chapter, you will be on the right road to becoming a real chemical wizard.

Understanding Chemical Use

Just as there are guidelines to follow for using the chemicals you find around your home (especially in the laundry room and kitchen), there are rules for using aquarium chemicals as well. After all, you wouldn't even think of mixing ammonia and chlorine to help whiten your laundry unless you wanted to spend five days in an oxygen tent at the Cloud Nine hospital, right? Well your fish really don't cope well with excessive mixtures and overuse of chemicals either.

Chemicals are chemicals. I cannot stress this point enough! Any chemical can be dangerous if it is mixed with the wrong substance. Although this is not a common hazard with aquarium chemicals, certain mixtures and overdoses can be lethal to your fish. Before you use any type of chemical, read the bottle very carefully.

A few species of aquatic animals cannot tolerate certain chemicals. For example, most invertebrates in a marine system die if you use a copper-based chemical to treat fish disease.

Overdosing — adding too many chemicals at one time, or even adding too many chemicals over a long period of time — can affect the water conditions (pH and so on) in your aquarium. Dumping bottle after bottle of treatments into your tank also makes your fish look like they're swimming around in a swamp, and I guarantee that they'll end up hating you for it. The point is that you shouldn't just dump 15 bottles of chemicals into your aquarium hoping one of them will work. (If you have to step carefully while walking across your fish room to avoid crushing discarded chemical bottles, you're probably overdosing.)

When should I use chemicals?

When you treat diseases, use chemicals only as a last resort. Try one of the many more natural ways available to help your fish though an illness. (See Chapter 16 for more detailed information.) If you're just starting or maintaining an aquarium, you can use chemicals a little more frequently (because you need to dechlorinate your water and condition it). But you still don't want to over do it. Too much of anything is usually bad in some way or another.

Following instructions to the letter

Always follow all the manufacturer's *instructions* on the label! Don't skip any steps, and follow through on the entire recommended treatment or usage time! It's the safest way, believe me.

If you don't understand the instructions or the ingredients on a chemical's label (sometimes they seem to be written in some weird alien dialect), don't hesitate to contact the product's manufacturer and have someone there help clear up your questions. If you're in a hurry, ask your local dealer for help.

Chemicals to Start Your Aquarium

When you first set up a brand new aquarium, certain chemicals can help you out a great deal. You can purchase most of the chemicals mentioned in this section at your local pet shop, and the other ones you can most likely find around your own house. (If not, sneak over to your neighbor's house and rummage through his cupboards until you find them.)

Glass cleaner

You can use a *household glass cleaner* to clean the **outside** of your aquarium. Standard window cleaning products such as Windex work very well. Cleaners that have a citrus base seem to work the best. They leave the glass clean and streak free and also help to keep fingerprints from reappearing on the glass. (This is especially useful when you have small children in the house.)

Never use a household glass cleaner on the inside of your tank! Glass cleaner residue can kill your fish very quickly.

The only thing that should be used to clean out the inside of an aquarium is fresh water. Never use soaps or any other types of chemicals on the inside glass.

Dechlorinator

When you first add water to your aquarium, you have to remove the chlorine from it. Chlorine will kill your fish. *Dechlorinator* usually comes in liquid form, and removes harmful chlorine instantly. With most brands, you need to add only a few drops per gallon to do the job. Basically, the main purpose of this type of product is to make the aquarium water safe for your fish without your having to wait for the chlorine to dissipate naturally (which usually takes 24–48 hours). Check out Chapter 6 for more on dechlorinating water.

Water conditioner

Water conditioners often combine a declorinator with other chemicals that instantly detoxify the heavy metals in tap water. You can use a conditioner when you are setting up a new aquarium, changing water, or adding water. Many sources of water (old wells and the like) may contain harmful metals that a water conditioner can detoxify.

Cycling chemicals you can use

I know it can be really hard to wait around for an aquarium to complete the nitrogen cycle. Depending on the type of system you have — freshwater, saltwater, or brackish — and the overall size of your aquarium tank, the entire nitrogen cycle can take weeks or even months to complete. *Cycling* products have been around for a long, long time. (I'm really not that old, I think someone told me about them!) As discussed in Chapter 8, during the nitrogen cycle, beneficial bacteria convert harmful ammonia (produced by fish waste) into less toxic nitrites. Following this conversion, another group of beneficial bacteria convert the nitrites into even less harmful nitrates. The nitrates are only harmful to your fish after they begin to build up in large quantities. The nitrates can be removed from your aquarium water though water changes.

Some cycling products can start your nitrogen cycle and speed it up as well. The appealing idea behind this particular product is really very simple. The faster your tank cycles, the faster you can add more new fish to your aquarium. (Hey, I like that speedy idea!) The sooner you have fish in your aquarium, the sooner your neighbors will envy you.

If these products speed up the cycling time and give your starter fish that extra edge, why not use them? The only danger that I can see is looking at this product as a cure-all for a tank you overstocked. Remember that these products are an aid to the nitrogen cycle, not a substitute for it!

Put it this way: If you set up a 55-gallon freshwater aquarium, and toss in a couple of tablespoons of cycling formula in an attempt to offset the 75 gold-fish you started your tank with, you are in for some serious problems. These products have a *specific purpose,* and should not be pushed to the limit.

Bacteria in a bottle

Some products speed up your aquarium's cycling time because they contain massive amounts of various *beneficial bacteria* held in a dormant state. After you add the bacteria formula to your aquarium water, the bacteria becomes completely regenerated, and rapidly consumes ammonia and nitrites. These different types of *micro-organisms* combine to create a powerful biological reduction team. Most of these products are *nonpathogenic,* and won't harm any of the plants or fish in your aquarium. It is impossible to overdose your tank with this type of product.

Bacteria on a medium

You can purchase a variation of the bacteria product mentioned in the previous section which comes as a rapid-action *biological filter medium.* This type of medium is *precolonized* (already has the bacteria attached) with a multitude of nitrifying bacteria which, in some cases, can cut your cycling time in half. The medium prevents clogging and helps maintain good water circulation in your filtration unit. This type of bacterial medium is designed to have a maximum surface area to encourage the largest supply of beneficial bacteria.

Bacteria in a box

Certain bacteria come in dry form and have an *unlimited shelf life*. The thing I like about this product is that you can keep it with your aquarium supplies and use it whenever you decide to set up a new tank. In fact, buy a couple of boxes. They look professional because they usually have weird scientific names written on the label that no one can understand. This is one great way to impress your fish buddies without spending a lot of money. You may never get around to using the bacteria, but the packages look cool.

Water clarifier

A *water clarifier* removes excess cloudiness in your aquarium caused by *bacterial blooms* (growth spurts) that have gotten out of control. Blooms are usually a result of too much organic matter in your tank.

Plant Chemicals

For all you hobbyists out there with a green thumb, I present several chemicals you can use to help your living aquarium plants thrive and grow to their full potential. (Don't try them on plastic plants, because they may turn funny colors or something.) It is important to remember that the living plants in your aquarium system have special needs that you need to meet. Your plants deserve the very best, just like your fish do.

Creating your own rainforest

If you have plants in your aquarium that come from the *Amazon region* (Amazon swords, for example), you can purchase chemicals to help create a rainforest condition in your tank. These products increase lush plant growth (without nitrates or phosphates), discourage algae and parasite growth, detoxify ammonia and nitrites, and help your plants create beneficial oxygen for your fish. They also give your plants a better chance of obtaining nutrients from the aquarium water and enhance biological filtration.

Helping your fish out at the same time

Amazon products (products that are manufactured to create a water conditions that are similar to that found in the Amazon region) provide essential macro-nutrients without stimulating algae and give your aquarium water the natural look of "peat" (yellow tinted water that is native to Amazon fishes).

You can also use these products for soft-water fish such as discus, angelfish, neons, barbs, and gouramis to create a yellow color to the water, which simulates their natural environment. This type of product often contains trace elements, vitamins, bark, and wood.

Reef Chemicals

Another category of chemicals useful in aquariums includes several different products known as *reef enhancers*. Reef enhancers are designed to encourage the rapid growth of invertebrates (which promotes good health) living in a marine aquarium. Reef enhancers also help regenerate new coral polyps (brand new corals). Using this type of product can make all the difference in the world as far as establishing proper invertebrate growth and providing your reef (live rock and so on) with a real "living look."

Potassium iodide concentrate

This product replenishes a large part of the iodide that gets stripped away through the processes of protein skimming (the removal of harmful protein from a marine system). Iodide is very beneficial to macroalgae (beneficial algae), coralline and calcareous algae (good guy algae), hard corals, and any soft corals living in your aquarium system, as well as to your fish.

Calcium chloride concentrate

A *calcium chloride concentrate* supplies the calcium necessary for any reef organisms that have shells or skeletal structures. This product deposits calcium that has been removed from the aquarium water (it's been used up by the invertebrates in the tank for growth) and helps maintain the proper water quality needed for optimal growth of soft and hard corals, mollusks, tubeworms, and calcareous and coralline algae in a marine system. Using calcium chloride may drop your pH levels, so you probably need to use a *buffer* to readjust them.

Trace element concentrate

This chemical replaces trace elements lost due to heavy filtration, use of protein skimmers, and ozonation devices. *Trace elements* are very important for the growth and overall health of invertebrates that contain symbiotic algae in their tissues.

Growth enhancers

A marine *growth enhancer* formula is designed to give you a more colorful and balanced reef. If you use this product on a continual basis, the chemicals overtake green, brown, and red algae (bad algae) so that they do not get out of control. Growth enhancers help corals and other invertebrate marine life achieve consistent reproduction and growth, which is essential to filter feeders.

Growth enhancers provide compounds that allow tiny micro-organisms to grow thickly all over the surface of your live rock. This product also provides *pigmentation priming* (helps to promote good coloration) of coraline algaes, anemones, sea mushrooms, sponges tunicates, feather dusters, live rock, and other organisms. After continual use, your corals begin to really open up, and the organisms living on your live rock display brilliant color.

Growth enhancers work in the process of breaking down organic wastes, ammonia, nitrates, nitrites, and phosphates.

Prevention and control treatments

Several chemical treatments protect the *slime coat* (a natural coating that helps to protect it against disease) on your fish's body. These products (Stress Coat is a good example) also help relieve stress and deter the onset of disease. Slime coat products are important for your fish, especially if they have just been transported or netted. Your fish's natural slime coat can easily be worn off and leave bare patches open to attack by various diseases.

Snail control products destroy snails in your freshwater aquarium, and help you keep them from coming back. Most snails are brought into the aquarium system on live plants. Snails are very sneaky and very crafty (kind of like my kids), and they have the ability to slip by even the most experienced eye. (Snails can multiply faster than your household bills and can ruin the appearance of an aquarium as they get out of control.) Once your aquarium is overrun with snails, they are almost impossible to get rid of, and they often carry diseases that can damage you fish's health.)

Chemicals for Medication

No matter what you do, disease is going to strike. Even the most experienced fishkeepers must deal with aquatic health problems from time to time. The following list gives you a few examples of products you can use to fight back when all other methods have failed. Chapter 16 has more info on keeping your fish healthy.

- ✔ **Formalin** is used to treat fish that have contracted external parasites. A formalin bath helps alleviate problems such as skin flukes.

- ✔ **Antibiotics** treat bacterial infections, fungus, ulcers, gill disease, popeye, and dropsy.

- ✔ **Malachite green** is often used in the treatment of ich *(Ichthyophthirius multifilius).*

- ✔ **Paragon** treats inflamed gills, anchor worms, copepods, open sores, hemorrhaging, and hole in the head disease.

Medications can be very confusing. Many manufacturers combine medications to treat a variety of illnesses. The label of most medication bottles lists the types of illness the product treats. These label listings help you wade through the confusion, and choose the right product for the job.

Keeping a clear head

In order for your fish to keep a clear head, you have to do the same. If you get carried away and turn your aquarium water into a chemical nightmare, your fish are going to start acting funny, suffer health problems, and face the possibility of death from toxicity. Make sure you check your water conditions are correct for your system (temperature, salinity, pH, nitrate levels) and equipment (make sure pumps and heaters are running properly, and filter pads are clean) before you add medications.

Remember, many chemicals claim to cure just about any problem under the sun. Always take each product's claims with a grain of salt until you check them out yourself!

Chapter 8

The Nitrogen Cycle and Water Testing

*W*ater quality is an important element in maintaining a successful aquarium system. Excellent water conditions allow your pets to live long and healthy lives. Poor water conditions can leave your fish in poor health or cause their demise. Fortunately, monitoring and maintaining proper water conditions can be easily done with a few simple test kits.

Take the time to monitor your water conditions on a weekly basis so that you can correct any problems with ease. Remember that your fish have to live in their aquarium water 24 hours a day. Make sure that you provide them with the best conditions possible.

Eliminating Fish Waste

Your fish are gonna look great swimming around in your new tank. The water and the decorations are going to look sparkling clean and will impress everyone. But it won't stay that way without proper biological filtration and cycling because your fish have to settle themselves with Mother Nature each and every day. Depending on the total amount of fish that you have in your tank, that can quickly add up to a whole lot of waste being excreted. This waste takes the form of *ammonia* (a dangerous chemical), which in high amounts can be lethal to your fish. Don't worry; for every aquarium problem there is always a solution.

Your fish look great swimming around in their new tank. The water and decorations are sparkling clean and the whole setup is very impressive. But your fish have to live in harmony with Mother Nature to keep their home happy and healthy. To do this, your fish and you join forces to provide proper *biological filtration* (living bacteria that remove waste) and *cycling* (converting ammonia to nitrites and then to less harmful nitrates.)

If you keep a large number of fish, they can generate a large amount of waste. This waste produces ammonia, which can be lethal to your fish in large amounts. (If you have ever taken a whiff of an ammonia bottle, you can understand why immediately!) But don't worry, for every aquarium problem, there is a solution.

Now for the good news: Certain *bacteria* (tiny organisms), which are present in the water to start with, help take care of excess ammonia buildup. Now, I know that the word bacteria is usually associated with bad and scary things such as infections, but in an aquarium system, bacteria actually act as the good guys and save the day. (There are bad bacteria as well, which I discuss in Chapter 16.)

To understand all the weird and wonderful processes taking place in the water of your aquarium system, you need to know about ammonia, bacteria, cycling, and the nitrogen cycle.These systems may seem a little complicated at first (only because they are!), but the tips and explanations in this chapter can help you cut a clear pathway through the darkness which continually lingers in the area of water conditions.

A new system is not as biologically stable as an old one *(conditioned aquarium)*, but in time even a new system becomes old.

Conditioning Your Tank

You need to condition your new aquarium to provide your fish with the best possible chance for good health and survival. *Conditioning* sets up a bacterial colony to get rid of the nasty waste products your fish excrete. You have to be patient during this conditioning cycle because it does take time.

Rushing headlong through this vital conditioning process will undoubtedly lead to quite a bit of heartache as you lose your fish to a condition known as *new tank syndrome*. (For the particulars, see the "New tank syndrome" section later in this chapter.)

The main danger in any new aquarium is the rapid build up of ammonia in the water through excretion and the decay of *nitrogen products* such as fish food and waste. As your aquarium begins to age, beneficial bacteria begin breaking down the ammonia so that the levels do not become too high. Bacteria are always present in your tank, but not enough in the beginning to take care of the problem.

Generally, conditioning takes about four to six weeks, but the time needed depends on the temperature of the water, the type and number of filtration units, the size of your system, and the number of livestock (starter fish) doing the backstroke around your tank.

Starting the Nitrogen Cycle

The nitrogen cycle plays a very important role in your aquarium system. During the nitrogen cycle, beneficial bacteria (nitrosomonas) convert lethal ammonia to less toxic nitrites. During the second part of the cycle, another beneficial bacteria (nitrobacter) convert nitrites to less harmful nitrates. Nitrates are harmful at high levels but can be removed though frequent water changes.

About two weeks after you add starter fish to your aquarium, the ammonia buildup in your tank begins to peak. (You won't really have any ammonia in your aquarium until after you add your fish and they start excreting waste.) You're probably wondering what to do with the ammonia, right? Well, just sit back, because your friendly neighborhood bacteria take care of everything.

During the weeks of the conditioning period, several types of bacteria multiply rapidly in order to remove toxic chemicals from the water. As the number of bacteria increases, they render larger amounts of waste product less toxic by converting them to less harmful substances in the nitrogen cycle.

Encouraging nitrosamonas (good bacteria number one)

During the first phase of the nitrogen cycle, the *nitrosomonas bacteria* in the aquarium water increase to detoxify the ammonia into less harmful *nitrites*. High levels of nitrites can still harm your fish, but they're not as bad as ammonia. Nitrosomonas bacteria require a good oxygen supply (which can be provided though filtration and airstones) in order to multiply and grow correctly.

Promoting nitrobacter (good bacteria number two)

In a short time, the nitrites produced by the nitrosomonas bacteria begin increasing toward toxic levels. When nitrite levels begin to climb, a second type of bacteria known as *nitrobacter* converts them to less deadly *nitrates*.

So far, the ammonia produced by waste has been converted to nitrites, and then to nitrates. Now what happens? Nitrate levels continue to increase slowly over time, but you can maintain them at proper levels through *frequent water changes*. If you don't change your water, the nitrates build up to the point where they are just as toxic as the ammonia you got rid of. (The only difference is that it takes much longer for nitrates to become deadly.)

During the conditioning period, you need to monitor pH, ammonia, nitrite, and nitrate levels using standard test kits. Notice that the pH level decreases a little during the conditioning process. This is normal. Don't use chemicals and medications during the conditioning process, because they can potentially damage proper bacterial growth and, in turn, interfere with the nitrogen cycle.

Speeding things up a bit

If you're short on patience (and after all, you got an aquarium because you like watching fish, not water), you can speed up the nitrogen cycle by adding one or more of the following substances:

- **Starter fish.** Adding one or two fish is a good way to provide a minimum amount of waste to your tank so that essential bacteria can multiply at a normal rate. Using a couple of guppies (freshwater systems), a few damsels (saltwater systems), or a few mollies (brackish systems) to start the maturation process is one of the best ways to begin your nitrogen cycle.

- **Mature gravel.** Gravel from a *mature* (and disease-free) aquarium already has a large bacteria population on its surface and acts as an excellent starter culture.

- **Food.** Adding a small amount of food to the tank each day can help begin the nitrogen cycle. The only problem with this method is that it is very unreliable and can lead to water fouling if food is not added in the correct amounts.

- **Commercial additives.** You can purchase additives such as *freeze-dried bacteria* at your local pet store to help speed up the nitrogen cycle. I never had much luck with the older products. However, many new products, such as *pre-colonized mediums* (you add them to your filter box or canister), can significantly increase cycling time.

The best way to begin the aquarium maturation cycle is by adding a small amount of mature gravel and a few starter fish.

Despite the fact that your starter fish start the process of proper bacterial growth, you must remember that it takes time to build up a well-established biological colony. Don't add too many fish right away because they can overload the biological filtration system and result in new tank syndrome (see the self-named section later in this chapter). Instead, simply wait a couple of weeks, then add a few small fish each week to the aquarium. This gradual increase in livestock keeps ammonia levels within an acceptable range.

Remember to check your water conditions (ammonia, nitrites, nitrates, and pH levels) after you add fish. Leave these few fish in your aquarium for a few weeks so that the bacteria grows at a steady rate. If you add too many fish at the same time, the waste produced can overload the growing bacteria colony, leaving you with new tank syndrome.

Frequent water changes (5 percent per day) help lower any excess waste buildup.

During the cycling period, you may notice a *cloudiness* in the water. Don't worry; it isn't a sign that all has gone wrong. The cloudiness is a beneficial bacterial bloom and is perfectly normal. If your aquarium has adequate filtration, the water should become clear again within a few days.

Preventing new tank syndrome

The nitrogen cycle plays a very important role in the overall biological stabilization of your aquarium. As time passes, waste is going to build up in your tank and will need to be eliminated. After a month or two, the significant amount of bacteria living in the substrate bed and filters (or any surface they can attach themselves to) take care of any fishy waste products.

New tank syndrome occurs when ammonia or nitrite is not properly converted to less harmful substances (nitrates). *Overstocking* (putting too many fish in your aquarium) when you first set up your tank usually causes new tank syndrome.

New tank syndrome is a silent killer, often striking without warning. It causes extreme physical ailments or even death. Your fish may look a little out of joint one day and be dead the next. You must learn to recognize the symptoms of this problem: Fish suffering from new tank syndrome often lose some of their coloring, hide in corners with clamped fins, and lie near the bottom of the aquarium.

If you notice *any* of these unusual behaviors, immediately test the ammonia and nitrite levels and carry out water changes as needed.

Testing Ammonia, Nitrites, and Nitrates

To maintain healthy water conditions throughout the life of your aquarium system, you need to test your water's ammonia, nitrite, and nitrate levels frequently. Keeping these levels where they should be helps your fish stay much healthier overall.

Changing the water frequently

One of the best (and oldest) methods of keeping your ammonia and nitrate levels down is to change the water frequently. Water changes help remove unwanted waste, and at the same time replace depleted trace elements. Besides, if you change your aquarium water frequently (yes, that means more than once a year!) your fish will love you for it.

Research shows that fish that live in aquariums where the water is changed often, display better coloration, live longer and healthier lives, and fight off disease with super human (I mean super fishy) strength. Water changes also help your filtration system function better.

You may wonder how much water you should change. I prefer to change about 15 percent of the water in my tanks every week. I know that this may sound like a chore, but it really isn't. You can get special hoses, called *pythons,* to help you out. You can also do it the old-fashioned way, using a bucket.

Do not do lift heavy buckets of water if you have any health problems. Get someone to do it for you. One of your neighbors probably owes you a favor anyway.

If you don't keep changing the water in your aquariums, your nitrate level may rise to the point where it becomes lethal. There is really no practical way to get rid of excess nitrate levels without water changes. Sometimes some of the oldest methods are still the best.

The only practical way to keep nitrates at an acceptable, non-lethal level is to change your aquarium water often. (Sometimes the old methods are still the best.)

As your aquarium system matures, the pH level drops due to acid buildup. Water changes help eliminate this problem as well.

Maintaining proper pH levels

When you set up you new aquarium, you need a *pH test kit,* available at almost any pet store. One is shown in Figure 8-1. Don't be afraid; they're really quite simple to use. Special test kits for freshwater aquariums test in the lower to neutral range; test kits for marine systems test the higher alkaline ranges.

Figure 8-1:
A pH test kit.

One type of kit consists of a simple *color card, plastic measuring tube,* and *chemicals* that either lower or raise the pH. Usually, you fill the measuring tube with water from your aquarium and add a few drops of *regent* (a water color changing chemical supplied with the test kit). Then you compare the resulting water color to the color chart, which indicates the pH value of your aquarium water.

Other types of pH test kits have strips (composed of *litmus paper*), which, when you dip them into your aquarium, change color to indicate the pH level. You can also have your pH level read electronically by inserting probes attached to a machine into the water.

The type of test you choose depends on how much mad money you have to blow when you find yourself picking up supplies. Buying a simple, inexpensive test kit is fine, though.

Check the *pH level* (a scaled measure of alkalinity or acidity) of your aquarium water when you first set up your tank and at least once a week after the nitrogen cycle is complete. Many species of fish prefer to live in alkaline water (marine species), others like to hang out in acidic waters (tetras), and some like to remain in between (neutral). So the pH level you need for your particular system depends on what species of fish you have.

The pH values in a freshwater system fluctuate very rapidly compared to those in saltwater tanks, which have a much higher mineral content and a more stable pH range. Even the smallest change in pH level can really stress out your fish and make them much more susceptible to various diseases.

The pH scale you get when you purchase a pH test kit ranges from 0 to 14. Zero, the lowest value on the scale, represents the highest acidic level. So the *acid scale* runs from 0–6.9. The number 14 is the highest value on the scale and represents the highest level of alkalinity (also known as basic). So the *alkaline scale* runs from 14 down to 7.1. A pH of 7 is halfway between acidity and alkalinity and is always considered *neutral*.

A pH of 5 is ten times more acid than a pH of 6. So don't let the little numbers fool you — they can change your water chemistry drastically.

Most freshwater fish prefer a neutral pH balance. Marine fish live in an alkaline condition (usually 8.2–8.4). So, when you purchase your fish, make sure that your various species' pH requirements are compatible.

Remember that ammonia is more toxic in a system with a higher pH.

If there are any fish in your aquarium, change the pH level gradually. Changes of more than one range value per day can shock your fish and result in their death.

Acidity (in your aquarium water, not your in-laws)

If, after testing, you find that the pH level of your aquarium water is too low (acidic), you can raise it by adding *sodium bicarbonate* (also known as baking soda) from the test kit, adding dolomite or coral pieces to the water, or running the water through limestone added to a mechanical filter. The easiest way is to add chemicals.

Alkalinity

If you find that the pH level of your water is too high (alkaline), you lower it by adding the *sodium biphosphate* from the test kit, or by adding *demineralized water*. Another way to lower the pH is to filter the water through *peat moss*. Adding aged peat moss (highly valued by aquarium keepers) to your filtration system softens your water and reduces the pH balance very gradually. Check your peat moss carefully before using it because peat moss that has not been aged can drastically change your pH in a short period of time and threaten the health and happiness of your fish.

Testing hardness and salinity levels

The *degree of hardness* (dH) in water refers to the amount of dissolved mineral salts in your water. You don't have to worry about your water's degree of hardness unless you live in an area where the water is very hard (150+), or very soft (0–4). (You can test for hardness by using a simple test kit that you can purchase at your local fish store.)

One way to dilute hardness is to add rain or distilled water to your tank. This also lowers the pH levels. Extreme hardness is found in alkaline (high pH) waters. *Reverse osmosis* units soften aquarium water, but these units tend to be expensive and use a lot of tap water in order to produce a small amount of mineral-free water. You can also use a water softener, add water from a *deionization unit,* or add peat moss to your filter.

To harden your water, soak it in crushed coral or dolomite.

Testing *salinity* levels is important only if you have a marine or brackish system. Freshwater does not have any measurable salt content, so you can skip this step if you keep a freshwater tank. You measure salinity with a hydrometer, which I discuss in more detail in Chapter 6.

Monitoring Water Conditions

During the conditioning period, closely monitor pH, ammonia, nitrite, and nitrate levels using standard test kits. Take daily readings. The pH level goes down as a normal part of the conditioning process. You can raise it again through frequent water changes if you live in an area with harder water (hard water and high alkaline levels go together). Allowing the pH to decrease over a long period of time during the conditioning process keeps helpful bacteria from multiplying to its full potential. When nitrite and nitrate levels begin to overstep their limits, daily water changes help alleviate that problem.

Do not use an excess amount of chemicals or medications during the conditioning period because they can potentially damage bacterial growth.

When the conditioning process is complete, you can begin adding a few fish every week to allow the bacteria bed to increase at a normal rate. If you make the mistake of immediately overstocking your aquarium, ammonia levels will gradually build up. To correct this situation, reduce the number of fish in the tank or add more filtration.

Chapter 9

Putting It All Together

. . . .

In This Chapter

▶ Setting up a freshwater aquarium

▶ Setting up a saltwater aquarium

▶ Setting up a brackish aquarium

. . . .

*I*f you are reading this chapter, you have probably purchased most of the equipment for your new aquarium. If you haven't, take a look at the first eight chapters of this book, which cover equipment, substrate, and tanks. But I'm sure many of you are wondering in what order all those hoses, funny looking pieces of tubing, and gadgets all fit into your system. That's what this chapter is for.

You are probably crossing your fingers in hopes that I talk about the type of system that you want to set up. Never fear! I'm going to show you how to set up a freshwater system, a saltwater system, and a brackish system. You can't beat that with a stick!

The setups that I cover in this chapter are my *own personal choices* for a beginning hobbyist. You can find many other types of equipment, substrates, and so on that can be put on these systems, but I want to lead you though the simple steps of putting together a minimal setup that will work fine and not cost you mega bucks. Later on, you can add more equipment if you choose to do so. But part of the excitement of the hobby is learning and trying new things, and I would not want to take that opportunity away from you by giving you system setups that are set in stone. Begin with the basics, and let your imagination lead you from there.

How to Proceed

Before you get going, I better take a few moments to explain how this chapter works so that you stay on the correct path for the system that you have chosen. If you want to set up a freshwater system, just follow all of the instructions labeled "for all systems" and skip the ones that say "for marine systems" or "for brackish systems." If you want to set up a marine system, follow the instructions and add the extra steps labeled "for marine systems." If you want to set up a brackish tank, just follow the regular type and then add the extra steps labeled "for brackish systems." Simple, eh?

Setting Up Your System

What follows are the basic steps you need to take to set up an aquarium.

1. **Find a good location (for all systems).**

   Choose a place that has a solid floor and is away from windows, doors, and high traffic areas. Make sure that you have adequate electrical outlets and a handy water supply.

2. **Set up the stand (for all systems).**

   Place the stand so that it is stable (that is, it doesn't rock). Make sure that you leave room for hanging equipment and leave enough room for yourself to do cleaning and maintenance.

3. **Clean out your tank (for all systems).**

   Clean out your aquarium with clear water and a soft sponge. Do not use soap or other chemicals!

4. **Place the aquarium on the stand (for all systems).**

   Make sure that the tank fits properly on the stand. Do not allow any of the tank's bottom edges to hang over. If you want, you can place a thin sheet of Styrofoam underneath the tank to cushion it.

5. **Add a background (for all systems).**

   If you want to add a background, now would be the time to tape it onto the back of the tank so that you don't have to work it around the equipment and cords later.

6. **Install an undergravel filter (for all systems).**

   Lay the perforated plastic plates on the bottom of the tank. Put the plastic uplift tubes in place over the large holes in the plate. Put an airstone connected to air-line tubing down inside of the plastic uplift tubes. Place the caps on top of the uplift tubes. Connect the air-line hosing to an air pump. *Do not plug in the pump yet!*

7. **Add your substrate (for all systems).**

   - **Freshwater:** Wash gravel with clear water. Put 2 inches of gravel over the undergravel filter plate. Slope the gravel so that it is about one half an inch higher in the rear.

   - **Marine:** Do the same as for freshwater, but use dolomite instead of gravel.

- **Brackish:** Do the same as for freshwater, but use pea gravel.

8. **Add a powerfilter (for all systems).**

   Place the filter on the tank by hanging it on the outside of the rear glass. The intake tube should hang inside of the aquarium. Rinse the filter pads under clear water and place them in the slots inside the filter. *Do not plug in the pump yet!*

9. **Add protein skimmer (for marine systems).**

   Follow the manufacturer's instructions. *Do not plug the skimmer in yet!*

10. **Install the heater (for all systems).**

    Install submersible heater at an angle along the rear piece of glass. *Do not plug in the heater yet!*

11. **Put thermometer on the tank (for all systems).**

    Hang or stick the thermometer in one corner of the tank.

12. **Add decorations (for all systems).**

    - **Freshwater:** Add rocks, plastic plants, driftwood, and ceramics.
    - **Brackish:** Same as for freshwater.
    - **Marine:** Add coral skeletons and seashells.

13. **Fill the aquarium (for all systems).**

    Add water.

    For marine tanks, the water should be already mixed with synthetic sea salt to a density of about 1.023. For brackish tanks, shoot for a density of about 1.015. Pour the water into the aquarium by letting it splash on top of a plate that is resting in the gravel. This will make sure that the water does not move the gravel and decorations all around while you are filling the tank. Make sure the water is the correct temperature for your species.

14. **Add dechlorinator to the water (for all systems).**

15. **Check pH (for all systems).**

    If it's okay, continue on. If not, adjust it.

16. **Plug in all the equipment (for all systems).**

    Add water from the tank to the powerfilter to prime it if necessary; set the heater and adjust the protein skimmer.

17. **Put the hood on top of the tank (for all systems).**

18. **Add lighting (for all systems).**

    Place the light on top of the tank and plug it in.

19. **Let the aquarium run for 24 hours (for all systems).**

20. **Do final pH, temperature, and salinity checks and adjust as needed (for all systems).**

21. **Add live plants (for freshwater and brackish systems).**

    Bury plant roots in the gravel. Place taller plants in the back and shorter plants up front. You may have to take a little water out of the tank so that it doesn't flow over while you are planting.

22. **Add live rock (for marine systems).**

    Remember that you may have to take a little bit of water out of the tank to prevent overflow if you have a large amount of live rock.

23. **Put in your starter fish (for all systems).**

    Just a few small ones! Don't go overboard!

Well, there you have it in a nutshell. Remember that you must monitor your water conditions daily to keep an eye on ammonia, nitrite, and nitrate levels. You can start to slowly add more fish after the chemical levels stabilize. Be patient during this process!

One Last Thing

The color section of this book has some great pictures of setting up freshwater and marine tanks. Go ahead and take a look.

Part II
Plants and Invertebrates

The 5th Wave   By Rich Tennant

In this part . . .

Aquariums are more than just fish tanks. The next couple chapters describe why plants, invertebrates, and other organisms are important to the maintenance of a healthy, beautiful aquarium.

Chapter 10

Live Plants for Freshwater and Brackish Aquariums

- -

In This Chapter

▶ Looking at plant types

▶ Transporting plants

▶ Recognizing plant problems

▶ Keeping your aquarium in tip-top shape

▶ Experimenting with planting techniques

- -

*L*ive plants are one of the most overlooked but truly wonderful aspects of the aquarium hobby. They come in a wide variety of sizes, shapes, colors, and densities. Living plants offer a unique and natural beauty that cannot be achieved with artificial substitutes. All that you need to enjoy live aquatic plants is the proper water conditions, good lighting, and a little bit of patience. Take the time to bring your fish one step closer to their natural environment with live plants, and they will love you for it!

Live plants are a lot of fun, look cool, and help to boost your image as a professional hobbyist. What better reason can you think of to keep them in your aquarium? Actually, there are a lot of other good reasons to keep live plants, but looking cool in front of your friends and family is the most important one.

Unfortunately, many small fish shops don't carry live plants, and if they do, they may have limited stock. But, as usual, the Internet can save you! You can find an entire aquatic forest just by cruising the cyber highway for an hour or so. If you don't have a computer, borrow your neighbor's for a while. (Tell her that you're doing international biological research, so that she willingly forks over her mouse and keyboard.) You can find a list of convenient Web sites in Chapter 26 to help get you started on your way to purchasing good aquarium plants.

What Live Plants Do for Your Aquarium

You can use live plants to enhance the natural look of your freshwater or brackish aquarium, and they can be very beneficial and beautiful at the same time. Plants can produce a calming affect (both for you and your fish), and help maintain a natural balance in your aquarium. Besides, having live plants sprouting out of your tank makes you look like a pro.

Don't get me wrong. Many hobbyists aquascape their aquariums with artificial plants and are perfectly happy with the outcome. But, many hobbyists use plastic plants because they don't have the knowledge they need to maintain live aquatic plants successfully. Certain species of fish destroy any live plants that you may put into your tank, so in certain situations artificial plants are much more beneficial than the "real McCoy." Artificial plants and live plants are generally about the same price, so don't let cost affect your decision.

If you do choose to use artificial plants, try not to get too carried away in the color department. Plastic plants are manufactured in every color under the sun. If your tank ends up with shocking pink on one side, black in the front, and red and green striped plants in the back, your fish may think they've been aboard a time machine and have crash-landed smack dab in the middle of Woodstock. They may die from sheer fright or become colorblind. Even though they pose no real physical danger, loudly colored plants can keep your fish from spawning on a continual basis and may cause them to hide in the corners of your aquarium.

A well-planted aquariums can provide numerous benefits:

- ✔ They offer good shelter for pregnant females who wish to escape from aggressive mates.
- ✔ They supply shade and cooler temperatures during the warmer months.
- ✔ They help protect small and shy fish from bullying tankmates.
- ✔ They provide a safe refuge for all your delicate and long-finned fish that may otherwise end up on the aquatic lunch menu.

Live plants can condition the water in your tank by removing carbon dioxide, sulfur substances, and other wastes. The biological filtration on an aquarium breaks down existing ammonia into less-harmful substances that live plants use for food. By utilizing light during a process known as *photosynthesis*, plants also create food within their own cells, releasing oxygen, which is very beneficial to your fish, during the process. This process is illustrated in Figure 10-1. When you turn off your aquarium lights, plants start absorbing oxygen. They then release carbon dioxide in a process similar to your fish's respiration process.

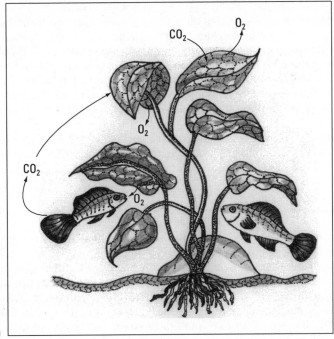

Figure 10-1:
Plants
absorb
carbon
dioxide and
create
oxygen.

Living plants can be a food source for fish that prefer a high amount of vegetation in their diet (of course you'll have to continually replace plants as they get munched). Your fish's color is much more intense in a naturally planted tank. Because they provide security, your aquatic pets also act much more confident in a planted tank. (They won't have to spend the entire day trying to dig an escape tunnel.)

Plant Types

You can find three basic types of plants in an aquarium shop: marginal, aquatic, and terrestrial. Unfortunately, many dealers sell terrestrial (earth-based) plants as aquatic plants. Each type of plant is unique in its requirements for survival and growth, so you need to know exactly which species you can accommodate before you purchase any plants. (Make sure each plant type is labeled correctly before you take them home!) A good plant book with pictures can help you through this dilemma.

Aquatic plants can be entirely submerged beneath the water line of your tank and still survive. These plants die when they are removed from the water. Sagittaria *(Sagittaria natans)* and pygmy sword *(Echinodorus quadricostatus)* are two good examples of aquatic plants. *Marginal plants* spend only part of their time submerged beneath the water. These types of plants flower and seed out of water during the dry periods of the year. Examples of marginal plants include cryptocoryne *(Cryptocoryne balansae)*. Marginal plants require special handling and should be left in the hands of expert hobbyists.

Terrestrial plants live on land and do not survive very long if they're completely submerged. I do not recommend them for use in the home aquarium.

Floating plants

Floating plants do not anchor themselves and drift around the top of your aquarium. Floating plants can grow very quickly, so you need to thin them out — or prune them — when they become too thick and bushy. If you don't, they may block out the light that enters your aquarium from the hood. The resulting loss of light can lower the temperature of your aquarium water, which has a devastating effect on your fish's and plants' health. One plant in particular, duckweed *(lemna)*, multiplies so rapidly that your tank may look like the lights have burnt out permanently. Avoid buying duckweed, and save yourself a lot of hassle.

Floating plants reproduce easily by sprouting young daughter plants and propagating new plants from severed pieces. Use floating plants in spawning tanks to hide young fry. One floating plant is the water lettuce *(Pistia stratiotes)*.

Rooted plants

Rooted plants anchor themselves in the substrate and draw part of their nourishment through their leaves, and part through their roots. Rooted plants reproduce by creating runners (slender plant shoots) that branch off of the main stem. These runners eventually reroot and form new plants or sprout young shoots out of existing leaf surfaces. Many species of rooted plants can grow very large, so use caution when choosing the correct species for your particular tank.

Basket plants come with a small receptacle around the roots and are often raised in humid nurseries. With this type of plant, you have the option of submerging the entire basket in the substrate or removing the basket and planting the roots directly. If you leave the basket intact, the plant's roots will grow through the basket's holes and then anchor themselves in the substrate.

TIP

I remove the baskets so that they don't show above the substrate level when rooting fishes begin digging around them. Unless you have ten feet of gravel in your tank, these horrid baskets always seem to find a way to show off and emerge into the limelight.

Removing the basket often reveals several small plants combined into one tight group. Carefully separate each individual plant from the others around it. Plant each of these little cuttings in the substrate separately. Remember that these plants are not full-grown, so you need to allow ample space for them to spread out.

Cuttings

Many varieties of plants are sold in aquarium stores as *cuttings*. Two examples of cuttings are *elodea,* and *cabomba*. Cuttings often grow very rapidly as they gather nourishment through their leaves. A small group of cuttings (plants too small to stand alone) can be bunched up together with aquarium weights (which you can purchase from your local fish dealer) and planted until they begin to root on their own. After they begin to grow a bit, you can separate them from each other.

Easy plant species

Some plants are a little more difficult than others. The following list gives you a few suggestions on plants that are good for beginners.

Easy-to-keep freshwater plants:

- **Dwarf Swordplant (Echinodorus tenellus):** Use this in the front area of your tank to create a carpet effect.

- **Corkscrew Val (Vallisneria spiralis):** Corkscrew val's light-green leaves are twisted like a spiral staircase. Val needs quite a bit of light.

- **Hornwart (Ceratophyllum demersum):** Hornwart has very stiff leaves.

- **Hairgrass (Eleocharis acicularis):** Hairgrass resembles the grass in your yard but is longer. (My house is an exception).

- **Amazon Sword (Echinodorus grandiflorus):** Amazon sword has heart-shaped leaves

and is very tolerant of beginner mistakes. This plant enjoys soft water.

- **Java Fern (Microsorium pteropus):** Java fern has large leaves that form a point at the top and requires only moderate lighting conditions.

Easy-to-keep brackish plants:

- **Green Cabomba (Cabomba caroliniana):** A plant with soft leaves and foliage that resembles feather wisps.

- **Mangrove (Brugiuera species):** Usually purchased in pots, this plant spreads out all over the tank.

- **Giant Hygrophila (Nomaphila stricta):** A beautiful plant that produces a purple flower.

Aquarium Conditions

To keep your plants healthy, you need to provide them with the proper temperature, nutritional food, proper substrate, good water conditions, and adequate lighting.

Temperature requirements

Plants have temperature requirements just like your fish do. Check each species' temperature requirements before you purchase them, so you know whether they're compatible with your fish's needs. A large majority of aquarium plants are tropical and need to be kept warm — they eventually die in cold water. While you're checking out a shop's tropical plants, see whether they are being kept in warm tanks. If they're kept in cold water, they probably won't survive very long after you place them in your home aquarium.

Substrate for rooting

Live plants prefer a substrate that consists of fine gravel or coarse sand. This type of substrate allows water to move through plant roots so that they can gather nutrients. It also provides plants with the space they need for their roots to fork out as they grow.

Filtration

Clean water is very important for successful plant growth in your aquarium. Dirt and debris settle on the surface of the leaves and clog the plant's pores. Keep plant leaves clean by gently brushing them with a soft toothbrush. If your aquarium water gets too dirty, the amount of energy-giving light is drastically reduced. Water changes help correct both problems.

Feeding

The tap water in your aquarium doesn't have the necessary trace elements and nutrients your plants need for proper growth. You can put tablets and liquid feeders (which can be found at your local pet shop) in the gravel near the plant's roots for fertilization — best done after a water change. You can also place a single cutting in the center of a *plug*, which provides nutrition on a continual basis. You then bury the plug in the gravel.

Lighting

Tropical plants require a constant source of light during the day in order to grow properly. Most tropical plants should receive at least eight hours of light each day. Planted tanks require more intense lighting than fish-only aquariums, but your fish probably won't mind an opportunity to get a bit of an extra tan now and then. Remember that some plants prefer low lighting situations. Check the requirements of each species before you buy.

You can use a *plant-growth light*, which provides the proper light spectrum plants need. You can also control the amount of light your plants receive by using a simple *timer* on your aquarium light so that peak intensity remains the same each day.

One way to compensate for the different lighting requirements between species is to place taller plants so that they shade the shorter species which thrive in low-light levels.

Purchasing and Transporting Your Plants

If you're fortunate to live in an area where the local pet shops stock a wide variety of live plants, you need to know which plants to buy and how to get them home safely. If possible, always purchase your plants from a reputable dealer (in town, or on the Internet).

Taking from the wild

You can collect plants from small bodies of water, such as ponds, but take a few precautions if you choose to do this. Any plants you take from the wild must be carefully cleaned to avoid introducing disease and aquatic pests such as snails. Wild plants should be suitable for aquarium conditions as far as temperature requirements go.

Before you go yanking up any plants at your local stream, make sure that their removal won't have any detrimental effects on the natural environment. You should also check with local authorities to ensure that your liberation of the plants doesn't cause your own removal from home to the town jail.

Buying from a dealer

Before purchasing any live plants, you should have a good idea of which types and sizes best suit your project. Write out a list which includes the total number of plants you need to reach the design effects you desire. It is possible that your local fish shop won't have all the plants you're searching for. Include substitute species on your shopping list just in case.

Start out by purchasing just a few of the plants on your list. Remember that plants usually grow very quickly. If you buy too many in the beginning, your aquarium may end up looking like an Amazon rainforest in a couple of weeks. Or, if your gardener has to come in to trim your aquarium plants back so that you can open your front door, you may want to start thinning them out a bit. One general formula to obtain the total number of plants for your aquarium is to calculate one plant for every six square inches of gravel area. Simply multiply the length of the aquarium by the width (in inches) and divide by six to get the number of plants you need.

You also need to use a little common sense when you buy your plants. Some species are naturally "fuller" than others and take up quite a bit more space. After you become familiar with a particular plant species, you have a better idea of how much room the plants occupy when they are full-grown.

Getting plants home in once piece (without a green thumb)

To maintain your plants' good health, you need to make sure that they don't dry out on the way home from the shop. Ask your dealer to bag your plants in water or you or he can carefully wrap each one in wet newspaper. Transport your new plants in a cooler so that the water remains warm.

Achieving acclimation

When you arrive home, place your plants in a shallow pan of water that contains a 10 percent solution of *potassium permanganate*. Potassium permanganate is a substance that kills unwanted germs and disinfects your plant surfaces. Trim all cuttings to the correct height and remove any dead or wilted leaves by using a sharp pair of scissors.

Never pinch off dead plant pieces with your fingers — you may damage the delicate tissues!

Plant Problems

Even the best hobbyist's green thumb turns black once in a while. Hey, no one is perfect! But, plant diseases are really rare, so don't get too worked up at the thought of all your beautiful sword plants kicking the bucket at the same time. If your plants are growing at a normal pace and are developing new shoots and buds, they're probably in good health.

Signs of poor plant health

Knowing how to recognize and cure foliage problems before they become too severe can help you to avoid losing your new aquatic plants. The following list lets you know what to look for when you are carrying out your daily aquarium maintenance routine:

- **Your plants have holes in them.** This problem is often caused by fish nibbling on the leaves. If your fish are vegetarians, and you provided the plants as a food source, use your new plant money to go bowling and don't worry about it. If your plants begin to fall apart after the holes appear, they may be suffering from *cryptocoryne rot,* which is usually caused by excess nitrates in the aquarium. Water changes help correct this problem.

- **Your plant leaves are turning yellow.** They may be suffering from an iron deficiency. Aquatic plant fertilizer solves this problem.

- **The leaves have turned brown or black.** This indicates decay, probably caused by *too much* iron. Water changes help this problem.

- **Some plants are dying, and some are surviving.** Remember that hard-water plants are able to extract CO_2 from the water, whereas soft-water plants have a more difficult time doing this. If you want to keep both types of plants together, try adding CO_2 to the tank. To avoid this problem, keep plants with similar requirements together.

Algae

No matter what you do, you always have some type of algae in your aquarium system. Algae is often introduced into your aquarium by fish and live food. But, if you keep strong, healthy plants in your system, algae doesn't stand much of a chance.

If your algae gets out of control, however, look out! Blue-green algae (caused by poor water conditions) can form a layer on all of your decorations and substrate. If your fish decide to stop swimming for a few minutes, they start to resemble a moldy cupcake. Red algae, which is caused by a lack of carbon dioxide in the water, is really nasty and hangs in threads all over your aquarium. Extra oxygen can be added to battle the red algae, but often a tank must be cleaned and restarted if it gets out of control. Brown algae (caused by inadequate light) forms huge brown layers in your aquarium. Green algae (caused by too much light) makes your aquarium water look like pea soup.

Algae grows quickly in a cycled tank, but eventually the plants declare war on it and remove the nutrients that it needs to survive. Do not change your water when algae becomes very intense — that can lead to an even bigger problem. If your plants are in good condition, they will eventually win the algae war. Don't depend on algae-eating fish to solve your problem. They couldn't eat that much algae in a million years.

Planting Techniques

It is a whole lot easier to put live plants in your tank after you add the water. Arranging plants in a dry aquarium can be a very difficult job. All they do is look limp and fall over. Besides, you don't want your friends to see your plants in that condition. Lock your front door until all the decorating is complete. That way, you can work undisturbed, then look cool when all is said and done. A full aquarium allows you a better view of the plants after they spread out into the water.

Do not push a plant into the gravel below the *crown* (the area between the plant's stalk and the roots). Space plants far enough apart so that they have plenty of room to spread their roots and grow properly. The distance between each plant should be approximately equal to the span of one leaf. Remember, a tank crammed too full causes the plants to wither and die. Stagger each plant row so that each plant has a leaf-span space on all sides.

One of the best strategies is to place all of your tall plants near the back of the tank. Fill the center of the aquarium with short or bushy plants. Use taller plants that spread out (such as elodea) to hide heaters, under-gravel filter tubes, and other unsightly equipment. Place small plants near the front of the glass. Try to arrange your plants so that they don't look too symmetrical (the same on both sides of the tank) because they normally don't grow that way in nature.

Sketch a picture of how you want your tank to look before you start planting, so that you have a simple plan to follow.

Growing your own

You can remove and replant the little shoots that grow out of a main stem. If you continually remove and replant new shoots, the parent plant grows at a much more rapid pace.

Chapter 11

Invertebrates for the Marine Aquarium

*P*eople who decide to set up a marine aquarium for the first time are often overwhelmed the first time they go shopping for aquarium plants. Sales clerks immediately start talking about invertebrates and using strange words that most people have never heard before. They often end up sounding like politicians on a caffeine rush. As a result, customers can easily become so confused that they often leave without buying a thing.

But I'm here to help explain the fascinating world of invertebrates to you simply and clearly. Soon, you'll be using the same lingo that seasoned marine hobbyists and aquarium suppliers use.

What Invertebrates Are

Invertebrates are animals that have no backbone. Have you ever called someone a jellyfish? (My ex-mother-in-law considered this a compliment because she thought it meant that she was nimble for her age.) Basically, you are calling that particular person spineless. Invertebrates are spineless, too. Because marine aquarium owners really have very few cool plants to decorate their saltwater tanks, they add invertebrates, which can be more easily obtained in most pet shops. Invertebrates are really animals even though many of them look like living plants. Invertebrates make saltwater aquariums look cool. They are also one of the most fascinating groups of animals on earth.

Many people mistakenly assume that some invertebrates are a type of fish. For example, have you ever seen a crab crawling along the seashore? Or a jellyfish floating majestically along with the tide? At first you might view these beautiful animals as fish. But they are actually invertebrates. Invertebrates make up a surprisingly large number of the total animal population. About 2 million species of animals inhabit the earth. Roughly 97 percent of these animals are invertebrates.

Often *pros* (aquarium hobbyists who are very opinionated) will tell you that you should not start with invertebrates if you are setting up your first marine aquarium. Although some invertebrates may be difficult to keep, the same rules apply to marine fish. There are easy fish to keep and difficult fish to keep. A little research can make a big difference in how successful you are at keeping any type of aquatic animal, be it fish or invertebrate.

Invertebrates have a slower *metabolism rate* (the speed at which an organism consumes food) than fish do and do not create as much waste. When you start adding fish to the tank, you may encounter a few problems. Fish begin to add waste to the tank and may affect the overall health of your invertebrates. Invertebrates also have a lower tolerance to poor water conditions, so you must kept them in a tank with excellent filtration.

Many fish and invertebrates do not mix well at all. Marine fish such as the parrotfish enjoy eating several types of invertebrates. So until you learn which fish and invertebrates can *coinhabit* (live together in relative harmony) a tank without destroying each other, you should stick to a fish-only tank or an invertebrate-only tank. As you gain experience, you can begin to introduce the invertebrates and fish to each other.

The best approach to starting an aquarium is to start with a few invertebrates and then add fish later on after you have learned how to care for the invertebrates properly.

Types of Invertebrates

So many different types of invertebrates inhabit the world that covering them all in this book is impossible. This section describes some of the most common invertebrates sold in fish shops. This overview gives you a good idea about specific groups of invertebrates and how they function in a marine tank.

Phylum Porifera

The *phylum* (a classification term meaning a large group of related organisms) Porifera is made up of sponges. These animals are so cool that they just had to have this category all to themselves. Many marine invertebrates (crabs and nudibranchs, for example) live inside or on sponges.

Sponges are *sessile,* which means that they don't move around and that their body is just one massive blob of cells. (Now I know where my landlord's genetic roots are from!) Sponges have a skeleton made of small *spicules* (calcium- and silicon-based skeletal bodies), but they don't have internal organs, a nervous system, or muscles. They feed by filtering particles through their pores from the current around them. While in the water, sponges are often very colorful and come in shades of purple, red, orange, and green, just to name a few.

Never remove a sponge from the water because this can cause air bubbles to get trapped inside of the animal, possibly affecting its ability to gather food. Sponges need to have a good filtration system to thrive. Most sponges prefer dimmer lighting. Also make sure that the tank's lighting does not produce so much algae that the sponges become clogged with algae. If your sponge looks like the mold-covered doughnut that fell unnoticed under your stove last year, then you need to cut down on your lighting a bit.

Phylum Cnidaria

The Cnidarians are a fascinating group of animals that includes the jellyfish, sea pens, anemones, hard corals, and soft corals. These animals have a basic sack that serves as a stomach, and they have two openings for collecting food and removing waste. Many Cnidarians have tentacles that contain *nematocysts,* or small stinging cells. The Cnidarians use these nematocysts to defend themselves and to capture prey.

Jellyfish

Jellyfish are cool-looking invertebrates that usually resemble an umbrella. These animals have a body that is composed of 90 percent water. Jellyfish often drift with currents in the wild, but they can move their body in a home aquarium by contracting their shape. Most species are carnivorous and attack other animals in the marine tank. Jellyfish require optimal water conditions and do not generally live long in captivity. I recommend that you leave these animals in a public aquarium or in the hands of an experienced species hobbyist because they are quite difficult to keep successfully.

Sea pens

Sea pens are interesting animals that resemble a feather's quill. These invertebrates are brightly colored and anchor themselves in one spot through the use of a burrowing foot. They capture detritus (small debris) for their main diet by filtering water.

Anemones

Anemones are one of the most common invertebrates that you can purchase at your local fish shop. You often see anemones with clownfish or damselfish living happily inside of them. (The anemone is the one that looks like a blob of spaghetti fell into the tank from someone's dinner plate.) This type of harmonious living is known as a *symbiotic* relationship. Both animals benefit by living together. (In some other cases in which animals live together, only one animal may benefit. A good example of this other type of relationship is your relatives coming to live with you.)

Fish that inhabit anemones receive protection not only for themselves but for their young as well. Clownfish have a body coating that is not affected by the anemone's sting. During an interesting acclimation process, the clownfish makes several passes or dips toward its intended anemone until it is ready to enter. After the acclimation rite is complete, the anemone usually receives food that the clownfish often carries to it.

Anemones stick to the substrate though the use of a suckerlike disk on their bottom side. They can use their tentacles to capture prey or small pieces of food that are carried by the water currents around them. If conditions are not optimal, the anemone is able to move to other locations within the tank. Never attempt to pull on an anemone when it has attached to a solid surface. You may accidentally damage its delicate tissues when you try to remove it.

Many species of anemones contain *zooxanthellae* (a minute algae) in their tissues and require good lighting for survival. If you want, you can feed your anemones once a week with a small piece of frozen brine shrimp. You can carefully spray food into the center of an anemone with a pipette or rubber bulb. But anemones are generally hardy and can survive on liquid invertebrate food and live brine shrimp.

Anemones are great invertebrates for beginning aquarists. Popular species include the carpet *(Stoichactis sp.)*, the Florida anemone *(Condylactis sp.)*, and the malu *(Anthopsis sp.)*. Most anemones prefer a temperature of around 71 degrees F.

Hard and soft corals

Corals are generally divided into two groups. Hard corals (for example, brain and staghorn) secrete a calcium-based skeleton, and soft corals (for example, gorgonians, leathers, and sea whips) do not. Many hard corals do not do well in a home aquarium unless conditions are above reproach, meaning that you must have the proper lighting, low nitrates, high dissolved oxygen, and good water current.

Hard corals are best left to experienced hobbyists. However, if you're determined to add these animals to your tank, the best way to find out about them is by working side by side with an experienced aquarium hobbyist or store owner who can help you with your tank's progress. Besides, shop owners might throw in some free junk if they feel sorry for you.

Soft corals are very popular in the marine hobby and are easy to obtain. Most of these animals are rather hardy and do well in a beginner's aquarium. Sea whips grow rapidly and come in a wide variety of colors. You can feed these animals with liquid invertebrate food. Often whips come attached to live rock. Popular species of sea whips include *Plexaurella* and *Muricea.* Many gorgonians look like branches or twigs and give an invertebrate aquarium a surrealistic effect.

Phylum Platyhelminthes

This unusual phylum contains good invertebrates and bad invertebrates. Parasites (bad flatworms) such as tapeworms and flukes belong to the *platyhelminthes.* You want to avoid them!

However, thousands of different *Tubellaria,* which are nonparasitic flatworms that come in many beautiful colors and patterns, are suitable for aquariums. Fish, shrimp, and crabs eat flatworms. Most species of flatworms are nocturnal. Good flatworms are not readily available in live form unless you purchase them on the Internet because few pet shops carry them. They can be quite beautiful if you get a healthy specimen. But if you get too many and they overrun your aquarium, you will never get rid of them. That can be a real bummer.

Phylum Annelida

The phylum Annelida includes the marine tubeworm and the common earthworm that always manages to fall off your hook when you go fishing.

Tubeworms are segmented worms that construct tubes from many different materials, such as sand and shells. They use these tubes (which can be soft or rigid) as their home. Their feathery crowns can usually be seen above the opening. These feathery appendages are actually tentacles that gather food and aid in respiration. Probably the most beautiful and famous of the tubeworms is the Christmas tree worm *(Spirobranchus giganteus),* which resembles its name.

When their crowns are spread out, tubeworms sway beautifully in the current. If they become frightened, they quickly retract into their tube. Tubeworms can gather debris with their feathers or can be fed invertebrate meal and live brine shrimp.

Many fish such as puffers and triggers may destroy tubeworms, so make sure that you don't add them to a tank full of these animals. But an aquarium with tubeworms is a sight to behold! Your friends will be impressed with your aquatic skills (even though tubeworms are a cinch to keep). Besides, the best reason to buy tubeworms is that they look cool.

Phylum Crustacea

The phylum Crustacea includes the shrimps, lobsters, barnacles, and crabs. This group includes many beautiful animals, but many of them can wreak havoc on other animals in the tank.

Shrimp

The shrimp that you keep in an invertebrate tank are quite different from those that you find sitting on your plate at Red Lobster. Live shrimp are usually very colorful and have long antennae, which they use to detect food and explore their environment. Shrimp are very hardy invertebrates and the ultimate survivalists. They are perfect for the beginning hobbyist.

Shrimp play important roles in the marine aquarium. They gather debris from the bottom of the tank, and many species will "clean fish" if you have them in your aquarium. They do this by attaching themselves to a fish and picking the skin and scales clean of parasites. Fish actually seem to enjoy these "cleaning stations" where they can go for service.

The coral-banded shrimp *(Stenopus hispidus)* is one of the most popular shrimp on the market. This beautiful animal resembles a candy cane and can grow quite large. When the coral-banded shrimp sheds its *exoskeleton* (outer covering), it leaves a perfect image of itself. So if you own one shrimp and wake up in the morning and find that a new shrimp has suddenly joined your tank, don't make an appointment with your therapist. It's probably a skeleton that has been left behind. This species of shrimp is not very compatible with its own species, so it is best to keep only one per tank.

Lobsters

Aquarium lobsters are quite different from the monstrous animals you eat at your local seafood restaurant. They are available in many different colors at your pet store. However, you usually must special-order lobsters if you want an unusual color.

Lobsters are nocturnal and can be kept with most other invertebrates. The problem is that many grow to 7 inches or more in captivity and can do quite a bit of damage to other delicate invertebrates if they happen to rush over them too quickly. In fact, your invertebrates will look like they have been hit by a semi when a lobster gets in a hurry.

Lobsters also can make short work of fish and crabs, so you should not try to mix lobsters with other species unless you have a large tank with plenty of hiding spaces. Popular species include the purple lobster *(Panulirus versicolor)* and the dwarf red *(Enoplometopus occidentalis)*.

Crabs

Marine crabs are some of the most diverse and colorful creatures in a salt-water tank. Crabs and their shells come in almost every color under the sun, and many have comical faces that would make Bozo jealous.

Boxing crabs *(Lybia tessellata)* use anemones as a weapon for defense. This type of crab picks up two small anemones and holds one in each of its front claws. When danger threatens, the boxing crab jabs at its opponent with the captive anemones like a deranged cheerleader.

The arrow crab *(Stenorhynchus seticornis)* is a spidery-like invertebrate that looks like it is walking on several pairs of stilts. These crabs are very peaceful and elegant despite their looks. This species does not get along with its own kind, so keep only one unless you have a large aquarium.

Phylum Chelicerata

The phylum Chelicerata includes the king crab and the horseshoe crab. These animals are characterized by the fact that they have six pairs of appendages. Although difficult to find in many aquarium stores, they can usually be ordered on the Internet and are well worth the extra time that it often takes to obtain them. These animals can be kept easily if they are provided with an aquarium that has plenty of filtration.

Horseshoe crabs

The horseshoe crab *(Limulus polyphemus)* is an invertebrate that looks like a knight with armor. These fascinating invertebrates spend most of their time digging through the substrate, which can help with natural biological filtration. You can feed pieces of crustaceans or fish to horseshoe crabs. King crabs are rarely kept by hobbyists, but like everything else, there is always an exception to the rule.

Phylum Mollusca

The *mollusks* belong to a phylum in which none of the animals seem to resemble each other at all. But despite their cosmetic differences, they still have many physical traits in common. All members have a mantle, which forms a shell in some species.

Clams

Clams make a great addition to the invertebrate tank (if you happen to have won the lottery) and are available in many species and many beautiful colors. Clams have two shells that are bound together with muscle tissue. A clam feeds by filtering suspended debris from the water around it. Most of the coloring in a clam's mantle is due to *zooxanthellae,* which is an algae that lives within its tissues. Proper lighting allows the algae to produce food for the clam through photosynthesis.

The main problem with clams is that they are very, very expensive. I'll put it this way: You can probably get that new car you want with the money you saved up to buy a couple of clams. You can lose a lot of money quickly if your clams die because your aquarium conditions were not correct. The most popular clams in the hobby are the giant clams *(Tridacna sp.),* which are native to the South Seas.

Sea snails

The most interesting member of the *sea snail* family is the cowrie. These invertebrates have smooth shells with a glasslike appearance that make them among the most beautiful shells in the entire world. Cowries are very easy to keep but are nocturnal and may nibble on corals. They feed on debris in the aquarium. Popular species include the map cowrie *(Cypraea arabica)* and the tiger cowrie *(Cypraea tigris).*

Nudibranchs

Nudibranchs have many different names. Some hobbyists call them sea slugs or sea hares, but I think a more fitting description is "flying pancake." These animals move through the water in a flapping motion that is quite extraordinary.

Nudibranchs have appendages that run along the dorsal area and that are used in respiration. The main problem with keeping these invertebrates alive is that they require optimal water conditions and must have plenty of vegetable matter in their diet for survival. Problem number two is that a pancake breakfast sounds pretty good to most other fish and invertebrates as well. The best way to insure success with nudibranchs is to keep them in an aquarium by themselves or provide plenty of decorative shelter such as coral caves and ledges.

But nudibranchs are totally cool-looking and will impress your family and friends. Popular species include the Spanish dancer *(Hexabranchus imperialis)* and the striped nudibranch *(Chromodoris quadricolor).*

Scallops

If you lived in the '60s and enjoyed beads and fringed pants, you will probably like scallops. These fascinating animals have a shell-encased body that sports wild-looking threads. Scallops can move by opening and closing their shells. They jet around the tank to escape from predators, which include just about any large fish, crab, or other moving invertebrate that you put into the tank. Scallops require optimal water conditions for filter feeding and do not live long in uncycled tanks. The bright red flame scallop *(Lima scabra)* is probably the most sought-after species in the aquarium hobby. Groovy!

Oysters

If the Munsters (you know, Herman, Lilly, Eddie, and Grandpa) dumped Spot at the Humane Society and then bought an aquarium, thorny oysters are probably what they would keep in it. The thorny oyster *(Spondylus americanus)* is an odd-looking creature that has thorny extensions on its shell that makes it look like it is ready for battle. Actually, oysters are peaceful filter feeders that require dim lighting. Oysters are very easy invertebrates to keep and can grow quite large (over 8 inches in diameter). These animals are expensive, so save your money.

Octopus

Don't even think about adding an octopus to your tank. See Chapter 23 for more information.

Cuttlefish

Cuttlefish are large, expensive, hard to find, and will eat everything in your tank. Enough said. Oh yeah, one more thing. Forget about them.

Nautilus

The nautilus is really a lovely creature but is not really recommended for the beginning hobbyist. This invertebrate is hard to obtain, very expensive, requires a vast amount of space, and is rarely seen in an aquarium during daylight hours due to its nocturnal feeding habits.

Phylum Echinodermata

Echinoderms are interesting invertebrates that can be easily maintained by most beginners. The echinoderms include starfish, sea urchins, and sea cucumbers.

Starfish

Starfish rule. You can choose from many shapes, sizes, and colors of starfish, which spend their day moving slowly across your tank in search of food. Unfortunately, this food also includes any bivalves (two-shelled animals such as clams and scallops) that you happen to have in your aquarium. Starfish have arms that can be regenerated if they are torn off. They keep your tank clean by removing debris, algae, and other undesirables, and they also readily accept bits of shellfish and crustacean meat. Popular species include the red-knobbed *(Protoreaster lincki)* and the orange star *(Fromia monilis)*.

Sea urchins

A sea urchin looks like a pincushion moving around your tank. Urchins have a soft underbelly, which is protected by numerous spines that are very sharp and can inflict a painful wound! If you have anything in your tank that even resembles vegetable matter, the urchin will eat it. If you want a lush green aquarium full of gorgonians and other pretty invertebrates, don't buy an urchin. In a few weeks, your tank will look like the aftermath of a nuclear explosion. "Devoid of life" is another way of putting it. These animals are better off left in the hands of experts. They are interesting invertebrates but do require suitable tankmates.

Sea cucumbers

Sea cucumbers are neat little animals that are very good "starter" invertebrates for the beginning hobbyist. Cucumbers have feathery tentacles that gather in organisms that are floating in the water (including brine shrimp). The most easily obtained species is the feather cucumber *(Cucumaria miniata)*.

Fish for an Invertebrate Tank

Some risk is always involved when you mix fish and invertebrates. In the wild, organisms have more room to move around and escape from their predators. When you confine these same species to a small aquarium tank, then you create an unnatural environment. But, with a little preplanning and care, you can have a peaceful fish and invertebrate aquarium. The following list provides you with a few good ideas for peaceful starter fish.

Damsels

Damselfish (family Pomacentridae) are a diverse group of easy-to-maintain species that live in harmony with most invertebrates. These small fishes come in a wide variety of colors and patterns. Damselfish live long lives, are relatively inexpensive, and are commonly used to cycle a marine aquarium. If you have plenty of hiding spaces (such as coral), you should not have any problem with territoriality. These fish are best kept in groups of at least three. Popular species include the domino *(Dascyllus trimaculatus)* and the blue damselfish *(Pomacentrus caeruleus)*. Most damsels tolerate varying water conditions but prefer a temperature of 75 to 80 degrees F and a density of 1.023.

Clownfish

Clownfish are famous for their symbiotic relationship with anemones. These beautiful fish are relatively hardy and get along well with most invertebrates, especially damsels. Clownfish are more expensive than damsels, but they are still within a reasonable price for even a modest budget. Popular species include the tomato *(Amphiprion frenatus)*, the percula *(Amphiprion percula)*, and the sebae *(Amphiprion sebae)*. Clownfish prefer a temperature of 75 to 82 degrees F and a density of 1.023.

Basslets

Basslets *(Grammidae)* are hardy fish for an invertebrate tank. The basslet spends most of its time searching for food along the substrate and in coral. The most popular of these species includes the royal gramma *(Gramma loreto)*, which is magenta and yellow, and the blackcap gramma *(Gramma melacara)*. This species can be aggressive toward its own kind, so keep only one unless you have an extremely large tank. Grammas live in harmony with most invertebrates and other fishes and adjust to most aquarium conditions.

Gobies

Gobies *(Gobidae)* have modified pectoral fins so that they can hang out on rocks and coral. Gobies, a hardy species that are easy to keep, are famous for their cleaning abilities. They freely clean parasites from other fish in your aquarium. Popular species include the neon goby *(Gobiosoma oceanops)* and the yellow goby *(Gobiodon okinawae)*. You may find yourself spending hours watching these fascinating little animals if you decide to purchase them.

Blennies

Blennies *(Blenniidae)* are scaleless fishes that live on the substrate area of an aquarium. Most species have modified pectoral fins that are designed to help them prop their bodies up. A few species are carnivorous and feed on small invertebrates. If you have an invertebrate tank, consider adding the bicolor blenny *(Ecsenius bicolor)*, which feeds on algae. I can think of no other species that has a more charming personality. Other popular species include the peacock blenny *(Blennius pavo)* and the carmine blenny *(Blennius nigriceps)*.

Setting It All Up

If you refer to Part I for information on equipment, tanks, and setup, you can get an overall picture of the particular aspects of starting an aquarium. In this section, I give you a few details about modifying a setup for a invertebrate tank.

The tank

Start with a larger tank if you want to keep invertebrates. For beginners, I recommend a 55-gallon tank. These animals are not tolerant of bad water conditions, so a larger aquarium gives you better biological stability. A 55-gallon tank is a great starting size because it allows you to keep many invertebrates and a few small fish together safely. As with other marine aquariums, the tank should not contain any metal.

Heating

The best type of heater for an invertebrate tank is a submersible one. You can angle the heater along the back of the glass to make sure that no cold pockets occur. If you have a large aquarium, you can use two heaters. Be careful with heater placement so that you do not burn any invertebrates that may settle on rock or coral near the equipment. If you see melted blobs that resemble Play-Doh all along the back of your tank, move your heater to another location.

Lighting

Proper lighting is one of the most important aspects of an invertebrate tank. Many invertebrates (which have tiny organisms within their cells) use light to manufacture food for proper growth. I recommend *actinic light* (long-wave untraviolet radiation light that can penetrate the water well) for anemones and corals. Your aquarium should receive eight to ten hours of light per day, but lighting depends a lot on what you have in your tank and the tank size. Experiment a little for the best results.

Filtration

Filtration type is really a matter of personal choice. One hobbyist swears by one system, while another disagrees with its performance. I recommend at least two filtration systems for an invertebrate tank. A good undergravel filter coupled with a strong powerfilter is a good combination to start with. Canister filters are another good option, but they can be quite expensive. You can always add more filtration later or switch to a bigger and better system. In addition, use a protein skimmer on your invertebrate tank to keep water conditions at their best.

Live rock works as a natural filtration system and gives your invertebrates places to settle on. Remember that the filtration systems that you use should be able to carry out mechanical, chemical, and biological filtration when combined in one aquarium. Make sure that you choose filtration systems that can cover those three areas. (See Chapter 5 for more information on equipment.)

Water conditions

Water conditions should be optimal in an invertebrate tank. Nitrate and ammonia levels must be kept low. Most invertebrates tolerate temperatures between 71 and 75 degrees F. But always check the individual requirements of each species that you buy.

Feeding

One great way to feed many invertebrates is to use bottled food. You can choose from a variety of invertebrate foods (such as premixed vitamins and seafood). All you have to do is follow the manufacturer's instructions on the label. You usually add this type of food to the tank by the teaspoon, but you dispense liquid invertebrate food by squirting it directly into an animal through the use of a bulb or pipette.

Another method of feeding involves placing a small piece of frozen food in the center of invertebrates, such as the anemone, once or twice a week. This method of food supply supplements their filter feeding. Most invertebrates gather live brine shrimp, which is a welcome addition to their diet.

Substrate

One good way to build a substrate for an invertebrate tank is to start with a layer of dolomite and then add live sand as a top cover. The live sand (which usually contains tiny crustaceans and worms) aids in filtration and provides soft spots for burrowing invertebrates and fish.

Part III
The Fish

The 5th Wave   By Rich Tennant

"Honey! I think the angelfish have outgrown the neon tetras!"

In this part . . .

Most aquariums aren't complete without fish. The next few chapters describe how fish live, eat, sleep, and breathe, and they tell you what fish might be suitable for your aquarium.

Chapter 12

Fish Anatomy

· ·

· ·

*F*ish are truly amazing creatures. They have been roaming the earth's water for almost 450 million years and have adapted themselves over time in order to live and survive in their watery environment. A species' body shape, fin length, and other physical characteristics have been specially formed to meet the needs of different types of habitats. As you find out more about a fish's physical makeup, you increase the odds of becoming a successful fishkeeper with that species.

As you read through this chapter, refer to Figure 12-1 as I mention various fish anatomical features.

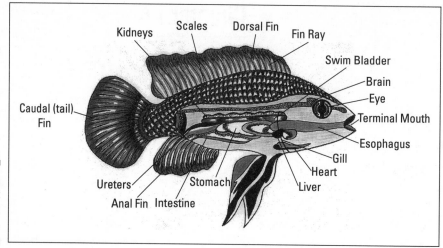

Figure 12-1:
Important
parts of a
fish.

What Really Makes a Fish Go?

At one time or another, everyone stands transfixed, watching aquarium fish glide effortlessly through the water and wondering how they navigate through their liquid environment with such ease. Humans flail at best with water wings; or if you're like me, you look like a pregnant whale while struggling to do a few simple laps at the local pool. So what makes a fish swim better than we do? The answer is really quite simple.

Fish have a set of *fins* (six or seven depending on the species) that they use for locomotion. They also have a cool organ called a *swim bladder* that helps them stay afloat. Fish have evolved to conquer their watery environment with adaptations that have led toward creating the perfect aquatic swimming machine. Unfortunately, even swimming numerous laps and using rubber fins, humans achieve only a pale imitation of the perfection of their aquatic friends.

Fish fins and what they do

In order to understand what makes a fish go, you must first understand each fin's function. Each individual fin has a specific job to do, and the combined effort of all a fish's fins is what propels her through the water and helps her navigate smoothly. Fin functions are an interaction of muscle power combined with agility and sheer grace.

The dorsal fin

The *dorsal fin* is located along the back of the fish between the tail fin and the head. This is the classic fin you see rapidly slicing through the water in the movie *Jaws*. If you happen to see a *Jaws*-type fin while swimming in the ocean one morning, you may want to take up beach volleyball for a while. Fortunately for your peace of mind, the dorsal fins on your aquarium fish generally remain underwater.

The dorsal fin provides lateral stability so that your fish can swim in a straight line (controlled swimming conserves energy) instead of looking like a staggering drunk trying to navigate his way home after slamming one too many at the local pub. A fish that cannot swim well will not live very long because it will not be able to compete for food with its tankmates. Each fin consists of a series of individual *rays* (some soft and some hard) loosely bound together by a membrane web. A few aquatic pets, such as some species of goldfish, do not have dorsal fins. They have great difficulty swimming normally because they cannot keep their movement in a straight line.

Marine filefish and triggerfish have dorsal fins that are doubled. Part of this fin is a nasty little spine that resembles a straight razor and can easily inflict serious puncture wounds. The other dorsal acts as a stabilizer. When confronting an adversary, a triggerfish raises her dorsal fin, using it to both intimidate and threaten. (Unfortunately, a triggerfish's adversaries include you and your family.) A fish with this double dorsal can also use an erect and locked fin as a wedge to jam herself into a tight area of coral so that a predator cannot pull it out.

The saltwater lionfish has adapted venomous dorsal spines. Each fin contains poison glands which can produce painful wounds when inserted into flesh (such as your fingers.) These elegant-looking fins stick out all over a lionfish's body and make him look like a floating pincushion. Always use extreme caution when handling this type of fish.

The caudal fin

The *caudal fin* (tail fin) is responsible for sudden forward movement (bursts of speed) and for very fast swimming patterns. Fish also use their tail fin to slow forward movement and to help make turns. This fin produces the majority of a fish's physical power.

Lengthening the caudal fin of many species (such as the goldfish and betta) through *artificial selection* (breeding for a specific trait) has produced a slower moving fish used for show purposes. These long-finned types probably would not survive long in the wild. A three-inch goldfish with a six-inch caudal fin dragging on the gravel like the train on a wedding dress is bound to cause a few unsightly swimming problems.

Sadly, many species of fish have been selectively bred to have fins that are so long or unusually shaped that the fish struggle just to stay upright in the water. Breeders, fish buyers, and fish lovers (sometimes all one person) need to take a close look at the type of fish being produced.

The anal fin

The *anal fin* is located on the underside of a fish between the pelvic and caudal fins. The sole purpose of this fin is to provide stability — it keeps your fish from rolling over in the water and going belly up (and no one wants to see her fish belly up in the water). In some species, the anal fin has developed into a double set of fins that are fused together at the base of the fish's body.

In species such as the freshwater guppy, the male's anal fin acts as a sexual organ and is known as a *gonopodium*. This rod-shaped organ inserts sperm into the female's vent during spawning. Many species of Characins, such as tetras, have small hooks on their anal fins that attach them to their mate during breeding.

The pectoral fins

Pectoral fins provide stability as a fish moves through the water, hovers, and makes slow turns. These paired fins are located near the bottom of the fish, directly beneath the gill openings (one on each side). Pectoral fins are used for navigation and are constantly in motion.

Many species use the pectoral fins to incubate their eggs with water during the brooding period. Many flying fish have adapted their pectoral fins into wings so that they can take short flights through the air.

The pelvic fins

Pelvic fins aid fish in braking, stabilizing their bodies, and changing directions. These fins are located in front of the anal fin on the abdomen of the fish (one on each side). Other uses of the pelvic fins include searching for food, carrying eggs, and fighting. These fins are usually smaller in open water species like the freshwater platy, and larger in bottom-dwellers such as the marine mandarin.

The adipose fin

A few species of fish such as tetras have an extra, *adipose fin,* located on the back between the dorsal and tailfins. Hobbyists often refer to it as the second dorsal fin. Scientists have not found any physical reason for this fin to exist. At this point, it has no known use. But, it looks cool, so why not?

Swimming movement

The special body shape of fish helps increase the overall efficiency of their swimming movement. A fish's body is usually tapered at the head and tail and bulky in the middle (kind of like me when I hit midlife). This tapering allows fish to slip through the water without much effort. So, maybe if I can find a way to live in my bathtub, I'll have it made.

Looking carefully at your fish, you may notice that most swim with little or no effort, which is surprising because water is much more resistant than air. But water's liquid form supports a body's weight as it moves. Because your fish's weight is suspended in water, he needs only a small amount of energy to overcome the force of gravity — as opposed to the effort we humans must put out as we move through atmospheric air on dry land.

A fish's muscle force is achieved though energy created by short fibers that run throughout the entire body. These numerous fibers move in sequence and create physical energy in a series of s-shaped curves. This energy is then transferred to the tail to provide locomotion. Finally, the tail fin pushes all the water surrounding it backwards, which in turn propels the fish's body in a quick forward motion. This sequence of events allows the fish to move through the water without creating any turbulence — which would slow it down.

Respiration

Just like humans, fish require oxygen for survival. Fish use oxygen that they strip from the surrounding water and produce carbon dioxide as a waste product. Any living plants in your aquarium use this carbon dioxide, and eventually expel oxygen back into the water.

The gill method

Unlike mammals, fish don't get their oxygen from air. Instead, fish take their oxygen directly from the water through their *gills*. Gills are lined with a large number of blood vessels that help retrieve oxygen.

Gills are very similar in structure and form to human lungs, except that they are a whole lot more efficient: While fish remove up to 85 percent of the oxygen from the water, humans obtain only about 25 percent of the oxygen in the air. (Of course, if you live in Los Angeles, your oxygen consumption drops to about 2 percent.)

Water enters a fish's mouth and passes across the gills where up to 85 percent of the oxygen is extracted by the gill filaments. The oxygen-depleted water is then quickly discarded.

Fish with high energy levels who are very active, like the freshwater danio, must constantly keep swimming in order to force water through their gills and obtain oxygen. Species of fish with high energy levels would eventually suffer asphyxiation if kept in a small aquarium that restricted their swimming movement. I doubt that you want to live in a sealed elevator with 20 other people. Neither do your fish.

When moving fish from one location to another, you must remember that gills are made out of fine tissue that can collapse if removed from water. The gills are structurally supported by the weight of the water itself. So it is very important that you keep your fish in water while moving them, to avoid causing any damage to their gills and other body parts.

The labyrinth organ method

A certain group of fishes (known as the Anabantids), found in Asia and Africa, are able to breathe air directly from the atmosphere, using a specialized organ called the *labyrinth*. The labyrinth, located inside the head behind the gills, has evolved over time to take oxygen directly from the air as a supplement to extracting it from the water.

Anabantids include bettas, gouramis, and paradise fish. In the wild, these fish live in dirty, poorly oxygenated waters full of strange-looking creatures. Hey, that sounds like a good day at our public pool!

The physical shape of the labyrinth organ gives rise to its name, which literally means "maze." The labyrinth contains rosette-shaped plates that have thousands of oxygen-absorbing blood vessels, which gather air that is inhaled. The inhaled air is then trapped inside a group of folds (which resembles a sponge) and is eventually absorbed into the main bloodstream.

Anabantids can survive in a smaller aquarium space than that which is normally provided (usually ten or more gallons) because they can extract oxygen from the air. However, this does not mean that anabantids can or should be kept in very crowded conditions or extremely tiny tanks. Even though they have the ability to breathe "extra" air, these fishes still add as much waste to the water as their tankmates, and need proper space and filtration for healthy living.

Anabantids can develop diseases brought on by crowded tanks with bad water conditions, just like other species. Take my word for it, they'll be healthier and happier in a proper aquarium. (Anabantids should be provided with the same high quality filtration, heating, and other proper conditions as is standard with other tropical fish.) They will like you a lot better too.

The Senses

Like humans, fishes have five senses: taste, sight, hearing, touch, and smell. Fish use all these senses to locate food, communicate with one another, attract mates, and avoid bigger and meaner fish. Fish have been known to learn to do without one or more of their senses when they've been injured or born with a physical defect. I've seen fish in the worst possible physical condition continue to survive. Think how great they can look and feel if we keep them in the _best_ possible condition!

Sight

Following are some fun facts about fish eyes:

✔ Fish have the ability to see in two directions at the same time. This physical phenomenon is known as _monocular vision._

✔ Fish can't completely focus both their eyes on a single object at the same time.

✔ Fish do not have eyelids, and sleep literally with their eyes wide open, resting in a hypnotic state.

✔ Fish are nearsighted and see clearly only about a foot away.

So, if you stand across the room, smiling and wildly waving both your hands to entertain your fish, don't hold your breath waiting for them to respond.

The lateral line system

Fish have an interesting system known as the _lateral line,_ which helps them locate objects in their path and in their surrounding environment that they cannot see normally due to their limited eyesight (see Figure 12-2).

The lateral line is located on both sides of their body and runs from the back of the eye to the base of the tail fin. These lines are composed of small _neuromasts_ (tiny stinging cells), which contain _cilia_ (very fine hairs) in fluid-filled canals. These canals detect vibrations in the water, and the vibrations form an "image" inside the fish's brain.

The eyes

A fish's eyes are often large to compensate for the poor lighting conditions that exist under water. Usually the eyes are located on the sides of the head, and in the case of the seahorse, can be rotated 360 degrees. In certain species that live in areas of total or semi-darkness (such as the blind cavefish), the eyes are absent all together. Over time, they have been selectively removed through the evolutionary process.

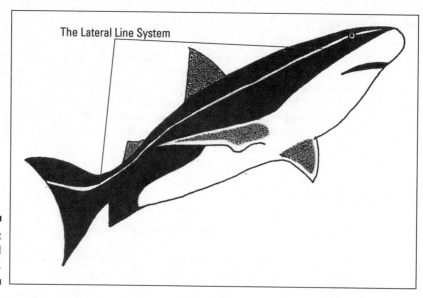

Figure 12-2:
The lateral
line system.

Some fish do have the ability to see a few colors at various depths, but have great difficulty adjusting to rapid light changes because their iris works slowly. For this reason, fish act "shocked" and begin to panic when an aquarium light is suddenly turned on or off without warning in the form of an accompanying change in the room lighting. So if you turn on your aquarium light right after you get up in the morning, then notice that your fish are stuck to the ceiling, you probably frightened them a little bit.

Within the human eye, the shape of the lens is constantly changing in an effort to achieve proper focus. The lens in a fish's eye remains the same shape, but focuses with help from special ocular ligaments that actually move the eye forward and backward in its socket.

Hearing

Fish do not have complex ears like we do because sound travels in water much faster than in air. Fish ears are composed of a simple inner chamber. Vibrations picked up from the environment are passed over sensory components, which generate sound. Most *ichthyologists* (fish experts) believe that a fish's swim bladder works together with the components of the inner ear to distinguish specific sound patterns. This is similar to the human ear working in harmony with the stomach so that you always know when it's time for dinner.

Smell

Smell plays an important role in detecting food and prey, and in locating a suitable mate. Fish take in smells through their nostrils, which are connected to their olfactory system. This olfactory system is not completely joined with the respiratory system and acts as a separate unit.

Taste

Fish have taste buds on their mouths, lips, and, in special cases, on their fins. The complete range of taste for fish is very short, so they must constantly forage through their environment in hopes that they can "stumble across" the food they need to survive. Catfish have evolved *barbels* that contain taste buds for locating food in cloudy or dark water.

Feeling

The old argument as to whether fish can feel pain or not has been at issue for many years. I, for one, would really hate to find out that my fish could feel pain if I did something that caused them harm. The safest bet is to assume always that your fish can feel pain and treat them with respect and great care.

Osmosis (And Other Complicated-Sounding Words)

Osmosis is a simple process by which a fish maintains the correct salt to water ratio in his body. Through osmosis, water molecules constantly pass through semipermeable membranes in the fish to equalize the amount of salt water throughout his body. Osmosis is one of the main reasons freshwater fish cannot live in saltwater and vice versa. (As with every other rule, there are a few exceptions to this one.)

Fish that don't drink water

The salt concentration in the body fluids of freshwater fish remains at a higher level than the salt content of the water in which they live (see Figure 12-3). For this reason, water is always being drawn into their cells by osmosis. If they did not have a means of getting rid of this excess water baggage, they would burst like a balloon that has been filled to a point where it has exceeded its air capacity, or resemble the human body after Thanksgiving dinner.

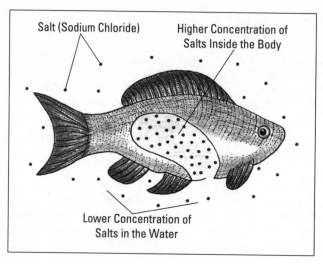

Salt (Sodium Chloride)

Higher Concentration of Salts Inside the Body

Lower Concentration of Salts in the Water

Figure 12-3:
Osmosis in a freshwater fish.

Water is removed by the kidneys in the form of a very dilute urine in freshwater species. Specialized salt absorbing cells that are located in the gills, move sodium chloride (salt) from the water into the blood. Very small amounts of salt that are present in commercial fish foods, will also help aquatic species to remain in balance. The amount of salt passed into a fish's body is so small that it does not require much energy to get rid of it.

Fish that need to drink water

Marine fish have the opposite problem when it comes to balancing water and salt in their body's cells. Saltwater fish have a lower salt content in their bodies and must constantly "drink" water to replace that lost by osmosis to the saltier environment around them. If saltwater fish do not constantly drink water, they eventually die from dehydration.

Saltwater fish excrete small amounts of urine. They also rid their bodies of excess salt to maintain their overall osmotic balance.

Recognizing Traits to Identify Fish

A fish's life, habits, and movement are completely dependent upon its overall body form and size. When you look at the individual mouth structure and fin design of each species, you can discover many clues to help answer questions about the way a fish survives, eats, and moves along through the watery environment in which it lives.

Discovering how a fish's physical form evolved over a long period of time to guarantee its survival in many different types of aquatic environments around the world helps you recognize unfamiliar species and can give you an immediate idea of what their aquarium requirements probably are. Although this is not a scientific rule, it works about 95 percent of the time.

Body shape

The specific shape of a fish's body can give you several clues as to its natural habitat and swimming range. The streamlined body of a zebra danio, for example, allows this fish to slip smoothly and effortlessly through open water. So, you won't find danios living in stagnant swamps in the wild. See what I mean?

Other types of fish have different body shapes that help them in their native environments. For example, the tapered shape of a discus lessens water friction and helps the discus conserve its energy as it quickly slips through obstacles to catch its prey. You find this fish living in areas with sunken tree roots and other types of natural barriers.

Round-shaped aquatic species, such as fancy goldfish, are slow swimmers and tire quite easily. You find these species living in slow-moving waters. Hey, now I know why I couldn't finish that second lap at the pool!

Fish that are flat on their ventral side (bottom side) such as the cory, spend the great majority of their time moving along the substrate bed in your home aquarium.

Taxonomy

If you ask a group of people what guidelines they would use to define and describe exactly what a fish is, you would probably end up with quite a long and varied list. People tend to forget that mammals such as whales and dolphins are not fish because they are warm-blooded and are required to come to the surface in order to breathe. Fish do not need to breathe our air because they have the ability to extract oxygen from the water around them.

Cold-blooded creatures

The fish in your aquarium are cold-blooded. All this means is that their body temperature depends on the temperature of the water around them. Metabolic rate also plays a role in body temperature — active fish have a slightly higher body temperature than lethargic fish.

Because lay people generally cannot decide unanimously on any subject, a group of scientists got together and decided to classify animals into large groups that they believed had similar physical attributes. Lo and behold, *taxonomy* was born. *Ichthyologists* (people who spend their time studying fish), place individual aquatic species into several categories (physical traits) so that they can differentiate fish from other types of animals.

Scientists classify bony fish as having a backbone (vertebrae), a small skeleton that protects and supports it body weight and internal organs; fins, rays made of cartilage or bone; gill respiration; separate sexes; and a brain case.

Mouth location

The way a fish's mouth is shaped and the direction it points have quite a lot to do with the manner in which it feeds and the range (bottom, middle, or top) of aquarium water in which it spends most of its time.

Aquatic species such as the hatchet fish have an upturned mouth, indicating that they are top feeders, and scoop up flakes and floating food on the water's surface in the aquarium. This upward-turned mouth is also known as a *superior position.*

A turned-down mouth is known as an *inferior position,* and can be found in many bottom-dwelling species such as catfish. These fish feed along the gravel bed and off of flat rock surfaces and plant leaves.

When the mouth faces straight away from the fish's face, this is known as a *terminal position* and is common in species that swim in mid-water such as goldfish and platys. These species feed by "picking off" food as it sinks to the bottom.

Scales

Most fish have a body that is covered with *scales* that overlap each other in a manner similar to the way shingles are nailed to the roof of a house. Scales are formed of transparent plates that protect the body from injury. These thin scales also serve as streamlining for efficient gliding through the water. A slimy mucus layer covers the tops of the scales to provide smoothness and add extra protection. The slimy feeling produced by the mucus also protects against invading parasites and infection.

Not all fish have scales, however. As usual, there are a few exceptions.

There are two main types of scales found in bony fishes:

 ✔ **Ctenoid scales** have tiny little teeth on their outer edges.

 ✔ **Cycloid scales** are smooth and round.

Scales grow out from the skin and generally have no color. Scale color comes from *pigment* cells located in the skin itself.

A quick guide to aquatic anatomy terms

The following terms are used quite often by hobbyists when they talk about the physical aspects of their fish. You can use this table as a handy reference guide until you become familiar with these terms.

- **Adipose fin:** An extra fin, found in some species of fish, located directly behind the dorsal fin.

- **Anal fin:** Located between the pelvic and caudal fins.

- **Caudal fin:** The tail fin, which provides the muscular force required to move the fish though the water.

- **Caudal peduncle:** The muscular stalk that connects the body to the tail.

- **Dorsal side:** The top of the fish.

- **Dorsal fin:** The fin between the head and caudal peduncle, which is used for stabilization.

- **Gill slit:** An opening behind the eye that provides a large area for absorbing oxygen during respiration.

- **Gonopodium:** A male sexual organ that some species developed from the anal fin.

- **Labyrinth organ:** A specialized organ that allows fish to breathe air.

- **Lateral line:** Fluid-filled canals that function as a sixth sense.

- **Operculum:** Bony plate covering the external gill cavity.

- **Pectoral fins:** Located behind the gill slit and in front of the anal fin; used for steering.

- **Pelvic fins:** Located between the anal and pectoral fins and are used for control of motion and propulsion.

- **Posterior:** The tail end of the fish.

- **Ray:** An individual section of a fin.

- **Vent:** The digestive and reproductive tract opening.

- **Ventral:** The bottom side of the fish.

The swim bladder

Hypothetically, most fish should sink to the bottom of your aquarium because they are slightly heavier than water. Their muscle and skeleton mass is made up of substances not found in great quantities in the environment around them. A swim bladder is an organ that helps them overcome this problem.

A swim bladder is one of those funny-sounding terms that you hear hobbyists use quite often. But what exactly is a swim bladder, and what does it do? The swim bladder is an organ filled with gas and helps fish maintain their vertical position in the water. Without a swim bladder, most fish would sink to the bottom and end up as a permanent tank decoration. (However, this organ may be lacking in some bottom dwellers.)

Internal gas adjustments through the use of a specialized duct allow fish to remain suspended with little or no effort. When a fish moves to the bottom of an aquarium, its swim bladder automatically compresses and the fish sinks. To correct this problem, gas must be added to the swim bladder to achieve buoyancy again. When a fish decides to move toward the top of the tank, its upward movement releases gas from its swim bladder. Otherwise, the fish would be forced to expend too much physical energy to move to a deeper depth.

Coloration and its purpose

Pigment cells (known as *chromatophores* in the snob zone) in the skin are responsible for the production of color. Different shades of colors in fish warn off predators and attract mates. This social use of a physical attribute has not been lost in the captivity of the home aquarium. Many species of freshwater and brackish fish have adopted new colors that have appeared through selective breeding, and have used them to their own advantage in mating and aggression displays. Hey, maybe I'll try that!

Chapter 13

Species Guide

● ●

In This Chapter

▶ Looking at freshwater fish

▶ Looking at marine fish

▶ Looking at brackish fish

▶ Purchasing captive-bred species

● ●

When you go to purchase your new fish, you need to have a general idea as to which species can survive in your particular type of system. Otherwise, you may end up with a bunch of marine fish floating at the top of your freshwater aquarium or a group of freshwater fish becoming lunch for your saltwater species — neither situation looking at all cool. You simply can't mix apples and oranges in aquariums. Save that combination for Sunday's fruit salad.

This chapter gives you a general overview of major fish families and shows you where they fit in each type of aquarium system. This chapter also helps you understand special dietary and social needs of many species. *Most* of the fish listed in this chapter are excellent choices for beginners. (I give you plenty of warning about those that aren't.)

This chapter presents you with many *scientific names*. A scientific name is usually based on Greek or Latin, and uses two words. The first word is the *genus* (a group of related species) that the fish fit into. The second word is the *species* (a group of animals that can interbreed) within that genus. The species name is often the same as the person who first described the fish. A named ending in *"I"* means that a man first described the fish. A name ending in *"AE"* means that a woman first described the species. Because no one could pronounce half of these strange names, a *common name* (like guppy) was given to each fish. Now that you have the scientific information, let's move on to the important stuff.

All you need to do is to memorize a few common scientific names so you can look cool around other hobbyists.

Key terms to remember

Carnivor: Any organism that eats animals as the main portion of its diet.

Herbivor: Any organism that eats plant material as the main portion of its diet.

Omnivor: Any organism that eats both animal and plant material as the main portion of its diet.

Community tank: An aquarium where many different species of fish are kept together.

Freshwater Tropical

As you already know, the freshwater tropical aquarium system does not contain any marine salt and generally requires some type of heater. This type of system usually contains live plants and has gravel for substrate.

Anabantids

The *anabantids* are a group of fish native to African and Asian waters. These fish have a specialized *labyrinth organ* that helps them breathe atmospheric air in the low-oxygenated waters of their native environment. This doesn't mean you should keep them in an aquarium that lacks aeration. If you do, all your fish will turn one color: Blue. Anabantids are generally peacefully species that swim in the mid to upper levels of the aquarium tank and are easy to breed.

Climbing perch (Anabas testudineus)

This amazing fish can live several days without water, and has been known to travel across land in its native environment as it moves from pond to pond. Keep *climbing perch* in water near 80 degrees F, and provide plenty of shelter for them (rock caves, and so on). This fish should be kept with its own kind. The climbing perch is carnivorous and swims in all levels of the tank.

Siamese fighting fish (Betta splendens)

The Asian *Siamese fighting fish* has been bred for years to develop strains that have long flowing fins and bright colors. Males of this species are aggressive toward each other, and must be kept singly. You can keep Siamese fighting fish in a community aquarium as long as the other fish are not fin nippers. Bettas build bubble nests to spawn and should be kept at a temperature of 76 to 83 degrees F. The betta is omnivorous and swims in all levels of the tank.

Paradise fish (Macropodus opercularis)

The beautifully striped and speckled *paradise fish* is native to China and Korea. When frightened, the paradise fish loses its color quickly. Paradise fish build bubble nests for spawning, and prefer a temperature of 75 degrees F. The paradise fish is aggressive, and should be kept with hardy species of its own size. Some males constantly fight with each other. The paradise fish is carnivorous and swims in all levels of the tank.

Cyprinodonts

The *cyprinodont* group is also known as *toothcarps* because they have tiny teeth. This group contains both live-bearing and egg-laying fish, and contains some of the most popular and classic community fish (guppies, platys, and swordtails). This group of fish are friendly, easy to breed, and swim in all levels of the tank.

Killifish

Although most killifish prefer soft, acidic water, a few species can be kept in a community aquarium. The killifish swims in the upper to middle levels of the tank, and is carnivorous. These species should be kept in schools.

Medaka or rice fish (Oryzias latipes)

Keep *rice fish* in a *school* (three or more fish) to ensure their survival in a community aquarium. Rice fish prefer a well-planted tank and they fertilize their eggs internally. This species has been known to jump out of a tank, so a tight-fitting hood is a must. The rice fish is carnivorous, requires live food, and swims in the upper level of the tank.

Striped panchax (Aplocheilus lineatus)

This great community fish is also an aquarium jumper, so make sure your aquarium hood is secure. This egg-laying species uses plants for shelter and to spawn, so provide plenty of plants. The panchax is carnivorous, requires live food, and swims in the upper level of the tank.

Livebearers

The *livebearers* (fish that give birth to fully formed young) are some of the most commonly purchased fish and are recommended for beginning hobbyists. These fish are peaceful and very hardy, so they tolerate many beginners' mistakes. The livebearers in this family are also relatively inexpensive.

Guppy (Poecilia reticulata)

The Central American *guppy* is an amazing little fish. It has been the staple of many community aquariums since the hobby began. Guppies are now available in a wide variety of colors and fin shapes. The male's anal fin has evolved over time into a specialized organ called a *gonopodium* (a rod-like extension), which it uses to internally fertilize a female's eggs. These fish are best kept in a well-planted tank in a ratio of one male to every three females. The guppy is omnivorous and swims in all levels of the tank.

Swordtail (Xiphophorus helleri)

The *swordtail* (native to Mexico, Honduras, and Guatemala) is a brightly colored fish that makes a good addition to any community aquarium. The males of this species have an elongated caudal fin extension that resembles a sword, and, like the guppy, have a gonopodium (see the preceding "Guppy" section) and prefer heavily planted tanks. Swordtails are very active and should be kept in water that is slightly hard. The swordtail is omnivorous and swims in all levels of the tank.

Sailfin molly (Poecilia latipinna)

The *sailfin molly* is a beautiful species native to the brackish waters of the United States and Mexico. The male's dorsal fin, when erect, looks like the sail on a ship. Keep mollies in a well-planted tank, and provide extra vegetation in their diet. This species can be aggressive toward smaller fish, but generally makes a great community member. Mollies like hard water, so you can add about one teaspoon of salt for every gallon of water to make them happy. The sailfin molly is omnivorous and swims in all levels of the tank.

Make sure that the other species you keep can tolerate extra salt before you add it.

Platy (Xiphophorus maculatus)

Platys sport some of the most beautiful colors of all freshwater fish. This hardy species, which is native to Mexico, Honduras, and Guatemala, breeds easily in the community aquarium and is very peaceful. Platys have been developed extensively through commercial breeding, and can be found with different fin shapes and in almost every color imaginable. The platy is omnivorous and swims in all levels of the tank.

Catfish

Catfish play an important role in the aquarium system. These species generally feed off the substrate as they gather unwanted debris. Catfish often survive by using their *barbels* (specialized organs used for tasting) to locate the leftovers that fall to the bottom of the tank. Many species are *nocturnal* (more active at night), so feed them the sinking food formulated especially for them accordingly. Catfish can be aggressive if they are not kept with species their own size, and most are omnivorous.

Bristlenose catfish (Ancistrus temmincki)

The *bristlenose catfish* is a prehistoric-looking member of the Loricariidae family. Males of this species carry a double row of bristles on their snouts, whereas the females bear only a single row. The bristlenose's mouth is formed into a *sucker disk* that it uses to feed on algae in its native habitat. This peaceful South American catfish is herbivorous, lives in the lower level of the aquarium, and is peaceful.

Glass catfish (Kryptopterus bicirrhis)

The *glass catfish* is a fascinating animal with a transparent body: You can actually see this fish's backbone and internal organs through its body wall. Keep this peaceful Southeast Asian fish in schools (at least three). The glass catfish is carnivorous and swims in the middle and lower sections of the tank.

Upside-down catfish (Synodontis contractus)

True to its unusual name, the *upside-down catfish* often swims with its abdomen pointed upward. This beautiful little fish from tropical Africa changes its body shading according to its swimming position. The peaceful upside-down catfish is carnivorous and swims in all levels of the tank.

Suckermouth catfish (Hypostomus multiradiatus)

One of the most famous catfish known to the aquarium hobbyist is the *suckermouth*. This fish has a leopard-print pattern of spots and can grow to lengths over one foot. Constantly in search of food, the suckermouth may tear up vegetation if your aquarium is planted. The suckermouth is herbivorous and swims in the lower and middle levels of the tank.

Blackfin cory (Corydoras leucomelas)

Probably the most popular species of catfish for the home aquarium is the cory. Corys come in a wide variety of spotted and striped patterns, are inexpensive, and do a good job cleaning debris from the bottom of the tank. The friendly little *blackfin cory* from South America is omnivorous and swims in the lower levels. Corys should be kept in schools (at least three), and are easily bred by amateurs.

Characins

The *characins* are one of the most diverse groups of fish, including the small tetras and the big, bad piranha of movie fame. Members of this group are characterized by the bones that link their swim bladder and inner ear. Many characins also have a small adipose fin on their top side between the tail and dorsal fins.

Glowlight tetra (Hemigrammus erythrozonus)

The *glowlight tetra* of South America is an interesting little fish with a glowing line running from its eye to the base of its tail. The peaceful glowlight tetra prefers soft, acidic water and a well-planted tank. It is omnivorous and swims in all levels of the tank.

Bleeding heart tetra (Hyphessobrycon erythrostigma)

The South American *bleeding heart tetra* earned its name from its physical attributes. This silver-colored fish has a red spot on its chest that makes it look as if Clint Eastwood just shot it at high noon. The bleeding heart needs plenty of swimming room and is easily spooked. This semipeaceful fish (it may be aggressive toward fish that are smaller than it) is omnivorous and swims near the middle level of the tank.

Neon tetra (Paracheirodon innesi)

The South American *neon tetra* is one of the most recognizable fish in an aquarium. This peaceful little fish has a blue-green stripe that glitters down the side of its body. The neon is omnivorous, swims at mid level in the tank, needs to be kept in schools (at least six to eight), and is quite difficult to breed in captivity.

Serpae tetra (Hyphessobrycon serpae)

This fish takes it name from its color resemblance to a Mexican *serape* (large shawl). The peaceful serpae is a mid-level swimmer and is omnivorous.

Cardinal tetra (Paracheirodon axelrodi)

The *cardinal tetra* is similar in appearance to the neon tetra, except that it has a larger area of red coloring on its abdomen. The peaceful cardinal prefers soft, acidic waters and is omnivorous. This fish swims in all levels of the tank and should be kept in schools (at least six to eight).

Unusual characins

There are many different types of characins. The following sections give examples of some that are quite unusual in physical form.

Some of the many different types of characins are quite unusual. The following sections detail some physically unique specimens.

Blindcave fish (Astyanax fasciatus mexicanus)

The *blindcave fish* has no eyes and navigates in dark, underground caves using its *lateral line* (see Chapter 12). The body is pink, and a school of five members makes a great addition to the community tank. The blindcave fish is omnivorous.

Silver hatchetfish (Gasteropelecus sternicla)

The body of the *silver hatchetfish* body resembles the blade of a large ax. This peaceful South American fish eats live insects and should be kept in schools (of at least three), which will stay near the top of the tank. This fish can leap from your aquarium to your driveway in a single bound, so keep a lid on it.

Pacu (Colossoma bidens)

A pacu looks like a piranha, grows to the size of your mid-sized car, and can eat you out of house and home. This fish is suppose to be herbivorous, but don't bet the bank (or the smaller fish in your aquarium) on it. The pacu swims at mid level.

Red-bellied piranha (Serrasalmus nattereri)

The piranha is a dangerous, (often illegal to buy, sell, or own in many states) large predator. If you temporarily lose your mind and think about buying this fish, seek professional help immediately.

Silver dollar (Mylossoma pluriventre)

This neat fish resembles a silver dollar in form and color. The silver dollar is herbivorous and may destroy aquarium plants if you have them. These fish are generally peaceful, but a few bad apples can become quite aggressive when larger. For best results, keep silver dollars in a school of five to eight in a species tank.

Three-lined pencilfish (Nannostomus trifasciatus)

This South American species is probably the world's coolest fish. It looks like a swimming number-two pencil. You may not find it in stock at pet stores, but you can usually order it. The three-lined pencilfish is omnivorous, peaceful, and requires thick vegetation.

Loaches

Loaches are an interesting group of species from Asia and India. Loaches resemble streamlined catfish and, like catfish, are bottom dwellers that use barbels to search for food. These fish can also extract oxygen from the air by gulping it. Most species are nocturnal, so unless you work a night job, you may not see them too often. Loaches are carnivorous, swim in the lower levels of the tank, and are often shy by nature.

Clown loach (Botia macracantha)

The *clown loach* is striped like a tiger and spends most of its time peacefully foraging for food near the bottom of the tank. The clown loach is carnivorous and is best kept in a school of three to five.

Orange-finned loach (Botia modesta)

The orange-finned loach has a blue-gray body with bright orange fins. This species hides during the day and is very shy. The orange-finned loach swims in the lower levels of the tank, is carnivorous, and makes clicking noises to attract mates.

Cichlids

Cichlids are native to the Americas, Asia, and Africa. Most species (with a few exceptions) tend to be aggressive and are best kept in a species tank with their own kind. Some cichlids require special water conditions — I note them where applicable.

Small ones

Although many cichlids have a thick body that can grow quite large, a few small varieties are suitable for the home aquarium.

Kribensis (Pelvicachromis pulcher)

The West African kribensis is a generally peaceful, rainbow-colored fish. The kribensis is an omnivorous bottom-dweller.

Keyhole (Aequidens maronii)

The *keyhole cichlid* is a pale fish with a dark band running through its eyes. The keyhole prefers a heavily planted tank and is an omnivorous bottom-dweller.

Other cichlids

A brief overview of a few larger cichlids is in order because they consist of the most beautiful species in this group.

Angelfish (Pterophyllum scalare)

The *angelfish* is such a delicate-looking species, you can only wonder how it can possibly be related to other cichlids. Angelfish have long dorsal and anal fins they use for balance. A deep and long tank is best for this peaceful, carnivorous species. Angelfish are egg-layers and are easily bred in the home aquarium. Angelfish make great community fish.

Red oscar (Astronotus ocellatus)

The *red oscar* is a Amazonian giant who may quickly outgrow your tank. This animal is carnivorous and eats anything it can fit into its large mouth. One cool thing about an oscar is that you can hand tame it to accept food from you. Oscars spend most of their time swimming in the mid levels of the tank. You can easily fool your friends into thinking that you are risking life and limb by feeding them.

Convict (Cichlasoma nigrofasciatum)

If you desire to impress your friends with your breeding abilities, the *convict cichlid* is the fish for you. This hardy cichlid would breed in a puddle of water during an earthquake if given half a chance. Rabbits can't hold a candle to convicts. The convict is aggressive, swims in the mid to lower sections of the aquarium, is carnivorous, and should be kept in a well-planted species tank.

Discus (Symphysodon var.)

The *discus* is the king of the cichlids. This flat fish, which resembles a plastic throwing disk, has been commercially bred to produce stunning colors. These fish are carnivorous and should be kept in schools of at least three to five. Discus water must be soft and acidic. Discus can be very expensive, but are well worth the investment.

Cyprinids

The *cyprinids* are a diverse family that includes barbs, danios, and rasboras.

Tiger barb (Barbus tetrazona)

The *tiger barb* is an orange and black striped fish native to Southeast Asia. This fish is omnivorous and swims in the middle and lower sections of the tank. Tiger barb can become quite aggressive and should be kept in a species tank or with fishes of similar size and temperament.

Zebra danio (Brachydanio rerio)

The South Asian *zebra danio* is one of the most popular community fish. This little speed demon makes the top of your tank look like the Indianapolis 500 race. This omnivorous, torpedo-shaped wonder is gold with blue stripes and very hardy. It would probably survive a lethal injection. Keep danio in schools of five to seven in a tank with dense foliage where they can lay their eggs.

Harlequin rasbora (Rasbora heteromorpha)

The omnivorous *harlequin rasbora* from Southeast Asia has an unusual marking that makes it stand out in a crowd. The body is gold-green and has a dark blue patch that forms a triangle on each side. The rasbora should be kept in schools and swims in all levels of the tank.

Oddballs

Here are a few other tropical fish considered oddballs as far as physical characteristics are concerned. However, despite their unusual appearance, they can be real show-stoppers in your home aquarium. They can impress and amaze your friends as well.

Elephant fish (Gnathonemus petersi)

The African *elephant fish* is a carnivorous species with an extended jaw that resembles an elephant's trunk. The egg-laying elephant fish can emit electrical impulses and should be kept by itself it an aquarium.

Clown knifefish (Notopterus chitala)

The carnivorous *knifefish* resembles the curved blade of a Japanese sword. This fish is nocturnal and should be kept by itself or with larger fish. This species lives in the lower levels of the tank.

Leaf fish (Monocirrhus polyacanthus)

The carnivorous South American *leaf fish* has a blotched skin pattern that makes it look like a decaying leaf floating through the water. The leaf fish floats head down and snags its prey as it floats by. Keep it with fish of its own size or in a species tank. The leaf fish lives in all levels of the tank.

Freshwater Coldwater

Freshwater fish that live in coldwater tanks do not require heating. However, if you keep fish in an outdoor pond during the freezing winter months, you may have to move them into a warmer area such as a holding tank in your garage until the frigid weather passes.

Koi (Cyprinus carpio)

Koi is a highly colored omnivorous pond fish. Because of its large size at maturity, it is unsuitable for an indoor aquarium. The torpedo-shaped koi requires a good filtration system and many plants, which it uses for food and shade. Champion varieties can be very expensive.

Fancy goldfish (Carassius auratus)

Fancy goldfish have been bred for many physical characteristics including bubble eyes, split tales, long fins, and unusual head coverings *(wen)*. These species can be kept in either a coldwater aquarium or a pond. Either way, this omnivorous fish needs a good filtration system and plenty of foliage.

Tropical Marine

A tropical marine aquarium is similar to a tropical freshwater system in that it, too, requires heat. This type of system often has invertebrates instead of plants and dolomite or live sand as a substrate. Tropical marines are among the most beautiful and colorful fish on earth. Many larger species can be quite expensive.

Damselfish

Damselfish are among the smallest of the tropical marines. Most species are very hardy and can be used to condition the marine aquarium. They are excellent choices for the beginning marine hobbyist.

Domino (Dascyllus trimaculatus)

Despite the fact that this little fish has a big attitude problem (it is very territorial and aggressive), the domino damsel is an outstanding contender for the marine aquarium. This hardy fish is black with white spots that make it resemble a child's domino. The domino is omnivorous and usually hangs near the bottom of the tank to defend its territory.

Humbug (Dascyllus aruanus)

The omnivorous *humbug* is a little black-and-white striped fish with a lot of courage that swims in all levels of the tank. The humbug zealously guards its territory (real or imagined) with all its energy. This species is very hardy and is great for beginners.

Sergeant major (Abudefduf saxatilis)

This *sergeant major* is a real pain in the you-know-what. This fish attacks anything that even looks at it wrong. Toss a couple of these into your marine tank, then sit back and watch your new aquatic action movie — or a bunch of your other fish disappear, whichever comes first. The sergeant major is an omnivorous fish that swims in all levels of the tank.

Blue devil (Pomacentrus caeruleus)

Yes, this fish is blue. No, it does not act like a devil. The Indo-Pacific *blue devil* has extraordinary body coloring that makes it an appealing member of almost any marine tank. This little fish is fast and can survive in a tank with fish much larger in size. The blue devil is omnivorous and inhabits all levels of the tank.

Triggerfish

Triggerfish have a cool dorsal fin that they can lock into an upright position when defending themselves against predators. Triggers seem to show a higher amount of intelligence than other fish, and come in many beautiful colors. The only drawback is that they can be very aggressive. Triggerfish are carnivorous and swim in all levels of the tank.

Picasso trigger (Rhinecanthus aculeatus)

The carnivorous *picasso* resembles a painting by the famous artist whose name it carries. This fish is one of the more peaceful of the triggers and can be kept with fish its own size or slightly smaller. Unfortunately, the picasso can wreak havoc on many invertebrates (scallops and so on). The picasso should not be kept with other triggers or fish that look like it (such as the huma huma trigger or other picassos).

Clown trigger (Balistoides conspicillum)

Remember that big bully who made you eat dirt in the third grade? Well, he grew up and turned into a clown triggerfish. The *clown trigger* is probably the most beautiful fish on earth. (Its price tells you the same.) Unfortunately, it trashes just about anything that moves, breathes, or even pretends to be alive in your aquarium. A few cases of this fish cohabiting a tank peacefully with others have been reported, but don't count on yours swelling to those ranks. Get a large tank for a single clown triggerfish, and be the envy of your fellow hobbyists. The clown trigger is carnivorous and swims in all tank levels.

Surgeons and tangs

Surgeons and tangs are cool fish that are difficult to keep. Leave these breeds in the hands of experienced aquarists for now and put them on your wish list for the future. Surgeons and tangs need plenty of algae and other vegetable matter to graze on, and should be kept in a well-established aquarium tank. They tend to contract disease quickly, and so require an excellent filtration system. Most surgeons and tangs have a sharp spine (similar to a scalpel) near the tail, which can inflict quite a bit of damage to other fish.

Powder blue surgeon

The elegant Indo-Pacific *powder blue surgeon* has a blue body and yellow dorsal fin. This herbivorous fish is peaceful and needs plenty of swimming room. This species chomps on small invertebrates and gorgonians.

Yellow tang (Zebrasoma flavescens)

The brightly colored *yellow tang* is an instant hit in any marine aquarium. This peaceful species resembles a yellow throwing disk. Without proper filtration, and plenty of algae and other vegetable matter, the yellow tang slowly wastes away.

Wrasses

Wrasses are known for their ability to "clean" other fishes. Wrasses follow their tankmates around and pick small pieces of debris and parasites from their skin. Most other fish welcome this free cleaning job.

Cleaner wrasse (Labroides dimidiatus)

The *cleaner wrasse* is one of the most popular members of this genus. This cool-looking fish has a black stripe running the length of its blue and brown body. The carnivorous cleaner wrasse swims in all levels of the tank and pops in and out of coral nooks looking for food. This species is hardy, and great for beginners.

Angelfish

Angelfish are beautiful specimens. In the wild, these omnivorous fish feed on corals and sponges. This natural diet can be replaced with commercial foods in most cases. These species often change color between their juvenile and adult stages, and have a sharp spine near their gill covers.

Flame angelfish (Centrophge loriculus)

The *flame angel* is a peaceful and popular species with a bright red-orange body. The flame angel is hardy, and not difficult to keep. Keep it with larger fishes to curb its tendency to become territorial. The flame angel is omnivorous and swims in the lower levels of the tank in a peaceful manner.

French angelfish (Pomacanthus paru)

The omnivorous *French angelfish* is often seen swimming in films with scuba divers. This graceful black and gold fish is an elegant addition to almost any marine tank. However, they can become quite large (12 inches), and feeds on invertebrates. This fish is very expensive (you can probably afford a few if you tell your kids to forget about college). The French angel is omnivorous and swims peacefully in the middle and lower levels of the tank.

Clownfish

Clownfish are also known as *anemonefish* because of their special relation-ship with that particular invertebrate (see Chapter 11). Clownfish (which have a special *protective mucus* on their skin to ward off stings) use an anemone's tentacles for protection. In return, the clownfish chases off any predators that even think about coming near its anemone. Often several clowns inhabit one anemone together.

False percula (Amphiprion ocellaris)

The Indo-Pacific *percula* is one of the most readily available clownfish you can find in your pet shop. The body is orange-yellow in color with white stripes. This omnivorous fish usually hangs near the bottom or center of the tank. Good water conditions and live food are helpful in keeping this fish in prime health.

Tomato (Amphiprion frenatus)

The *tomato* clownfish is brownish-red in color, and is very peaceful. This omnivorous fish is hardy, and can live peacefully with most nonaggressive fish in all levels of the tank.

Butterflyfish

Butterflyfish are extremely difficult to keep and should not be on a beginner's shopping list. These species require optimal water conditions and specialized diets. Popular species include the raccoon *(Chaetodon lunnula)* and the cop-perbanded *(Chelmon rostratus)*. Butterfly fish are carnivorous and live peacefully in the middle to lower regions of the tank.

Oddballs

Just like the human world, the marine world has a few oddballs as well. The following section takes a quick look at these oddities, and I try to talk you out of purchasing most of them at the same time.

Polka-dot grouper (Chromileptis altivelis)

The polka-dot is really, really big. It looks like a swimming baked potato with the mumps. It can eat you into the poor house. This grouper is carnivorous, swims in the middle and lower sections of the tank, and will eat any fish that it can fit into its mouth.

Blue-spotted boxfish (Ostracion meleagris)

Again, the blue-spotted boxfish is really, really big. It looks like a box with mumps that is trying to swim. You can spend your entire existence trying to find food it will eat. The boxfish is omnivorous and spends most of the day, shyly hiding in the lower levels of the tank.

Batfish (Platax orbicularis)

One more time: The batfish is really, really big. It looks like a rusted UFO. You can spend lots of time and lots of money feeding it. The batfish is omnivorous, swims in the middle to lower levels, and is very peaceful.

Lionfish (Pterois volitans)

Well, the lionfish is really, really big. It looks like a floating pincushion, and may eat every moving thing in your tank if it gets hungry enough. This fish can inflict a painful wound with its spines and should be handled carefully. The lionfish is carnivorous and swims in all levels of the tank.

Seahorse (Hippocampus kuda)

The cool thing about this fish is that the male gives birth. Yeah! But forget about including a seahorse in any marine tank with other species because they all have a "kick me" sign on their backs. Seahorses also must have a constant supply of live food.

Snowflake moray (Echidna nebulosus)

The snowflake moray is large and long. A hungry moray can eat all your fish, then spend the rest of its time trying to get out of your tank. Oh goodie.

Mandarin (Synchiropus splendidus)

Cool fish. It looks like it's wearing something it bought at Woodstock. But, this is the type of fish you put into your tank and are lucky to see once every couple of months because it spends most of its time hiding in coral niches. This carnivorous species should be kept with less aggressive species such as clownfish.

Moorish idol (Zanclus canescens)

This is a beautiful fish that looks like a swimming lollipop with a dorsal fin the height of the Empire State Building. The drawback here is that this fish is a picky eater. Let me say that again: PICKY EATER.

Scorpionfish (Scorpaena species)

The scorpionfish is large, dangerous (to you and everyone else within a hundred blocks of your aquarium), and deadly. Enough said.

Brackish Fish

Brackish fish live in habitats that are somewhere between saltwater and freshwater. These animals are really unique, but can be difficult to find at times.

Archer fish (Toxotes jaculator)

This remarkable species can shoot insects out of the air using a jet of water from its mouth. The carnivorous archer fish can also leap from the water to capture its prey (even if that prey happens to be stuck to your ceiling). It must be kept in a well-covered tank.

Scat (Scatophagus argus)

The omnivorous scat spends most of its time swimming in the middle and lower levels of the tank. The scat should be kept in schools of at least three to five and requires vegetable matter in its diet.

Understanding Setups

When your aquarium setup is complete, make sure that you match your fish to it. Using this chapter as a rough guide gives you a good head start. When in doubt about an unfamiliar species, check with your local fish shop owner because some friendly fish have been known to go bad and vice versa. It is better to be prepared with knowledge than face instant disaster.

So, much of the road that leads to becoming an expert fishkeeper is dependent upon practical experience as well as knowledge. Sometimes when trying to choose compatible species, you have to experiment a little to see what works best for you and your individual setup. The size of your tank, the number of fish it contains, and the types of decorations in it can all have an affect on how well your tankmates get along.

Captive-Bred Species

People tend to think that the ocean is an endless realm overflowing with aquatic animal life. But as an ecologically concerned fishkeeper, you must remember that only a small percentage of the world's waters contain the fish that you put into your aquarium. Each year, fish populations decline due to overfishing, the curio trade, and other human interventions, such as pollution.

Often fish dealers offer both *captive-bred species* (fish or other aquatic animals that have been raised in hatcheries for the aquarium trade) and animals that have been caught in the wild. By purchasing captive-bred fish, you can help slow down the elimination of wild species. Most freshwater fish are now commercially bred to one extent or another, and are usually less expensive than those caught in the wild.

The real problem occurs in the marine side of the hobby. Few marine fish are bred commercially because they can be quite difficult to spawn. In the last few years, marine fish hatcheries have made great progress in reproducing many species of clownfish, wrasses, and other types of saltwater fish. At the present time, captive-bred marine species can be a little more expensive than those caught in the wild, but in the long run it is well worth the extra money to help save our natural aquatic resources.

The collection of live coral has also hit an all-time high in recent years. Many areas are now prohibiting collection of live coral because the world's reefs are beginning to disappear due to repeated harvesting for curio shops and the marine aquarium trade.

Many marine fish are caught by people using illegal practices and products such as cyanide, which also destroys large portions of any coral reef that it comes in contact with. Purchasing wild animals only encourages wholesalers to continue removing fish and invertebrates from their native habitat.

So if you have a choice, always purchase captive-bred species. That way your grandchildren won't have to have an aquarium with plastic fish suspended in it.

Chapter 14

Purchasing Your Fish

. . . .

In This Chapter

▶ Finding and keeping a reputable merchant

▶ Choosing healthy, appropriate fish

. . . .

*O*ne of the best ways to start out as a beginning hobbyist is to develop a good relationship with a local fish vendor. A quality vendor can help you make informed decisions on the type of aquarium best suited for you, the proper equipment for your new tank, and the best aquatic species for your system. A good vendor can also locate hard to find products (such as a filter for an irregularly shaped tank) and can help you with water testing on a regular basis.

Of course, there are many things that you can do as an informed hobbyist to help insure that you start off your fishkeeping adventure with success. Choosing healthy pets from your local vendor is the best way to start off right, and this chapter can help.

Choosing a Quality Dealer

The aquarium hobby is generally a lifelong addiction. (I promised myself that I will attend Aquariums Anonymous meetings just as soon as some burnt out and frazzled hobbyist starts a chapter.) It is really difficult to lay this fascinating hobby aside once you take the plunge. In the years to come, you will need to purchase fish, replace worn equipment, and keep stocked up on chemicals and food.

During the course of your hobby, you also need expert advice on fishkeeping skills once in a while, and someone to keep you informed on the newest trends in equipment and other aquarium-related paraphernalia. This is why you need to find a good retailer who specializes in the aquarium aspect of the pet industry.

A knowledgeable aquarium fish dealer, especially one in your neighborhood, can help you anytime you have a problem with your aquatic pets. Building a personal relationship with this merchant also helps you stay informed on aquarium-related issues. For these reasons and more, it is so important to make contact with an informed and trustworthy vendor. Besides, if you get to know a dealer well, you may be able to snag a few freebies.

The search

When you want to buy a house, you don't just purchase the first one you see, do you? No, you look around a bit first. The same principal applies to your aquarium hobby. Look for the best and don't settle for less. There's nothing wrong with checking the gossip in your neighborhood to determine whether the local dealers have a good reputation among other businesses and their customers. Friends, aquarium clubs, and family members are a great place to start asking questions. If your family is like mine, you'll not only hear all you need to know about local aquarium shops, you'll pick up a few juicy tidbits at the same time.

In today's consumer-conscious environment, you cannot afford to end up with mediocre service because you were afraid to investigate the references or character of a particular dealer. You can obtain valuable information through this age-old method.

The best strategy is to visit as many local dealers and aquarium shops as your time and budget allow. These fun little investigative trips provide you with a solid foundation on which you can compare dealers' overall quality of service, livestock selection and condition, and prices on fish and equipment. Of course, if you are visiting New York City, you may want to rent an RV for a couple of months until you get around to seeing all the retailers in the area.

In choosing a tropical fish dealer, take into consideration a few important factors before you formulate any final decisions to pledge your loyalty to one particular shop. I find it best to frequent at least two fish shops. It's kind of like having an ace in the hole (or up your sleeve) at a poker game: If one shop goes out of business, or has an internal problem that affects you, you're still covered.

After you compare all your local fish shops, choose the two retailers you think can satisfy all your aquarium requirements.

The importance of great service

When you revisit the two dealers you chose (see the preceding section for advice on choosing retailers), see whether the employees are friendly and offer good advice. Do the clerks make every attempt to help you out when you come in, or do they just stand around shooting the breeze?

Do the shop's workers take a personal interest in your aquarium? Are they willing to go out of their way to make sure that you find exactly what you need or are searching for? Is there adequate personnel to provide good service to you even during the peak hours of the day? If you feel like a first round draft pick on Monday Night Football because you had to blitz a clerk, tackle him, and threaten him to make him talk, then you need to find another place to shop. A reputable and caring owner who takes pride in her business and in providing customer satisfaction makes sure that her shop is well staffed with knowledgeable and caring employees.

Employees who stand around and do nothing generally do not have an interest in their employer's business, and probably don't have an interest in making sure that you get the proper equipment, livestock, and supplies for your aquarium, either. (Hopefully you won't see those clerks the next time you visit.)

The store's appearance

When you go to an aquarium shop (even if you're checking out a new one that just opened up in the neighborhood), carefully inspect all the display tanks for obvious signs of dealer dedication or apathy. (If the place looks like the owner couldn't care less about how the tanks look, he probably cares just as little about the rest of his business.) A visual inspection can tell you quite a bit about a shop's habits. As you look around the shop, check for clues that distinguish a good dealer from an uncaring one.

The tanks

Quality retailers understand that the overall condition of their shop makes a big difference as far as customers' first impressions are concerned.

The physical condition of the tanks is a good indication of how well the fish are taken care of on a daily basis. Are the tanks free from excess algae growth or do they resemble the Florida swamps? Are the proper mixtures of compatible species displayed in the tanks, or does it appear that a bunch of fish have been thrown in together to save space?

Do the tanks look like they have been properly vacuumed some time in the last five decades? Is the front of the glass clean or does it still bare smudges and fingerprints from the grade school class who visited the shop the week before? Someone who won't even take the time (maybe a couple of minutes) to clean the front glass doesn't care very much about presentation or the impression the shop makes on its customers, and usually does not care about the health of their fish, or their customers' best interests either.

The fish

A good quality retailer has good quality fish. No exceptions. If a dedicated dealer is not happy with his suppliers, he quickly looks for another who can ensure him high-quality fish. While you are browsing through a store, see whether the dealer's fish are swimming boldly (out away from the decorations) in the open spaces of the aquarium, or hiding in the corners. Fish that hide in corners usually have health problems after you bring them home. If the fish in the shop look like they just swam through a waste dump, find another pet store.

Do the dealer's fish look generally healthy? Are the fish's fins erect? Does the body display proper color? Does the fish have a good shape, and is the body correctly formed? Do all the merchant's fish appear to be in good health, or just a few? Has the dealer turned the lights off or put a sign on any tanks to indicate diseased fish — or is the store selling fish in bad condition?

The equipment

There are times when your equipment will wear out or fail, and you may need to replace it. Make sure that the dealers you choose have an adequate supply of equipment and parts. Nothing is more frustrating than having to run from store to store to find a simple piece of equipment (like a net, pump, or filter). Make sure that your dealer has a wide selection on hand. If not, make sure the shop can order needed supplies and get them in within a reasonable amount of time.

Chemicals and food

Does the shop have a good supply of chemicals and foods available? You may not have time to wait for a dealer to order medications if your fish are really ill — it's much better to have it available when an emergency arises. Check to see if the store carries a wide selection of frozen foods for your tropical marines, as well as food for fish with special or unique dietary needs.

Dealer Practices (The Good, the Bad, and the Ugly)

To be honest with you, there are good dealers (Do Bees), bad dealers (Don't Bees), and ugly dealers (Wanna Bees). I have seen all types during my years in the aquarium hobby. All I can do is give you a little personal advice as to what to look for when you are trying to determine who is the good guy and who is the bad guy.

Do Bee dealers

A Do Bee dealer helps you find success. Some of the signs of a good retailer are:

✔ Friendly, helpful, knowledgeable staff members who answer your questions willingly, go out of their way to help, and who are familiar with aquarium equipment, the different types of aquarium systems, and individual species of fish.

✔ A large selection of aquarium equipment, food, medication, and fish on hand — they carry more than one or two brands.

✔ Free services, such as water testing.

✔ Some type of guarantee on the fish they sell and the commitment to stand behind the equipment that they sell. A really good Do Bee offers free repair service on basic equipment.

✔ A willingness to tell you where you can get a certain species or piece of equipment if they cannot get it themselves. (This includes offering competitors' phone numbers.)

✔ Autopsies of dead fish to help determine the cause of the disease (if they have qualified staff) and medication advice to help prevent the need for an autopsy.

✔ A genuine interest in you and your aquariums.

✔ Clean tanks and shops.

Don't Bee dealers

Don't Bee dealers own aquarium shops you want to avoid. They are really quite easy to spot when you recognize the symptoms of their "I have no business being in the tropical fish trade because I don't really care about my job, or I am just in it for the money" disease. Avoid these dealers at all costs! You can recognize them by the following characteristics:

> ✔ A really bad attitude: They're willing to tell you to take a hike if you question the quality of their service or livestock; they let you stand around without offering to help you find what you are looking for; they spend a lot of time answering phone calls and leave you waiting for service until they finish yacking; they try to give you a snow job if you ask them a question they don't have an answer for.
>
> ✔ They try to sell you a bunch of junk you don't need because they believe that you don't know any better.
>
> ✔ They sell fish they know are diseased, just to get rid of them.
>
> ✔ They use the same net to capture fish in all their tanks without sterilizing it between uses.
>
> ✔ They have dirty aquariums and a filthy shop.
>
> ✔ They sell you fish that are not compatible just to make a few extra bucks (which they obviously they don't spend on the upkeep of the shop).
>
> ✔ They refuse to go out of their way to order any special equipment or fish for you.
>
> ✔ They don't keep any type of regular store hours and show up whenever they happen to feel like it.

Wanna Bee dealers

A Wanna Bee dealer is the owner of a pet shop that appears overnight and disappears within a few months because she didn't have the proper finances to keep it afloat long enough to establish itself. These dealers sell you poor quality fish and equipment at inexpensive prices in an effort to get some money coming in, and then simply fall off the face of the earth. If a new shop opens up and you are unsure as to whether you should purchase fish from the new owners, simply wait a few months to see if it stays open. During this time, keep your ear out for information from other customers concerning the quality of the shop.

Developing a Good Relationship with Your Fish Vendor

After you make your final decision and pledge your loyalty to a couple of dealers, try to become acquainted with as many of the employees in the shop as possible. Go out of your way to meet the owner or store manager. She can help you with any serious problems you may have.

Setting Up a Freshwater Aquarium

1. The first step in setting up a freshwater aquarium is to clean the tank with fresh water.

2. Place the clean tank on a stand.

3. Add an undergravel filter plate. The plate should cover the bottom of the tank.

4. Slip the airstones and hose inside the uplift tubes, add the carbon caps, and connect both sides to an airpump.

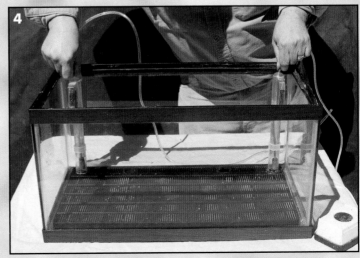

5. Place clean gravel in the tank and smooth it out so that there is a half-inch rise sloping toward the back glass.

6. Carefully place rocks, plants, and other decorations in the gravel bed.

7. Fill the aquarium with clean water. A plate can be used to break up the incoming stream so that it does not disturb the decorations.

8. Add a powerfilter to the back of the aquarium.

9. Place a heater along the back glass and add a thermometer in the front.

10. Add dechlorinator to remove chlorine from the water.

11. Put a hood and light on top of the tank.

12. Plug in all equipment, test the pH and temperature, and adjust as necessary.

13. Allow the aquarium to run for 24 hours, retest the temperature and pH, and then add your starter fish when water conditions are correct.

Egglaying Freshwater Fish That Are Easy to Keep

The red chromide is often found in freshwater, but it also does well in a brackish tank.

The male betta builds a bubblenest to hatch its mate's eggs.

Central American cichlids are hardy, but can be aggressive with tankmates.

The diamond tetra really sparkles in any aquarium.

Tiger barbs are active and interesting.

For Experienced Freshwater Fishkeepers

Experienced fishkeepers may want to
try keeping koi in an outdoor pond.

Pencilfish require good water conditions and
are better off in the hands of experienced
freshwater fishkeepers.

Freshwater Livebearers That Are Easy to Keep

A molly breeds rapidly but requires a slightly higher temperature.

A platy can adapt to many beginners' mistakes.

The guppy is very hardy and an excellent starter fish for beginners.

Swordtail are great community fish that come in many bright colors.

The discus is a popular fish.

Easy-to-Keep Fish for Brackish Aquariums

Monos are hardy and very active.

Puffers are easy to keep but require live food.

Setting Up a Marine Aquarium

1. After washing the tank and placing it on a stand, add an undergravel filter, airstones, tubing, and carbon caps.

2. Place clean dolomite on the bottom of the tank and slope it toward the rear.

3. Carefully place coral, shells, and other decorations in the dolomite.

4. Add heater to the rear of the tank, and place a thermometer on the front glass.

5. Place a powerfilter on the rear of the aquarium.

6. Fill up the tank with premixed water and marine salt.

7. Add dechlorinator, plug in all equipment, and then test the temperature, pH, and salinity. Adjust as required.

8. Place a hood and light on the aquarium. Allow the aquarium to run for 24 hours, and then retest the pH, temperature, and salinity. Adjust as necessary, and add your starter fish after all water conditions are correct.

Marine Fish That Are Easy to Keep

Most clownfish are easy to maintain
if provided with plenty of shelter.

A wrasse spends most of its time
darting between decorations.

A domino damsel may be small, but it can
terrorize larger fish that enter its territory.

A blue devil is a hardy addition
to any marine tank.

Marine Fish for Experienced Fishkeepers

A moorish idol requires precise water conditions in order to survive.

Lionfish have special diets and dangerous spines, and they can easily devour many tankmates.

Tangs and surgeonfish are quite susceptible to disease.

Flame angels do not fare well in poor water condions.

Invertebrates That Are Easy to Keep

Matte can form interesting colonies along the substrate bed.

Sea urchins are easy to maintain but may prey on other invertebrates and fish.

Tubeworms come in a wide variety of colors.

Soft corals develop well under the proper care of a dedicated hobbyist.

Invertebrates for Experienced Fishkeepers

A thorny oyster needs plenty of nutritional additives.

Many corals require precise lighting
and water conditions.

Christmas tree coral require good water conditions.

Flower pot invertebrates require
plenty of correct lighting.

For Inspiration...

This aquarium displays a beautiful community of freshwater fish.

A reef tank requires a lot of time and patience.

Marine fish, like this Mandarin, are known to exhibit extraordinary colors.

Koi are often found in cold-water ponds.

Interesting species can be seen at public aquariums like the John G. Shedd.

Many freshwater fish like the killi are becoming difficult to obtain.

A great majority of dealers are very enthusiastic when given the opportunity to work with regular customers. After the initial conversations, your aquarium may become as familiar to them as their own personal tanks. Many merchants beam proudly at a customer's first successful aquarium setup (after all, the merchant helped create it). A caring vendor also mourns with you at the loss of your favorite fish.

Making the effort required to solidify a personal relationship with your local dealer puts you in good position to receive quality advice and the highest degree of comprehensive service available. When a merchant is familiar with you, the type of systems you own, your special interests, and other personal aquarium specifications, he has a better opportunity to help you become a successful hobbyist.

Selecting Healthy Fish

Now, whether you find a good dealer or not, you still need to take responsibility for choosing the healthiest fish possible. Starting off with diseased fish is the quickest way I know to lose interest in the hobby. You always take a risk when you purchase a live animal because unseen problems may manifest later on. But you can improve the odds of success by starting off with the healthiest fish possible.

Don't buy the first fish off the boat

Avoid buying any new arrivals your dealer recently received. (If the fish are still in a packing crate, that should give you a clue.) You see a large number of bags containing fish floating in the aquariums on the days the store receives new shipments. Most dealers receive new fish on one or two specific days each week. Ask your dealer which days these are. A good dealer doesn't allow customers to purchase fish until she's had sufficient time to quarantine them. This quarantine period reduces the fish's stress from shipping, and allows the shop's personnel to treat any disease that shows up in the first few days after arrival.

If you happen to see some fish that really catch your eye, still in the bags, ask the dealer to hold them for you until a reasonable quarantine period has expired. Most dealers willingly agree to do that. Helpful merchants who take the time to grant such simple requests to provide customer satisfaction are definitely worth patronizing in the future. Stop for a moment and ask yourself one simple question. If I owned this fish shop, would I do this for my customer? If the answer is yes, then you should expect your dealer to do the same thing.

Don't be Doctor Doolittle

Never allow anyone (including your dealer) to talk you into buying a sick or ailing fish in the mistaken but honorable belief that you can quickly nurse it back to vibrant health. This is one of the biggest mistakes a beginning hobbyist can make. I myself have purchased fish that I wanted to save from destruction, but I was not a novice at the time. I saved these fish with round-the-clock care, but a lot of experience is usually required to get the job done. The ones I did save, however, quickly became my favorite pets.

Playing Florence Nightingale for aquatic pets only works when you have the proper knowledge and equipment to pull it off. Diseased fish can cause water problems and infect your other fish as well. Don't buy any fish from tanks that the dealer is currently medicating.

If you notice dead fish floating in a healthy-looking tank, avoid buying any of the livestock from that aquarium. Do not purchase a fish with an unusually humped back — this generally indicates old age. A good dealer never allows a customer to purchase old, dying, or diseased fish. She tells you that certain fish are being medicated and are not for sale until the condition clears up.

Just because a fish has been medicated, does not mean that it is completely well again. Let your eye be the best judge; carefully inspect any fish for signs of disease, such as torn or clamped fins, white spots or growths, or irregularly shaped bodies.

Start simply

If you are new to the hobby (still wet behind the ears), never buy hard-to-maintain species of fish such as marine tangs and freshwater eels. Fish that have special dietary requirements may be a little bit too much to handle in the beginning when you are still trying to get the hang of how your equipment works. Wait until you are completely familiar with your system before trying your luck with the harder-to-maintain species of tropical fish.

Go with what you know

Do not buy fish that you are completely unfamiliar with. Just because you are browsing through the marine section and happen to a see a cool-looking bamboo shark, doesn't mean you should take it home. These types of animals can be very difficult to feed and require strict water conditions to survive. Leave them in the hands of the pros to avoid heartache.

Look for physical characteristics of good health

You can look at several physical characteristics to determine whether your fish are in good health. There is never a guarantee of complete success, but if you follow these rules, you can increase your chances of getting a healthy specimen. Look for the following characteristics:

- ✔ Body color is rich, not faded or dull. The color should be complete and not missing in any areas (unless it is typical for the species).
- ✔ No open sores, visible ulcers, boils, or obvious skin problems, such as peeling scales or blemishes.
- ✔ Fins are long and flowing, or short and erect. The fish should not have any ragged, torn or missing fins.
- ✔ Scales are flat and smooth, not protruding away from the body.
- ✔ The stomach is well rounded, not sunken or concave.
- ✔ Girth of the entire body is of normal size, not bloated or emaciated.
- ✔ Visible excreta (fish waste) should be dark in color, and not pale.
- ✔ All the fins on the fish's body should not be collapsed or completely clamped shut.
- ✔ Eyes are clear, not cloudy or popping out of the sockets.
- ✔ No visible parasites, such as ich or velvet.

Know your fish's behavior

A few behavioral characteristics (how they act), combined with physical actions, are worth taking a look at. Your fish should exhibit the following behaviors:

- ✔ Swimming in a horizontal motion, not with its head up or down.
- ✔ Swimming with complete ease, not continually fighting to stay afloat.
- ✔ Swimming throughout the aquarium, not lurking in the corners or hiding behind decorations.
- ✔ Breathing normally, not gulping for air or hanging around the top of the tank with its mouth kissing the top of the water.

Getting the Right Fish

In order to be a successful hobbyist, you need to understand your purchases. What I mean by that is that you need to know which fish are best for you. You know how to spot a healthy fish (if you don't, read the preceding section), but there's a little more to it than that. You also need to pick fish that are compatible and won't tear each other to bits so that your aquarium doesn't look like a war zone. Making a shopping list and understanding a fish's ultimate size are two ways that you can avoid disaster.

When you go to purchase your fish, take paper and pen with you and write down the names of all the fish that appeal to you. By writing down the names of the fish, you don't have to remember names (scientific names and even common names can be a little confusing at times), and can backtrack to certain tanks quite easily. This can be a real advantage if the shop has several hundred display tanks.

When you finish your list, locate your dealer and check to see whether all the species you chose are compatible with each other, don't have unique dietary needs (diving in the Bahamas every week to pick up natural fish food gets old), and don't have special aquarium requirements.

Keep an eye out for other compatibility issues. For example, a marine triggerfish is a wonderful marine pet, but will destroy many of the invertebrates, such as coral and scallops, you may have in your tank.

Many shops have little stickers or labels to tell you which species are compatible and which are not. But not all fish stores offer the customer this courtesy.

Leave difficult species in the expert hands of experienced hobbyists who know how to take care of them properly. Start simple so you won't be disappointed.

A reputable dealer can answer all your questions about aquarium requirements and compatibility, as well as offer pertinent suggestions of his own as to which species may be more successful for a beginner.

How did this fish get so big, so fast?

The problem with many of the fish you see in pet stores is that they may be still in their juvenile stage of growth and have not yet reached mature adulthood. For example, I was at the pet shop the other day and saw a 2-inch marine grouper. It was so cute! But this fish can grow to lengths of 10 inches or more, leaving smaller tankmates to end up as Sunday's buffet!

Purchase a good aquarium book (like this one!) that gives you a good idea of just how big many species get in adulthood. If you have any doubts, consult your local dealer. Larger fish are great for some hobbyists, but they do tend to limit your aquarium space, and your choices of other tankmates.

Part IV
Caring for Your Aquatic Friends

The 5th Wave   By Rich Tennant

©RICHTENNANT

"Of course being clownfish, we supplement their feed with a little cotton candy, ice cream and a corn dog now and then."

In this part . . .

1 show you how to feed your fish and keep them healthy. From offering the right kind of food to providing the proper treatment for illnesses, the next few chapters are a primer on raising fish that you'll be proud to show off to your friends.

Chapter 15

Diet and Nutrition for Your Wet Pets

*J*ust like their human counterparts, your aquatic pets need proper nutrition so that they can remain active, healthy, and live long lives. A proper diet can be found by using most manufactured fish foods, but you can also increase your fish's good health by providing a variety of fresh vegetables and other household products.

Basic Nutrition

Unfortunately, you can't feed your fish the cheeseburger, fries, and apple pie that keeps many kids happy, so you have to supply other types of food to meet their dietary needs. Fortunately, you can combine many good nutrition sources to form a proper diet for your fish. Aquarium food can be quite varied, and includes brine shrimp, dry flake, fresh shrimp, algae, guppies, daphnia, tubifex worms, and beef heart — to name just a few. These foods are all good sources of nutrition, but only if they are distributed in proper amounts. Tossing an entire beef heart into the tank for your guppy's breakfast doesn't cut it.

When purchasing any type of aquarium food, the most important rule is to select the finest quality your finances can handle. Aquarium foods are not really that expensive when you look at the total amount of food you get for the price, so why not purchase the best? Top-quality commercial foods are enriched with vitamins and minerals and help keep your fish in optimal health. Low-grade food promotes poor health and disease.

Feeding your fish can be a really relaxing activity. What's more entertaining than observing a bunch of animals pigging out? Watching your aquatic pets interact socially (pushing each other out of the way, stealing food from each other, hoarding the choicest items, turning their noses up at others) can be very educational. If you're like me, you probably see the same thing at your own dinner table, but at least you don't have to cook for your fish.

What your fish need

What you feed your fish needs to contain the following components:

- **Carbohydrates** provide energy for your fish and also help them resist disease. But research shows that excess carbohydrates may be harmful.

- **Minerals** are important to your fish's health because they help to ensure proper growth. You can provide them in liquid form or through frequent water changes.

- **Proteins** help your fish to build strong muscle and tissue. Fish obtain proteins through a diet that includes meat, fish, insects, and manufactured foods. Proteins are an important factor in promoting physical growth, so it is important to remember that younger fish need a little more than full-grown adults.

- **Vitamins** are vital to your fish's good health. A balanced diet that combines live and processed foods easily supplies the necessary vitamins. A balanced diet includes vitamin A (egg, greens, crustaceans), vitamin B (fish, greens, algae, and beef), vitamin C (algae), vitamin D (worms, algae, shrimp), vitamin E (egg, algae), vitamin H (egg, liver), and vitamin K (liver, greens).

Experienced hobbyists realize that feeding their aquatic pets can be considered an art in itself (especially if you own an overgrown piranha). With so many different natural and prepared foods to choose from (not only in fish shops but on the Internet as well), beginning hobbyists can quite easily be confused about nutritional issues. Just remember that no one product can satisfy every fish in your aquarium. But, as this chapter shows you, learning to feed your fish properly is not as hard as it first seems. A little experience and practice can make all the difference in the world.

Overfeeding

You want to make sure that your tropical fish receive all the nutrition they need. But, danger lurks in the area of feeding. Many new hobbyists tend to *overfeed* their fish. Overfeeding can lead to obesity and other health problems. (If your fish resemble over-inflated tires, you may want to cut back on the grub a little.) Too much food in an aquarium tank can also build up and foul the water or increase the risk of disease.

Excess food around the edge of the substrate is one sign of overfeeding. This wasted food accumulates on the bottom of the tank, and begins to spoil. Spoiled food can cause health problems for your fish if they happen to eat it. If excess food piles up, decrease the amount you feed and try putting the food in a different area of the aquarium.

Remember that your fish's stomach is no larger than its eye. So, if you dump a half a can of fish food into the tank, you had better hope your fish has an eye the size of a dinner plate, otherwise, you're in for a few problems. Excess food breaking down on the substrate surface can cause an overgrowth of harmful bacteria. If you do happen to overfeed, remove the excess with a standard aquarium vacuum.

Underfeeding

Underfeeding can be a problem for certain species of fish. Saltwater fish require higher protein diets than freshwater fish, and many saltwater fish die in home aquariums due to starvation. Many saltwater species, such as seahorses, eat only live foods. So, it's important to check out a fish's dietary requirements before your purchase it.

Because so much emphasis is placed on overfeeding and its polluting effects, many hobbyists don't feed their fish enough. (Oops, I did mention that earlier didn't I?) Well, the point is, don't overfeed or underfeed. Feed the correct amount.

Just-right feeding

The general rule is to feed only what your fish can eat in a period of three to five minutes. Now, this does not mean that you have to stand around with a starter's whistle and stopwatch at every meal. Just check to make sure that your fish polish off most of the food within five minutes. Another option is to purchase a plastic feeding ring that keeps most dry foods confined to a small area on top of the water. A feeding ring can keep most of the food from falling to the bottom of the tank, where you cannot see if it has been finished off.

If at all possible, feed adult fish three small meals per day instead of just dumping a bunch of food in at one time. Juvenile fish and fry need be fed more often to insure that they grow properly.

When vacation time arrives

When you go on vacation, try to find a trustworthy person to feed your fish while you're away. A relative or mature neighborhood kid is usually a good choice. To make sure that they feed your fish properly, place individual servings in plastic bags so that your substitute knows exactly what to put into each tank. This may sound like a hassle, but it's better than returning home to find your prize goldfish has become the size of a basketball and is stuck on top of a mountain of uneaten food.

Another option is to purchase an automatic feeder from your local fish shop. These units automatically dispense a certain amount of food daily. Never add a bunch of extra food to the tank before going on vacation. Your fish won't eat the extra food before it starts rotting, and by the time you get home, you may have a serious water problem.

It's best to feed your fish at different times of the day (usually morning, afternoon, and night). Because many nocturnal fish feed only at night, make sure that they receive their fair share.

It's not a bad idea to make your fish fast one day a week. Going 24 hours without food keeps a fish's dietary tract in good physical condition.

What Type of Eater Do You Have?

One reason many aquarium species face starvation and poor health is because hobbyists who are unfamiliar with a particular species fail to provide the proper nutrition for individual needs. If you take the time to do a little research into a fish's natural habitat and feeding patterns, you quickly gain a better understanding of their individual dietary requirements.

For example, most marine fish need to be fed often because they have high metabolism rates. Their high activity level burns off food quickly. If you have a very clean marine system, there may not be adequate amounts of natural foods, such as algae, to provide the fish with something to tide them over until their next scheduled feeding.

Never feed your fish cat food, dog food, or other types of animal feeds. Non-fish food is difficult for your fish to digest properly, and it doesn't provide the essential amino acids and nutrients they really need.

Just like people, fish can be good eaters or bad eaters. The following hints provide you with a little ammunition to fight those fish that just don't want to jump on the scheduled feeding bandwagon.

A picky eater

There are times when your fish simply stop eating. After you panic, stop and ask yourself this question: What caused this sudden lack of appetite? Here are some possible answers:

- ✔ **Incorrect food.** When your fish stop eating, the first thing to do is check with a pro to make sure that you're giving them the correct food for their species. If you're feeding them the wrong thing, switch to the proper food immediately. If the problem persists, read on for other causes.

- ✔ **Crowded conditions.** Overcrowding causes stress and encourages excessive competition for food. Normal eaters may become shy or frightened and not get their share of the food.

- ✔ **Disease.** Fish stop eating regularly as they start to drop off physically.

- ✔ **Poor water conditions.** Incorrect salinity levels (for marine or brackish fish), polluted water, and other bad aquarium conditions can have a major effect on your fish's normal feeding habits. Also check the temperature and pH and nitrate levels if your fish suddenly stop feeding.

- ✔ **Temperature or weather changes.** Hotter weather may mean a decrease in oxygen in the aquarium's water. If this is a problem, add an extra airstone (to split the air into smaller bubbles) or install a power head (which you can purchase at your local pet shop) on your undergravel filter.

So remember, the fact that your fish are not eating may not be caused by improper feeding conditions. You need to take other factors into consideration.

Some fish refuse to eat just because they're picky. There may be no other reason than that. Don't hold your breath trying to please them! Just vary their food and hope for the best.

Carnivores

Feed *carnivores* (meat-eaters), such as piranha, small amounts of meat and insects. If you have carnivores, you need a good filtration system because this type of fish generally excretes a high amount of waste.

Vegetarians

Many freshwater and marine fish need vegetable matter in their diet to survive and achieve proper growth. For example, most species of freshwater catfish, marine angelfish, and cichlids need vegetables. You can purchase vegetable fish food at your local aquarium shop. Specific types of vegetable foods are manufactured to meet the needs of these types of fish.

If you feel the urge to get creative, you can try preparing a vegetable supplement at home. (If your creation turns out badly, just serve it as a surprise salad at your next family get-together.) You can boil lettuce and spinach leaves until they are soft; then put them on a special clip (available at your local fish store), which holds them at the top of the tank. Chopped up pieces of potato, fresh peas, and zucchini are also a welcome treat for almost any type of fish if they are cooked.

Algae as food supplement

The single-celled algae plant can provide an excellent food source for many fish that require veggies in their everyday diet. Almost every species of fish enjoys this treat once in a while, be they marine, brackish, or freshwater.

Aquariums with plant growth lights (actinic blue) or strong fluorescent lighting generate algae in the form of slime that attaches itself to every living and nonliving thing in your aquarium. If your fish start looking like mobile Christmas trees, you need to clean the algae out a bit.

Many species of fish, such as the marine tang and freshwater molly, feed continuously on algae, which is a main staple of their natural diet. Algae also benefits tropical marines in other ways such as maintaining good health (as an extra veggie supplement) and providing good coloration for defense and mating displays.

Of course, you don't want your tank to look like a sewage plant, so you have to remove excess algae from time to time. The easiest and quickest way to remove it is with an algae scraper that you can buy at your local fish store. You can leave a small amount of algae on the coral, gravel, and plants for your fish to graze on.

If you want an aquarium that isn't covered in funny-looking green stuff, you can culture algae in small jars. Here is a simple method to ensure a continual growth for feeding purposes: Put a piece of coral or hard rock in a small jar filled with water and place the jar near a window that receives intense sunlight for a week. Algae grows on the rock or coral, and after a while, you can remove the rock and place it in the tank for your fish to munch on when it is covered in green algae. Then, put another piece of coral or rock in the jar by the window to start new growth. The water in the jar should be changed periodically (once every two weeks).

Giving them what they really need

It is important to give your fish what they really need. The problem is making sure that everyone else in your family isn't doing the same thing. If other family members have a burning desire to feed your fish, set up a feeding schedule so that your fish don't end up with a 24-hour-a-day buffet. If you do have other people feeding your fish, show them ahead of time how much to put into the tank. Don't rely on their common sense to figure it out.

Fish recognize their feeder. They welcome and love you every time they spot the food can moving toward the tank.

If you give your fish fresh vegetables in this manner, make sure that you remove all the uneaten food at the end of each day. Fresh vegetables decay and foul the water when left in the tank too long.

Fish that eat anything that falls into the tank

There are sociable (and gluttonous) fish that continually try to mooch food by imitating a starving animal. (Nothing new there, my teenagers have that routine down to a science.) These fish also try to eat anything that falls into the tank, including pet food, sandwiches, toys, and your hand. Piranhas, tetras, and marine triggerfish are famous for this behavior. Overfeeding these fish can quickly become a problem, because they snag most of the food before the other fish even realize that it's chow time.

If you have a tank hog grabbing all the food, try feeding less food more frequently.

Types of Food

You have many types of foods to choose from in an aquarium shop. Most fish eat just about anything. Most fish can survive on any type of aquarium food, but that doesn't mean they will live up to their full potential if they are fed improperly. By combining different types of food, you can give your fish a head start on good health.

In the artificial environment of an aquarium, you need to provide the proteins, fats, vitamins, and carbohydrates that are a part of fish's natural diet. If you don't, your fish won't reach their full growth potential. Lack of proper nutrition also makes them more susceptible to contracting diseases. Most foods supply the essentials, but combining different products (such as flakes, cooked veggies, and fresh strips of fish) can ensure your success.

Prepackaged and frozen foods

Fish food manufacturers offer a wide variety of well-balanced foods that are easy to feed and store. Some are shown in Figure 15-1.

Prepackaged dry foods generally contain most of the nutrients your fish need to survive. (The exceptions to this rule are aquatic pets, such as the seahorse, that usually require live food.) You can purchase dry food in many forms, including flakes that float on top of the water, disks that sink to the substrate for bottom-feeders, and large pellets for koi and other types of pond fish. There are large-grained foods for big fish, and small foods for tiny fish. You can drop tablet foods to the bottom of the tank, or stick them to the aquarium glass at different levels to help ensure that the fish at all the different feeding levels get their fair share. Pretty neat, huh?

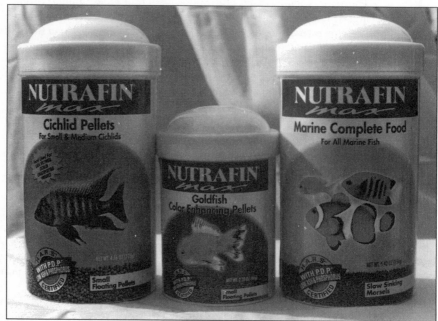

Figure 15-1:
Some prepackaged foods.

Flake foods are a good staple that can satisfy most of your fish. Your can purchase flakes to meet the need of your particular species. For example, some cichlid flakes contain high amounts of fat and protein for quick growth; and goldfish flakes often contain garlic, which inhibits parasites, and the extra vegetables that are a natural part of the goldfish diet. Flakes generally float on or near the water surface and sink as they become saturated. The only problem with flakes is that very few of the ingredients in the can are found in any fish's natural diet. But, despite this lack of natural nutrients, flake foods keep your fish healthy.

The moisture level in manufactured flakes should be less than 4 percent of the total product, because many nutrients dissipate quickly in aquarium water.

Floating pellets are made for surface feeders, and bottom feeders, such as pond fish, can gobble up sinking pellets. Granular foods sink quickly and are generally used to feed bottom-dwelling species.

Frozen foods are usually mixes of live food, such as brine shrimp, silversides, bloodworms, daphnia, meat, or vegetables. You can purchase this type of food in a variety of forms, such as sheets and cubes (see Figure 15-2). Little frozen cubes are a great way to keep an accurate account of exactly how much you are feeding at every meal. You must keep frozen foods from thawing before you need them because once they melt, they cannot be refrozen without a major loss of nutrients. Besides, melted brine makes your house smell like a shrimp boat.

Figure 15-2:
Some frozen brine shrimp.

Before feeding, take the frozen food and thaw it in a small cup of dechlorinated water. Dispersing the food in water allows the food to move throughout the entire tank so that aggressive feeders don't get a chance to eat it all before the rest of their tankmates get any. You can use a tool like the one in Figure 15-3 to disperse frozen food.

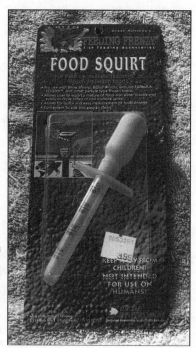

Figure 15-3:
An easy way to offer frozen food to your fish.

Spirulina

Spirulina is a natural micro-algae that is rich in proteins and helps enhance color and promote a healthy mucus layer on your fish's skin. Adding spirulina to all your fish's diets gives them healthier fins and increases their resistance to skin infections. Spirulina, which you can usually purchase in both flake and frozen form, has a soft cell wall and can be digested quite easily. Spirulina contains fatty acids that are important in proper development of the body's organs, and is also rich in A and B vitamins, iron, and calcium.

Research shows that most of a fish's color comes from the food it eats. Spirulina contains a high percentage of *carotenoid pigments* that give your fish outstanding color.

Ash alert

Manufactured fish food usually contains a certain amount of ash, which is inorganic in nature, and contains pieces of fish bone and scales. Aquarium food manufacturers are starting to reduce the total amount of ash in their products because it may be harmful to fish and can contribute to water fouling. (Ideally, the ash content should be less than 12 percent.) Check the can's label for ash levels in food products, or call the manufacturer if the content is not listed on the container.

Live food (the stuff they really love and want)

Very few aquarium shops carry live food, so it can be very difficult to find. Your best bet for locating live food is on the Internet. *Live food* includes fortified brine shrimp, bloodworms, silversides, feeder guppies, and feeder goldfish. Feeder guppies and goldfish are usually to feed large carnivores (such as pacu and Jack Dempseys).

Some people balk at feeding their aquatic pets live fish, but realistically, they're just going along with the natural pecking order in nature's food chain. Besides, feeder guppies and goldfish are raised in large hatcheries specifically for food purposes. If no one bought them, they wouldn't exist anyway. (Is that deep, or what?)

A few live foods should not be introduced into your aquarium because they may attack smaller fishes or fry. These predators include leeches, hydras, beetles, and dragonfly larvae.

Freeze-dried foods

Freeze-dried foods contain preserved small crustaceans, shrimp, larvae, and worms. This is one type of food that fish seem to either love or hate, so just keep a little bit around for a treat or emergencies.

Brine shrimp

Brine shrimp (Artemia) are tiny saltwater crustaceans appreciated by freshwater, brackish, and marine fish. Brine shrimp are available frozen, and a few pet shops carry live brine. But if you want to raise your own live food, you can buy a kit at your local pet store and hatch brine shrimp from dried eggs.

The only problem with hatching your own brine shrimp is the awful smell. Try raising them in a garage or basement — otherwise, your family and neighbors may move away without leaving a forwarding address.

One other important point about brine shrimp: Even though your aquatic pets are in a captive environment, they still enjoy hunting live food. Survival is an important instinct that cannot be removed by the presence of four glass walls, or by birth in a hatchery. Providing live foods keeps your fish more healthy and active, too. Think about it: If you had to chase down your own pig to snag a few pork chops for Saturday's barbecue, you'd probably work up a little bit of an appetite.

But, along with the good, comes the bad, as the old saying goes. Live foods have a higher risk of transmitting disease into the tank than manufactured products. Live brine shrimp at your local fish shop are pretty safe; however, if you go out to the ocean, a river, or pond to collect live food, you run the risk of introducing disease.

Infusoria

Infusoria (paramecium and amoeba) are small animal protozoans that make an excellent food for small, newborn fry. Infusoria are very tiny and form a cloud when added to your aquarium water. Infusoria can be cultured at home by soaking vegetable matter (such as a piece of lettuce) in a jar of water placed in direct sunlight.

Rotifers

Rotifers are small invertebrates raised on rotifer farms. You can find the addresses of these farms in most aquarium magazines, or on the Internet. Recently, rotifers have been used in the development and survival of captive-bred marine fry such as clownfish. If you plan to breed marines, then rotifers are a must. They also make a great treat for your other aquatic pets as well.

Predigested plankton (PDP)

Predigested plankton is an important new element (introduced a few years ago) in aquarium fish food. This natural food was first introduced in Nutrafin products and is available only from a U.S.-based manufacturer. According to Klaus Reimuller, an aquatic research and development manager at Rolf C. Hagen Corporation, PDP enhances fish colors, increases growth and survival rates, improves food digestibility, and is high in proteins.

Tubifex, bloodworms, mosquito larvae, and earthworms (yuck!)

I know these worms sound gross, but your fish will love them! You can purchase freeze-dried tubifex and bloodworms in cubes or shredded form to use as a treat periodically. They can cause digestive problems, so don't feed them to your fish regularly. Mosquito larvae provide good health and coloring for show fish, but can be difficult to find.

Fish readily accept earthworms, but clean the worms thoroughly with water and chop them up before serving.

Other cool foods

Live coral can be an excellent diet supplement for some marine fish. Many fish such as the marine parrotfish *(Bolbometapon bicolor)*, butterfly fish *(Chelmon rostratus),* and angelfish *(Pomacanthus imperator)* enjoy nibbling on live coral as a snack between meals. Young tropical marines retain better color and mature at a much faster rate if live coral is provided for food. The only problem with this diet is that it can cost you an arm and a leg. Live coral can get pretty expensive.

You can periodically give your fish many cooked household foods in small quantities, including thin strips of lean meat, lettuce, shelled peas, potatoes, shellfish, and spinach. These types of foods should be fed in moderation to avoid gastric problems.

Feeding Fry After the Stork Arrives

Young fry require a different type of diet than adults because their digestion systems have not yet matured. The good news is that you can feed many fry special foods available at your local fish shop. The bad news is that young fry need to be fed constantly, so swing by the pharmacy on the way home and grab some drops for your sleep-deprived eyes.

Microworms

You can easily culture *microworms (Anguillula silusiae)* at home and make a good starter food for young fry. All you need to do is mix a little oatmeal, yeast, and water in a bowl until it forms a paste. Add a small amount of microworms to the paste from an existing culture (which you can purchase on the Internet), and allow it to stand at room temperature for a couple of days. When worms appear on the sides of the bowl, you can transfer them to the fry tank.

Liquid foods

You can purchase manufactured fry food that comes in a tube that resembles toothpaste. Use this product sparingly, because it can foul the water.

Chapter 16

Diseases and Treatments

. . . .

. . . .

*I*f you want your fish to live long and healthy lives, then you need to make sure that they remain as disease free as possible. Many factors, including bacteria, fungus, parasites, chemicals, and poor water conditions cause disease. By monitoring your water conditions daily and checking your fish for signs of disease, you can stay ahead of the game, and keep your aquatic pets in prime condition.

How Stress Leads to Disease

In your home aquarium, your fish live in an enclosed ecosystem that is very different from and slightly imbalanced compared to the natural stability of their native environment. The majority of health problems tropical fish experience are the direct result of stress, which is often caused by poor environmental conditions.

Your fish are capable of carrying all types of diseases that generally are not a threat to their everyday health. These diseases usually remain dormant until your aquatic pets are weakened by fluctuating environmental factors such as temperature and pH. When environmental stability problems occur, your fish's latent disease can manifest quickly and cause health problems. Sick fish can be a real bummer, but this chapter helps you overcome most fishy health problems.

Stress Coat

One really cool preventative medication on the market is *Stress Coat*. A small amount of the protective coating on your fish's body is removed when you capture it using a standard aquarium net. This natural *slime coat* plays a very important role in preventing the loss of body salts from the gills and skin.

A dose of Stress Coat helps heal tissue damaged by the loss of mucus coating, and protects against bacterial and fungal attacks. Use this product each time you add new acquisitions to your tank or use a net on your fish.

Preventative Measures

Preventing disease is generally the best way to battle physical problems. Sounds simple doesn't it? It is. You can provide optimal living conditions for your tropical fish simply by following a few simple *maintenance routines*. (I promise, no 5 A.M. stuff!)

Keeping abreast of the water and equipment conditions in your aquarium, which takes only a few moments a day, gives you a safety margin to quickly correct any problems that show up. The following schedule gives you a few pointers on how to watch for signs of disease and other aquarium problems such as equipment malfunction.

Daily measures

Maintaining the following daily routine is not as difficult as it sounds. It takes only a few minutes a day, and after a week or so, it will become second nature — just like grabbing a midnight snack while your spouse is asleep.

Check the equipment

It is very important to make sure that all the aquarium's mechanical equipment is functioning properly each and every day. Are the filter systems putting out the optimal flow that the manufacturer suggests? Is the water flowing smoothly, or is it running too slow? If the water seems to have slowed down to the point where it resembles a still life painting, check to see whether the filter and tubes are clogged and make sure that the motor is not wearing down (water flow is slow, or the filter is making noise).

Many filter motors can be rebuilt with parts supplied by the manufacturing company that produced the product. If the filter pads are clogged or extremely dirty, replace them or rinse them gently under water until they're clean. The only real disadvantage to replacing or washing filters is losing the biological bacteria that lives on the pads.

Are the air pumps in your aquarium in prime working condition? Carefully inspect them to make sure that they are running properly and not overheating. If the pumps are not putting out enough air to run the equipment and decorations efficiently (you'll know when the little plastic diver turns blue and keels over), you can usually rebuild them by replacing worn diaphragms with parts you special order at your local fish shop. If your local dealer cannot find the parts for you, take a couple of aspirin, then call the manufacturer and ask the folks there to send you the parts you need. If the pump is very old and no parts are available, it's probably time to purchase a new one.

Check the water temperature

Monitoring water temperature is another important part of your daily routine. Any fluctuation in temperature more than two degrees from the norm can quickly lead to serious health problems. If the temperature is not within correct range (your fish are either floating around in the center of an ice cube or have melted into a blob), check to make sure that your heater is not stuck in the on or off position.

Always measure the water temperature at the same time each day to get the most accurate readings. Replace any faulty heaters immediately and install a heater that contains an *internal regulator* if your finances allow. An internal regulator lets the heater turn itself on and off automatically.

One common cause of overheated aquarium water is an excess of natural or artificial lighting. Check the amount of natural sunlight the tank receives every day. If too much natural light is causing the temperature to rise during peak sunlight hours, then you need to move the tank, block out the light with a thicker background, or cover the windows with heavy drapes or shades.

The duration and intensity of artificial lighting can be a problem as well. If a light is constantly overheating your tank, switch to a lower wattage bulb, or leave the light off for longer periods of time, or else your pets may end up looking like floating fish sticks.

Check the fish

After you get up in the morning and choke down a few dozen cups of coffee, make a quick inventory of all the fish in your aquarium. If any fish are dead, remove them from the tank and take them to the bathroom for the final flush. Rotting fish can cause serious biological problems and upset the balance of your tank.

If any fish seem to be sick or diseased, immediately transfer them to your *hospital tank* (I explain setting up a hospital tank at the end of this chapter) and begin treatment. If you check the health of your fish daily, you can remove them in time so that disease doesn't spread to other fish in the aquarium.

Check the overall health of your fish very carefully. Take a close look at their physical condition. Are they swimming normally, or consistently lurking in the corners of the tank? Are their eyes bright and alert, or clouded over? Are their fins erect, or clamped shut and drooping? Do they have a straight spine, or do they look like Quasimodo? Do their bodies have normal, well-rounded proportions, or are their stomachs swollen or sunken? If you can visually identify physical problems, you need to check the aquarium's water and equipment.

Weekly measures

Weekly routines are just like daily maintenance. Choose one day per week to carry out the following tasks.

Check the water

Change at least 15 percent of the water in your aquariums every week. Many large new filter systems and chemicals claim that you never need to change any water ever again if you purchase and use that product.

Cure-all equipment and medications pose a real danger to your fish. When you stray down untried paths instead of using the standard, proven road that you know leads you where you want to be, you run a serious risk of losing your fish.

The water in a fish's natural environment is constantly replaced by seasonal rains, tidal flow, and run-off. Take a moment and pretend that the water in your aquarium is your only drinking supply for the entire day. Would you be comfortable drinking it? Remember, your aquatic pets have to *live* in it 24 hours a day.

Carefully check your pH and nitrate levels with a test kit each week to make sure that they remain within the proper range required by your individual species of fish. If they are not correct, you can slowly change your pH by adding chemicals or carrying out water changes.

If chemical tests indicate that your nitrate levels are too high, the best way to fix the problem is to change 20 percent of the water daily until the nitrite levels return to normal. Don't forget to check your aquarium conditions, so that you can identify and correct whatever is causing your nitrate levels to soar higher than the national debt. A few causes of high nitrates include poor filtration, overcrowding, lack of water changes, and chronic overfeeding.

While you are doing your weekly maintenance routine, take time to siphon off any accumulated debris on the substrate's surface area by using a simple gravel cleaner or aquarium vacuum. Remove any dead vegetation, such as decaying plant leaves, from the tank. This type of living debris can quickly cause a large fluctuation in the water's nitrate levels. If you need to use searchlights to locate the gravel in your tank, then the water needs to be cleaned.

Make the fish fast

Ideally, your aquatic pets should *fast* (not be given any food for 24 hours) at least one day per week. I know this may seem difficult at first, but avoid the temptation to give them treats such as cinnamon rolls and donuts because you feel sorry for them. Fasting helps clean out your fish's digestive systems and guards against constipation problems that occur from time to time. Remember to fast your fish on the same day each week, so they don't go too long between feedings.

Give medications

Take a close look at all the medications you use for common illnesses such as ich and fungus and make sure you have all the standard treatments. Is there enough *dechlorinator* (which removes chlorine from your tap water) in your home to make daily water changes if they become necessary? Have you sterilized your hospital tank since its last use? Is it ready to be used, or is it holding last night's leftovers? Being prepared can make all the difference in the world between saving your wet pets and losing them.

Monthly measures

Monthly chores are much easier to remember if you mark them down on a calendar. Or you can simply tack a reminder note up on the fridge so that you remember these routines every time you go for a midnight snack.

Replace all filter mediums that contain *carbon*. Carbon loses its effectiveness after a period of time. If your filter isn't carbon-based, gently rinse it under water to remove debris. Don't use hot water for this task, as excessive heat can destroy the entire beneficial bacteria colony living on the filter.

Clean all algae from the glass so that your fish won't think they've gone blind.

Common Ailments and Cures

The list of common tropical fish illnesses in this section gives you general guidelines for identifying and treating various diseases. In addition, take a look at Figure 16-1 for an illustration of some of the symptoms mentioned on the following pages. Keep in mind that several common medications and salt treatments may be detrimental to live plants, some species of catfish, and other delicate or sensitive tropical fish. It is always best to treat sick fish in a hospital tank, away from the main population.

Copper-based medications used to treat marine fish can be lethal to invertebrates living in the same tank. So, always check the manufacturer's warnings on the medicine bottle's label very carefully if you plan to treat your fish without using a quarantine tank.

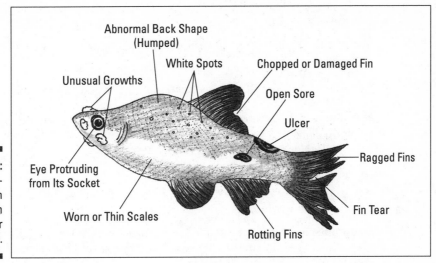

Abnormal Back Shape
(Humped)

White Spots

Chopped or Damaged Fin

Open Sore

Ulcer

Unusual Growths

Ragged Fins

Eye Protruding
from Its Socket

Worn or Thin Scales

Fin Tear

Rotting Fins

Common bacteria infection

Symptoms: Blood spots; open sores; ulcers; frayed fins.

Cause: Aeromonas.

Treatment: Antibiotics.

Constipation

Symptoms: Reduced appetite; little or no feces; swollen stomach; general inactivity. (If your fish haven't left the gravel for over a month, they may be constipated.)

Cause: Incorrect nutrition; overfeeding.

Treatment: Add one teaspoon of magnesium sulfate for every two gallons of water. Fast your constipated fish for several days. Improve your fish's diet by feeding live foods frequently.

Dropsy

Symptoms: Swollen body; protruding scales that make your fish look like a pincushion.

Cause: Organ failure from cancer and old age, or poor water conditions.

Treatment: Antibacterial given through medicated food. Improvement of water quality through water changes also provide a little relief to afflicted fish. Complete recovery from dropsy is rare.

Fin rot

Symptoms: Reddened or inflamed rays; torn, choppy, ragged, or disintegrated fins. Your fish may look like it just swam through an electrical fan.

Cause: Fin rot is a highly contagious bacterial infection that, in its advanced stages, can completely erode the fins and tail all the way down to the body. Bad water quality and fin injuries are usually the main causes of this disease. Fin rot is frequently followed up with a secondary fungal infection.

Treatment: Spot treat infected areas with gentian violet and use proprietary medication (a treatment that is labed for one particular disease, such as fungus cure, ich cure, and so on). Add 1 tablespoon of aquarium or marine salt for each 5 gallons of water to help your fish with body fluid functions. Remove activated carbon from all filters during the medication period. Frequent water changes are necessary to help improve water conditions.

Fish louse

Symptoms: Disk-shaped parasites are attached to the skin. Ulcers often develop close to the area of parasitic attachment. Bacteria or fungus problems may follow after.

Cause: Crustacean parasite. After feeding on the skin, the adult parasite leaves its host and lays gelatin-like capsules full of eggs on the substrate and aquarium decorations. Often the eggs don't hatch until the aquarium temperature rises, and may stay in the tank for extended periods of time.

Treatment: Remove all parasites from the afflicted fish using a small pair of tweezers. Dab any wounds using a cotton swab dipped in commercial

Mercurochrome. Remove water from the main tank and sterilize all decorations and substrate. In other words, start over.

Freshwater velvet

Symptoms: A golden-velvet or grayish-white coating on the body or fins. If your fish has velvet, it looks like it has been sprinkled with gold dust. This disease is very common among certain species such as bettas.

Cause: Piscinoodinium parasite. The adult parasites attach themselves to the skin of tropical fish and then fall off after seven days or so. These parasites immediately drop into the substrate and begin to multiply. The new parasites are then released into the water and move around until they re-infect the fish in your aquarium. If the parasites cannot find a living host within a period of two to three days, they die.

Treatment: Proprietary malachite green remedy. Add 1 tablespoon of aquarium salt for each 5 gallons of water.

Freshwater ich

Symptoms: The sudden appearance of small white spots, which look like little grains of table salt, on the body and fins. Fish infected with this disease continually scratch themselves on gravel and decorations during the advanced stages. (If your fish look like they are making love to the rocks in the aquarium, they probably have ich.)

Cause: Ichthyopthirius parasite. Adult parasites fall off of the host, and multiply in the substrate. Soon after, new parasites go searching for another living host.

Treatment: Proprietary ich remedy (formalin or malachite green). Even if you remove the infected fish to a quarantine tank, you must still treat the aquarium water in the main tank with medication to kill off any remaining free-swimming parasites.

Fungus

Symptoms. White growths on the body or fins that are fluffy in appearance and make your fish look like a cotton puff or a floating marshmallow.

Cause: Fungus often attacks regions where the mucus or slime coating on the fish has worn off due to damage by injury or parasites. Fungus is caused by Saprolegnia and Achlya species of parasites. Once the slime coat is damaged, the fish is more susceptible to all types of other disease.

Treatment: Spot treat with gentian violet, methylene blue, or use aquarium fungicide in extreme cases.

Gill parasites

Symptoms: Redness in the gill areas; labored respiration; scratching; excessive mucus coat; glazed eyes; inflamed gills; loss of motor control (your fish resemble slam dancers).

Cause: Flukes (Dactylogyrus).

Treatment: Sterazin or other proprietary treatment. Formalin baths can be effective as well.

Hole in the head

Symptoms: Pus-filled holes on the head, near the lateral line or the base of the tail. This disease is most common among cichlids.

Cause: Hexamita parasite.

Treatment: Flagyl. Recent findings show that Vitamin A and C supplements are effective in treating this disease (aquatic vitamins, not Flintstones Chewables).

Intestinal parasites

Symptoms: Worms sticking out through the vent; emaciation of the body.

Cause: Several different varieties of intestinal worms.

Treatment: Standard fungus cure or in advanced cases, veterinarian prescribed anthelminthic added to the daily diet. Add 1 tablespoon of aquarium salt for each 5 gallons of water to help your fish with normal body fluid functions. Remove any activated carbon during treatment. Change 15 percent of the water daily to keep environmental conditions optimal.

Large skin parasites

Symptoms: Scratching; visible parasites.

Cause: Fish Lice (argulus) and anchorworms (Lernaea).

Treatment: Remove large parasites with tweezers. Apply an antiseptic solution to the injured site.

Marine black ich

Symptoms: Small black spots appear on the body; scratching; paleness; decreased appetite.

Cause: Turbellarian worms.

Treatment: Formalin baths and copper-based medications.

Marine clownfish disease

Symptoms: Body lesions; excessive slime; increased respiration; pale color.

Cause: A ciliated (an organism made mobile by small hairlike projections) protozoan known as Brooklynella hostilits.

Treatment: Malachite green.

Marine velvet

Symptoms: White- or rust-colored dust on the body and fin areas; fish is scratching by rubbing its body on the gravel or decorations; increased respiration; pale color; excess slime; flared gills.

Cause: Amyloodinium ocellatum.

Treatment: Freshwater baths and copper-based medications.

Marine white spot

Symptoms: White spots, resembling small grains of salt, appear on the body.

Cause: Cryptocaryon.

Treatment: Place the afflicted fish in a freshwater bath for a few minutes. Copper-based medications are also effective.

Mouth fungus

Symptoms: White cotton-like growths around the mouth area (your fish looks like Santa Claus having a bad hair day) or patchy-white skin in the same region. In advanced stages, the jawbones begin to deteriorate badly.

Cause: Usually flexibacter, which follows after other infections have begun.

Treatment: Proprietary fungus treatment or methylene blue in the early stages. If this treatment is not effective and the fungus is out of control, consult your veterinarian about antibiotics immediately.

Pop-eye

Symptoms: Eyes inflamed and protruding from their sockets to the point where they almost "pop" out of the head. Often the fish's eyes develop a cloudy, whitish haze. Inflamed eye sockets are also common with this disease.

Cause: Parasites or poor water conditions.

Treatment: There are no known commercially packaged medications to treat or cure this disease. The only thing you can do to help your afflicted fish overcome pop-eye is to improve the aquarium's water conditions with frequent changes. It may also be beneficial to add 1 tablespoon of aquarium salt per 5 gallons of water to help with osmoregulation. Check and adjust all water conditions (pH, ammonia, nitrites, nitrates) with test kits to make sure that they remain within proper ranges.

Septicemia

Symptoms: Redness at the base of the fins followed by blood streaks that appear on the fins and body. Other symptoms include hemorrhages, loss of appetite, and general listlessness. This disease usually follows finrot or skin infections. Septicemia often results in major heart damage and blood vessel problems. These complications can in turn lead to fluid leakage in the abdomen, which in some cases causes dropsy.

Cause: Pseudomonas or streptococcus bacteria inflames body tissues made susceptible by a skin infection.

Treatment: Antibacterial Furan2 or Triple Sulfa. Change the water every 24 to 36 hours.

Skin flukes

Symptoms: Inflamed skin; excessive mucus coating (your fish looks like it was baptized in Vaseline); scratching.

Cause: Gyrodactylus.

Treatment: Proprietary medication.

Slimy skin disease

Symptoms: Gray-colored slime on the body or fins; scratching; frayed fins; excessive mucus coat; shimmying like a politician during questioning.

Cause: Costia, trichodina, cyclochaeta, or chilodonella parasites.

Treatment: Proprietary remedy of malachite green and frequent water changes. Short-term (5-minute) formalin and salt baths can be effective. Check and correct any poor water conditions.

Swim bladder disease

Symptoms: Abnormal or irregular swimming patterns (your fish do the doggie paddle upside down), and complete loss of physical balance.

Cause: Bacterial infection; physical injury to the swim bladder from fighting; breeding: netting; transportation from the dealer; poor water quality.

Treatment: Treat with an antibiotic in a clean, shallow tank (The water should be about 2 inches higher than the dorsal fin on the fish.) Carry out water changes as frequently as once a day if possible.

Tuberculosis (TB)

Symptoms: Fin deterioration; a paling of body color; clamped fins (fins are closed up or folded together); excessive weight loss; ulcers; and pop-eye.

Cause: A highly contagious bacterial disease caused by poor filtration or overcrowding in the aquarium.

Many medical personnel believe that this disease can be transferred to humans through contact with the infected areas on the fish.

Treatment: At this time, there is no known effective treatment of tuberculosis, and in my opinion *it is not worth risking your own health, or the health of your family,* to try treating infected fish. Use strict care when handling these infected fish! Use plastic gloves when removing any fish infected with tuberculosis. Any tropical fish that has this disease should be euthanized *immediately.* Do not leave the TB-infected fish in the main aquarium because other tankmates will probably eat it and may develop the disease shortly thereafter.

Frequent Causes of Disease

There are many causes of disease that are not related to parasites and infection, such as carbon dioxide poisoning, poor water quality, metal poisoning, chemical poison, improper diet, overfeeding, and fright. These important physical and social conditions should be monitored frequently.

Carbon dioxide poisoning

Symptoms: Listlessness; increased or rapid respiration — your fish may hang near the top of the water like an aquatic Christmas tree ornament.

Cause: Lack of oxygen; too much carbon dioxide in the water.

Treatment: Add more aeration to improve gas exchange at the water surface; cut down on plant fertilization; check and correct any poor water conditions; and carry out frequent water changes.

Poor water quality

Symptoms: The first sign is that your tropical fish are gasping for air at the water surface of the tank, and are generally inactive. Clamped or closed fins, overall bad health, and poor coloration are a few of the other symptoms of incorrect water quality.

Cause: Poor water quality due to infrequent water changes, poor filtration, and overuse of standard chemicals.

Treatment: Make daily water changes until any high ammonia, nitrite, or nitrate levels return to lower readings. Make sure that the aquarium has enough aeration, and add an extra airstone or bubble disk, if necessary. Make sure that the pH of the water is within the proper range.

Metal poisoning

Symptoms: Erratic behavior; paleness.

Cause: Metal objects coming into contact with the aquarium water.

Treatment: A complete water change. To avoid accidentally poisoning your tropical fish, never allow any metal to come in contact with the aquarium water. Metal hoods and metal equipment clips are two common sources of poisoning. To keep this equipment from poisoning your fish, use plastic clips and make sure that the glass cover on your aquarium fits properly so that no water comes into direct contact with the hood and light fixture.

Chemical poisoning

Symptoms: Erratic behavior; gasping for air; fish lying on their sides; paleness; clamped fins; refusal to eat.

Cause: Other common sources of water poisoning in aquariums are cleaning, cosmetic, and insect-control products. Never use insecticides, hair sprays, or mist cleaners near your aquarium. Small drops of these airborne products can easily fall through the small equipment holes in the top of your tank and poison your fish. If you have to use one of these products near your aquarium, tightly cover your tank ahead of time with plastic sheets or large towels to protect your fish.

Treatment: Complete water and filter change.

Improper diet

Symptoms: General poor health; paleness of color; inactivity.

Cause: Poor nutrition.

Treatment: An unbalanced diet doesn't contain all the vitamins and minerals important to your fish's health. Begin feeding a wide variety of commercially packaged flakes, small servings of fresh lettuce, peas, and other green vegetables, and live foods.

Overfeeding

Symptoms: Lethargic fish; excessive weight gain; and constipation.

Cause: Overfeeding your tropical fish on a regular basis.

Treatment: Fast your fish for two days. Improve poor or fouled water conditions caused by uneaten, rotting food before it leads to more disease problems. If your fish are beginning to resemble the Goodyear blimp and are bobbing up and down in the water like corks, start measuring each serving of food so that you don't feed them too much at one time.

Frightened fish

Symptoms: Your fish dash for cover when the aquarium lights are first turned on; constant physical injures from collisions with decorations.

Cause: Sudden changes in lighting.

Treatment: Gradually increase room lighting by opening drapes and turning on lamps before you switch on the aquarium lights.

Home Remedies

In this section, I give you a few good home remedies that you can try to avoid giving your fish large doses of medications. These methods work really well and can save you a lot of money.

Salt bath

A salt bath as a method of treating freshwater fish has been around since the aquarium hobby first began. Salt baths have proved effective over time to help cure problems such as fungus infestations, ich, and several other types of parasites such as gill flukes. Basically what happens during this treatment is that the parasites are submerged in the salt solution along with your fish and begin to take on water until they burst and fall off.

I have personally used this home-remedy method for over 20 years and have found that it has a very high rate of success in treating different types of diseases. (Don't try this in your home bathtub with your own sores, or you may end up peeling yourself off the ceiling — you've heard of salt in an open wound? Trust me, it's not good for nonaquarians.)

A salt bath is really very simple. All you have to do is add one teaspoon of table salt for each gallon of water in your hospital tank. Continue adding one teaspoon of salt twice a day for the first five or six days. If the infected fish is not completely well by the sixth day, continue to add one teaspoon of salt for another three days.

Freshwater bath

If you have a marine fish, you simply reverse the treatment and give them a freshwater bath for a couple of minutes, then return your saltwater fish to the main tank. Return the fish to the regular tank immediately if it shows any signs of distress.

Tell-Tale Clues and the Sherlock Holmes Method

Everyone wants to do a little bit of detective work at least once in their life-time. If you're like me, you couldn't find more than one pair of matching socks in the dryer even if your life depended on it. Fortunately, looking for clues that indicate the presence of a tropical fish disease is much easier to do than the laundry. To get started, all you need to do is find one of those cool-looking hats, a pipe, a long coat, and follow the clues I give you in this section.

I cannot overemphasize the importance of checking the overall health of your fish very carefully every day. Shimmying, abnormal loss of appetite, weight loss, paling or darkening of colors, increased or labored respiration, and miniature For Sale signs on the aquarium's porcelain castles are a few of the warning signs that disease or environmental conditions are causing them discomfort.

Other tell-tale clues to look for include: a bloated look, obvious visible damage to your fish's eyes, fins, or scale areas, and abnormal spots on the body. If your fish is hanging around the heater, continually scratching on tank decorations or substrate, or is a normally active fish that is suddenly moving slowly, it may have a serious problem.

If you notice any of these problems, don't panic. Take the time to make care-ful observations on the efficiency of the equipment, the condition of the water, and other disease-related factors. After you compile all the information you can, you're in a better position to make a sound judgment on the proper course of action. If you're unsure about what to do for a diseased fish, con-tact your local vet or fish dealer. The people there can give you good advice and help you with your fishy problems.

Using a Quarantine Tank

A *quarantine tank* helps you treat sick fish. A quarantine tank is simply a small aquarium that acts as a hospital ward for afflicted fish. You remove dis-eased fish from the main tank and place them in the quarantine tank for chemical or other types of treatment. It's as simple as that.

Purpose and advantages of quarantining

All tropical fish go through a tremendous amount of stress being transported to your home aquarium. Think about it — if someone snagged you with a giant pair of panty hose, and then stuck you in a large plastic bag, wouldn't you have a little bit of a problem with that? You'd need a little time to get your senses back in order, so that no one could accuse you of being a couple sandwiches short of a mental picnic.

Fish are really not that much different from us when it comes to mental stress. A quarantine tank can be the perfect way to provide your new tropical fish with a suitable recovery area — it gives them time to regain their strength before moving into their brand-new home. This recovery period also gives you time to see whether any latent diseases or physical problems manifest themselves.

Quarantine time

The very first thing that you need to do when you bring your new acquisitions home, (unless they are being used as a starter fish for a new aquarium) is to place them in a quarantine tank for one week. You don't quarantine starter fish because you need them to begin the nitrogen cycle.

Writing it all down

A simple journal can help you keep track of your fish's quarantine and health record. You can check these records for information on previous treatments. Keep a separate page for each individual fish and include the fish's name, date of purchase, size, health record, length of quarantine, and any other information you feel may be important in future medical treatments. If you want to look like a real pro, simply write something important looking like "Scientific Information" on the journal's cover. Your friends will be impressed.

The tank

I think a 10- or 20-gallon tank is a good size for quarantining unless you plan on purchasing some very large fish. All the equipment you need to get your quarantine tank going is a good-quality power filter and a submersible heater. Make your new fish feel secure by adding a small amount of gravel and a few plants. The last thing you need is for your new aquatic pets to be placed in a bare tank where they can easily be frightened.

Don't forget that a quarantine tank needs to be cycled just like your regular tank. A starter fish or two will help begin the biological cycle. When you go down to your local dealer to purchase starter fish for the main tank, pick up a couple of extras for the quarantine tank at the same time. The water conditions (pH, temperature) in your quarantine tank should be similar to those in your permanent aquarium. This prevents your fish from being stressed out further when you move them to the main aquarium.

Remember, it is much better to be patient and wait until your new fish complete their quarantine cycle than it is to place them immediately into a main tank where they can spread disease that could have been caught and treated. In the long run, treating disease can cost you quite a bit more money than setting up a simple and inexpensive quarantine tank.

Setting Up a Hospital Tank

Unfortunately, there is no 911 number for your aquatic pets should they become ill. So you need a hospital tank to help treat them when they become diseased. Hospital tanks are similar to quarantine tanks. The only difference is, hospital tanks are used to treat ill fish, whereas quarantine tanks are used to hold new acquisitions for observance. It is much more practical to treat diseased fish in a separate hospital tank because many common medications affect different species in different ways. For example, a malachite green formula used to cure ich in most species has the potential to destroy any tetras in your aquarium.

Treating diseased fish in a hospital tank also lowers the risk of the disease spreading to other inhabitants. Many antibiotic treatments destroy essential bacteria and cut down on the efficiency of a tank's biological filtration system. This can lead to even more health problems and outbreaks of new diseases. Using a hospital tank prevents these problems.

It really doesn't take much money to set up a hospital tank if you purchase a small aquarium (5- or 10-gallon) and a simple sponge filter to provide a good base for beneficial biological bacteria. Filtration systems that contain carbon don't work very well in a hospital tank because the carbon often absorbs the medication. The frequent water changes you need to do when treating sick fish are much easier to handle in a small aquarium. A good submersible heater with an internal rheostat lets you monitor water temperature as needed. Diseases such as ich can be treated more quickly if you raise the standard temperature by a few degrees.

Remember that overly bright lighting reduces the effectiveness of many medications. Try to use a lower wattage bulb for your hospital tank setup. Add a few extra airstones to the hospital tank to increase the oxygen supply because many medications tend to reduce the oxygen supply in the aquarium.

Understanding Medications

There are a large number of medications on the market, and many of them can be used to treat a variety of diseases, so deciding which one you should actually use can be very confusing. More often than not, the final choice of medication rests with you. Each case is unique, and many aquarists prefer one medication over another.

In time, you'll discover which medications work best on certain diseases and different species of fish. Until you reach that point, try to keep a wide variety of medications around so that your friends and family think that you have everything under control. The following list gives you an idea of how to use common medications, and the pros and cons of each drug.

- ✔ **Salt:** Common table salt or marine salt is generally used to treat ich and other parasitic diseases in freshwater fish. The normal dosage is one tablespoon per gallon of water in the aquarium. Salt is very inexpensive to use, but you can't use it in tanks containing certain species, such as catfish.

- ✔ **Methylene blue:** You often use this liquid to treat diseases such as ich, fungus, and velvet. You achieve the correct dose by adding enough methylene blue so that the water is difficult to see through, usually about 5 drops per gallon. The bluish cast in the water disappears with proper filtration, but stains decorations and gravel, and cannot be used with many species of living plants. Methylene blue is difficult to get out of clothes and stains everything it comes into contact with.

- ✔ **Copper:** This liquid treatment cures diseases such as flukes, velvet, and parasites that are characteristic of saltwater ich. Copper is one of the main medications used for many marine diseases, but can become expensive and is very toxic, especially for marine invertebrates.

- ✔ **Malachite green:** Use this wonderful medication to treat velvet, fungus, and ich. It is very effective in battling disease, but cannot be used in tanks that contain fry (newborn fish) or certain species of fish such as tetras. Malachite green can be very toxic if used in large doses.

- ✔ **Formalin:** This is a bath-type treatment only, and should not be used in the main display tank. This is a great remedy for parasites, but it doesn't work well on internal infections and can be very toxic.

- ✔ **Penicillin:** Penicillin treats bacterial infections and is nontoxic. The main disadvantages of this drug are the expense and the difficulty of obtaining it.

- ✔ **Tetracycline:** This antibiotic is great for bacterial infections and is nontoxic. The only problem with this medication is that it can turn the water yellow and cause unsightly foam to collect on the water surface.

- ✔ **Acriflavine:** Acriflavine treats ich and fungus, but may turn the water green.

Part V

Breeding Your Fish for Fun and Profit

The 5th Wave   By Rich Tennant

What exactly did you say you were breeding your cichlids with?

WOOF!

In this part . . .

Breeding your fish takes a little work, which is why we need a whole part of this book to cover the topic. You'd think that something that happens so naturally in the wild would be a piece of cake in your aquarium, but you'd be wrong. The next few chapters help you to set things up properly so that you can be the proud foster parent of a bunch of baby fish.

Chapter 17

The Breeding Room

*T*he first thing you need to know about breeding your fish is that there is no perfect way to breed any single species of fish. Sure, a lot of techniques are known to be successful and a lot of aquatic breeding methods are steadfast and true — but, what one hobbyist finds to be a successful method, others may have no luck with. Better methods are waiting to be discovered, and there is always room for improvement and new ideas when it comes to breeding fish.

Many hobbyists have bred fish accidentally, just by having the right combination in their aquariums! Whether it occurs by accident or on purpose, breeding is breeding. Don't let anyone tell you any differently! (If they do, tell them to come see me.)

When you're breeding your fish, take the time to observe everything going on:

✔ What are the *spawning pair* (male and female that you want to mate) doing about the other fish around them?

✔ Are there any changes in the pecking order?

✔ Have feeding patterns changed since the courtship started? Are the fish eating more or have they stopped feeding normally?

By making pertinent observations of all your fish's activities, you can gain a better understanding of how aquatic relationships work.

Keep a logbook so that you have a permanent record of your spawners' ages, successes, diseases, and brood sizes.

Make sure that you *exchange* information (call other hobbyists on the phone and brag, write an article and brag). Only by sharing information can breeding methods be refined and perfected. Never adopt the attitude of complete secrecy: You may hold the key to solving a very difficult puzzle for someone else. Besides, by exchanging information or asking for advice, you can avoid breeding hazards and unwanted mutations (no one wants to produce piranhas the size of the Titanic).

Deciding to Breed Your Aquarium Fish

Aquarists, like everyone else, have goals for their hobby. One of your first goals as a fishkeeper is to maintain a healthy and successful aquarium. After you accomplish that goal, then what?

You may decide to try another type of system (freshwater, brackish, or marine), or to investigate a few unfamiliar breeds. But when all is said and done as far as maintaining an aquarium is concerned, what does the future hold? (If you're like me, then the answer is: a lot of bills at the local fish shop!)

Impressing people

Breeding aquarium fish successfully is kind of like getting into a sport's Hall of Fame: There is no greater reward. So many species can be bred easily that you should have no problem getting into this fascinating and enjoyable aspect of the aquarium hobby. But, there are also many fish out there that have never been bred, which leaves the door wide open for you to become a pioneer. Just imagine what it would be like if you were the first person on earth to successfully breed a species. It can happen. Your friends and family would be so impressed.

Gaining new knowledge and enjoyment

Impressing people is a good reason to breed fish. The satisfaction of accomplishing something new (and perhaps snagging a little fame and money while you're at it) is another good reason. You can gain an overwhelming amount of wisdom, knowledge, and pleasure by partaking in this scientific aspect of the hobby. When you successfully breed a particular species, you also find out much more about that species than the average hobbyist learns in a lifetime.

Breeding fish is fun! Hey, if you think human courtship is a little odd at times, wait until you see your fish go a few rounds!

Conserving the environment

Probably the most important reason to breed fish is to contribute to the *conservation* (keeping species alive for future generations to enjoy) of our Earth's aquatic species.

At one time, freshwater fish were shipped from many countries around the globe so that the average hobbyist could enjoy them. Today, thanks to massive freshwater breeding programs, most of the species in this side of the hobby are captive-bred. If anything ever happens to them in the wild, aquarium hobbyists will be there to pick up the ball. Already, aquarists have saved many fish species from extinction by breeding them when their numbers reached alarmingly low rates in their native environments.

Although not many saltwater species have been bred, new advances are being made everyday. You, too, can contribute to this relatively new aspect of aquarium fish breeding. We all have a responsibility to put back what we take from the wild.

Every aquarist should attempt to breed some species, whether freshwater, brackish, or marine. Don't concern yourself with wondering whether it's already been done — just go out and do it.

Choosing Your Equipment

Before you set up a spawning tank, decide whether you want to breed a few fish in your main aquarium (in which case you don't need a breeding room), or turn out fry faster than your local greasy spoon.

A large-scale breeding operation requires space. Easy-to-breed fish multiply very rapidly. You may end up living on the back porch permanently to make room for your new arrivals. To breed fish in a serious way — to develop new colors, sizes, and/or fin shapes — you need quite a bit of room. An extra bedroom or office offers the perfect solution. But, if your whole house is the size of a small fishing cabin, you may want to look into the possibility of a heated storage shed. Make sure you have plenty of room before you start, or you may end up hastily trying to bamboozle your local dealer into buying them off you. (When you sell fish to a dealer, don't look desperate or they will cut your profit margin because they think you need money badly.)

It is important to keep all your fish stuff (tanks, nets, chemicals, and so on) in the same room if possible.

The aquarium

A 10- or 20-gallon aquarium is a good starting size for a breeding tank. You don't want to use a tank that is too large, because you might lose track of your spawners and their fry. In order to keep up with everything your fish are doing, you have to spy on them frequently. (Hey, aquatic voyeurism is a blast!) So, a smaller tank allows you to remain in control of the action at all times, and is much easier to work with and clean. As with any aquarium, thoroughly rinse it with clear water before you use it.

Putting a lid on the whole thing

When your fish are ready to breed, they get a little excited. Excited fish tend to jump very high. High-jumping fish can end up as decals on your room light or as an afternoon treat for Puffball the cat. A tight-fitting hood keeps your fish in the water where they belong, protects eggs and young fry from many unseen disasters, and keeps heat loss at a minimum. A good hood also prevents dirt and household chemicals (like your daughter's mushroom cloud of hair spray) from entering the water.

Decorations

Plenty of places to hide (rocks and plants work well) give your spawning pairs the opportunity to get used to being around each other before they start spawning. It's a fact of life, some couples just don't get along very well. (If you don't believe me, check out Ma and Pa during their next bridge game.) If your breeding tank has no hiding places, the male of many species may have to kill or maim his mate out of territoriality or frustration before any spawning has an opportunity to take place.

Many species of fish like to breed on pieces of shale, rocks, flowerpots, or plant leaves. In Chapter 18, I discuss these decorating options in further detail.

Don't laugh, but many hobbyists mistakenly place two aggressive males together in a breeding tank (it's more difficult to determine sex in some species than in others), which leads to total disaster. The loss of fish in this instance can be avoided with proper hiding places.

Substrate

Hobbyists disagree as to whether to use a gravel substrate in their breeding tank. I generally recommend using no substrate for several reasons:

- ✔ A tank with gravel or sand is much more difficult to keep clean.

- ✔ Most species are happy breeding in a tank that has no substrate and use rocks, plants, or flowerpots for protection and laying eggs if needed.

- ✔ The newborn fry of *livebearers* (fish that bear live young) often sink down to the substrate after birth. I have seen many fry trapped by gravel too large for them to navigate around.

- ✔ It is really difficult for you and the parents to see and keep track of the fry's health and growth with substrate in the breeding tank. For example, a betta male gathers eggs that fall from the surface and spits them back into the safety of his bubble nest. If the bottom of the tank is covered with gravel substrate, the young fry may fall between the individual stones and become unreachable.

Many hobbyists argue that a spawning tank is not natural without substrate, but I have seen most species of fish bred without it. If you feel the need to use substrate for species that prefer to spawn on it (like some killifish), a thin layer of fine sand is a good choice.

Spawning grates

Once in a while, you run into a species that likes to eat their own young or eggs. To prevent this, lay a spawning grate on the floor of the tank so that the young fry or eggs fall to the bottom through the holes. This allows you time to remove the parents before they can have their offspring for dinner. You can find woven lattice plastic mats that work well at most hobby or craft stores, and you can cut them to any shape you need. Just place the lattice sheet on top of marbles, and you have a made-to-order spawning grate for very little expense.

You know those cool green plastic containers that hold strawberries? (Remember you unsuccessfully tried to turn them into a Christmas ornament?) Laid end-to-end, they work well as a spawning grate! Sometimes a little imagination goes a long way. (Darn, that leaves me out.)

Turning up the heat

Use a good quality heater in the breeding tank to keep the water from chilling. This is especially important if your breeding room is not insulated as well as the rest of your home. Besides, many fish require an increased temperature to prepare them for breeding. Although it's possible to control the water temperature with the heating system in your home, this isn't a practical method. It's better to have a heater you can adjust as needed on each individual tank.

Filtration

Filters are important in breeding tanks, because they supply needed oxygen and produce the water movement that entices many species to mate. Filtration also keeps wastes that can destroy eggs and fry from building up.

A *sponge filter* is ideal for almost any breeding tank. This unit has a very simple design and is easy to use. A sponge filter provides simple biological filtration without the risks of mechanical filters (youngsters can be sucked up in the intake tubes). A sponge filter creates current, but doesn't cause the excess turbulence often produced by larger power and undergravel filters. If your spawners are stuck together permanently, you may want to cut down on the current with a valve or a smaller filter. Heavy turbulence from an extra air supply (bubble disks or airstones) can damage the delicate eggs or young fry.

If you decide to use a larger filter, make sure that it runs slowly. If you use a sponge filter, you can always do water changes to remove any mechanical debris.

Plants for safety, spawning, and inspiration

Plants have a wide variety of uses in a spawing tank:

- ✔ Plants look cool.
- ✔ Plants are inexpensive.
- ✔ Plastic and live plants provide privacy and offer security.

✔ Several species use live plants in the construction of their nests.

✔ Plastic and live plants serve as spawning sites for many species of fish.

✔ Live plants remove carbon dioxide from the water and replace it with oxygen.

✔ Live plants destroy bacteria present in the water.

✔ Live plants are a natural food source.

✔ A planted tank can make your fish think they're in a natural environment, which helps inspire and speed up their spawning plans.

✔ Plants can provide protection and shelter when a spawning partner becomes aggressive (and many do). You're wise to always have several thick plants to have on hand just in case the lovemaking reaches Round 15.

Well, if those aren't enough good reasons to use plants for spawning, I'll never be able to talk you into it!

Thoroughly clean any plants you choose for your spawning tank before adding them to the tank. Plants often carry snails and small nematodes (worms) that can potentially harm eggs and fry. To be on the safe side, you can set up a separate tank to grow plants that can be used especially for spawning.

In case you're wondering what types of plants to use in your tank, I provide you with a list to get you started in Table 17-1. Remember that many *freshwater plants* have different pH and temperature requirements. So, you can check the list below and match the plant to your individual aquarium setup accordingly. (See Chapter 10 for explanations of the terms I use to describe these plants.)

Table 17-1	Plants for Spawning Tanks				
Name	*Temperature Range (in degrees F)*	*pH Range*	*dH Range*	*Planting Method*	*Uses*
Amazon Swordplant *(Echinodorus bleheri)*	72–83	6.5–7.5	2–15	Planted or potted	For species that prefer to spawn on large plant leaves
Cryptocorn *(Cryptocoryne affinis)*	72–82	6.0–7.5	3–14	Planted or potted	For species that spawn on leaves

(continued)

Table 17-1 *(continued)*

Name	Temperature Range (in degrees F)	pH Range	dH Range	Planting Method	Uses
Hornwort (*Ceratophyllum demersum*)	60–84	6.0–7.5	5–14	Anchored or free-floating	For almost every type of freshwater fish
Java Moss (*Vesicularia dubyana*)	68–85	5.8–7.5	3–15	Anchored	For free-spawning fish (fish who let their eggs scatter anywhere)
Ludwigia (*Ludwigia repens*)	62–82	5.8–7.5	3–14	Planted or free-floating	For fish that like to spawn on leaves
Sagittaria (*Sagittaria subulata*)	68–83	6.0–7.7	2–12	Anchored, planted, or free-floating	For many varieties of bottom dwellers
Spiral Val (*Vallisneria spiralis*)	60–85	6.5–7.5	5–12	Planted, anchored, or free-floating	For species that spawn on leaves
Water Hyacinth (*Eichhornia crassipes*)	72–82	6.0–7.8	2–14	Floating	For bubble nest builders
Water Lettuce (*Pistia stratiotes*)	72–80	6.5–7.5	5–14	Floating	For bubble nest builders
Water Sprite (*Ceratopteris thalictroides*)	68–84	6.5–7.5	2–12	Anchored or free-floating	For fish that build bubble nests, such as bettas

Getting the Water Right

The water in your spawning tank must suit the species of fish you're trying to breed. Take a look at Chapters 6 through 8 for more info on getting the water right.

Transporting youngsters

When you transport your newborns to a *rearing tank* (also known as a *growout tank,* which is used to grow juveniles to adulthood), make sure that the water temperature and pH levels are identical to the tank from which you remove them. The growout tank should function like a normal aquarium system. Also keep a close eye on the youngsters while moving them because they are very small and can disappear faster than your kids when it's time to clean out the garage.

pH control

You must keep the pH level of your water under control in a breeding situation. Changes in pH are very damaging to your fish, and the ill effects double in intensity during the breeding ritual. Eggs and young fry are especially susceptible to even the smallest of fluctuations in pH level.

Water temperature

One important thing to keep an eye on, especially if you have *egglayers* (fish that don't bare live young, but lay eggs that hatch), is the temperature of the water. Eggs can be severely damaged in temperatures above 85 degrees F. You may end up with poached eggs at best. Higher temperatures also cause eggs to develop too quickly, which can lead to weak, deformed, or weird-looking fry.

Cleanliness

Young fry and eggs are much more susceptible than adults to problems resulting from too many *nitrogen compounds* (waste) in the water. Poor water conditions can destroy eggs or damage the growth cycle of newborns. Change at least one quarter of the water each day in a spawning or growout tank.

To avoid fouling the water in a breeding tank, feed the fish there small amounts of live foods instead of flake.

Conditioning the Love Birds

Many fish practically jump into the spawning tank from across the room in order to breed. Others, however, have a hard time adjusting to their new partners and your breeding goals. This section gives you some die-hard methods that you can try to help *condition* (get your fish in the mood to spawn) your aquatic lovebirds. (Don't bother with Mozart and a little wine in the water — I already tried that.) No lovemaking tricks are completely foolproof, but several tried over the years have proven to be quite reliable and accurate.

The way to the heart is through the stomach routine

Everyone loves to eat, right? (In the strange case of my teenagers, some more than others!) Fish are no different. You probably already picked up on that last time they jumped out of the water and into the open food can in your hand. So, it is simple to turn the tables and take advantage of the fact that your fish are real gluttons most of the time.

One change that commonly occurs during the breeding season in a fish's natural environment is the sudden appearance and overabundance of live foods. When seasonal rain storms sweep over ponds, lakes, and rivers, a large supply of live insects and fresh food drops onto the water surface. Offer your fish live foods such as brine shrimp and tubifex worms (okay, okay, so it's a bribe) to condition them for breeding purposes. Just remember to rinse all live food before feeding.

Fruit flies *(Drosophila),* mysis shrimp, live brine shrimp, and small earthworms make great conditioning food.

The old fake rainstorm trick

Weekly water changes are very important to the health of your fish, and you can use them to aid in the conditioning process as well. In the wild, seasonal rains (you know, when you walk outside in the morning to go to work and find that your car has floated down the block) usually signal the start of the breeding system. Now, I know that it's not practical to run outside with your fish tank in your hands every time it rains in your neighborhood. The only other option is to create a rainstorm in an artificial way.

In the home aquarium, you can duplicate a rainstorm to some degree by doing frequent water changes (about 20 percent per day in a breeding tank). Clean, demineralized water stimulates most species into entering their seasonal spawning cycle.

Another way to duplicate the rainy season is by showering the surface of the water in your spawning tank with drops of water. You can do this quite easily by using an inexpensive watering can purchased at almost any garden shop. No, you don't have to stand there all day imitating a stone fountain. Run one full can of water slowly over the surface each hour when you have time. (Don't forget to remove some water first!) You can also try pouring water slowly through a colander or plastic mesh.

The barometric pressure advantage

In the wild, an increase in _barometric pressure_ (ask a weather forecaster about that one) often makes fish more lovable. Many hobbyists report that their fish breed more actively right before or during a rain or snowstorm. Follow the local weather conditions and you may be able to introduce pairs to the breeding tank during a barometric pressure change and have a successful spawning.

The old change the temperature ploy

If you go backpacking out to your species' natural environment, you soon find that they do not live in an area that remains the same temperature 24 hours per day. (If you don't believe me, pitch a tent for one night by the river.) Try fluctuating the temperature of the breeding tank overnight. Drop the temperature 3 degrees at night, and then slowly raise it back up in the morning. Now don't get carried away and start tossing ice cubes into the tank or anything. All temperature changes must be done _slowly_!

The new guy next door approach

If you have a beautifully colored male that is being really stubborn and refusing to breed, you can always try introducing a second male (the meanest, ugliest one that you can find) in close proximity. (This is kind of like sending your fish to a downtown singles bar.) Placing the rival male in a glass holding container near the spawning tank often inspires the stubborn spawner to breed when he suddenly realizes that there may be competition for his female.

The absence makes the heart grow fonder routine

If a pair is being outright stubborn about getting along, you can always separate the male and the female with a glass partition until they decide to either breed or die of boredom. (You know the old saying: "Absence makes the heart grow fonder.") This method is illustrated in Figure 17-1. While separated, keep feeding them small bits of live food until they shows signs of mating such as displaying brilliant colors or excessive contortions and body movement. This method works best when you only have one pair of fish in the spawning tank.

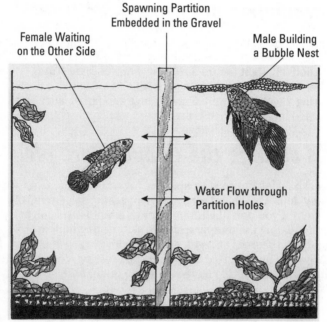

Figure 17-1: Using a breeding partition.

So What's Next?

This chapter goes into the equipment you need and how to condition your fish for spawning. In the next chapter, I examine individual courtship and breeding routines in more detail.

Chapter 18

Let's Spawn!

*B*reeding your fish is a great way to advance your fishkeeping skills. After you learn the basics and have successfully bred your first fish brood, there's no reason why you can't begin thinking about selling the excess off-spring to a local dealer. You may get lucky and find a dealer who needs a regular supply. This little bit of extra money can help offset some of the expense incurred with your hobby (and offset your spouse's financial wrath at the same time!).

After you have bred your fish, you are going to have an excess of fry that you may want to get rid of. Your local fish shop is a great place to make a few extra dollars off of your extra fry. Simply ask your local dealer if he or she would be willing to trade equipment or purchase your extra fish at a cost that will compensate both the buyer and the seller. You can also run an add in your local newspaper and sell your fry to other hobbyists.

Some fish breed in your community or species tank without any help from you. But if you want stay in control, set up a *spawning tank* (a tank designated only for breeding). That way, you can adjust the water quality and feeding schedule as necessary, as well as *cull* (separate the good from the bad) the fry of each species you're raising. Culling is simply the process of separating the fish you want to keep from the fish you don't. This ensures that you will be able to breed individuals with the characteristics you are looking for.

Introducing the Bride and Groom

With most species, it is better to introduce the female to the spawning tank ahead of the male. Males are more aggressive, and putting the female in first allows her to establish a little bit of territory for herself. Give the female plenty of time to become comfortable in the new tank (at least a couple of hours until she is swimming normally and not hiding in her new surroundings). When she looks like she has become "king of the hill," place her behind a tank partition before you introduce the male. This "prenuptial" separation lets the male get accustomed to the sight of his mate and give him a chance to calm down a little bit before he actually meets her. Leave the partition up until the male seems like he is calm. You don't need to do this with all species, but it is usually the safest way to go.

Dealing with aggressive males

Some males are naturally more aggressive (actually *nasty* is the word I was looking for) than others, and it's difficult to determine an individual's habits before you see him in action. I've had very peaceful males of one species, only to turn around and end up with one of the same species that was ready to take on Mike Tyson. (I'd bet my money on the fish, too!)

If your spawning tank is heavily planted and contains many safe areas where a female can hide, you may be able to introduce both partners at the same time. I personally do not use this method very often because I've seen too many females torn up by normally peaceful males that got a little too excited.

Setting up the second date

If a spawning pair seems to get along well on the first date, it's probably safe to put them back into the same spawning tank at the same time. But fish in love can be very unpredictable, so don't bet the farm on their getting along again, or you may end up sleeping in a borrowed haystack.

The art of love (Yes! My fish really like each other!)

If your fish are having a real romantic picnic, why spoil the fun? Let them continue to breed as long as they're in good health.

The art of war (Darn! My fish hate each other, now what?)

If your fish are throwing gravel at each other, they probably won't be in the mood to mate. Don't force something that isn't meant to be. Give them a little time away from each other and then try again. If they still try to kill each other, forget it and work with a different set of partners. I have witnessed a couple of instances where one male would refuse to mate with only one particular female out of a group of ten identical fish! Why they seem to turn on one individual is unknown.

Following are a few physical reasons why fish won't spawn.

- Their water looks like a sewer.
- Their tank is too small.
- They need more fish (for example, neons mate in schools).
- One of the partners is cradle-robbing, or is older than dirt.
- The fish have not been conditioned (been fed live foods prior to spawning) properly.

Strange rituals

Tropical fish have some really weird things they do when they make out. Here are just a few wild examples:

- Some killifish smash headfirst into the ground and then spawn. (Hey, what a great "I have a headache" excuse!)
- Marine damsels hit their partners in the face with their tails while backing up, and then do loop de loops that would put Space Mountain to shame.
- A Bichirs male catches his mate's eggs in a fin that he forms into a small pocket.
- Male seahorses carry the female's eggs and do all the work giving birth. (I like that idea!)

- Bettas wrap around each other so tightly, that you can't stick a pin between them.
- Some killifish carry their eggs suspended on threads (which are manufactured by their own bodies).
- Kissing gouramis often "kiss" each other while mating.
- Sicklebacks "yawn" to attract their mates.
- All clownfish are male until it is time to spawn, at which time one turns into a female.

- ✔ The fish may be sterile.
- ✔ You have two females in the spawning tank (not good).
- ✔ You have two males in the spawning tank (even worse).
- ✔ They just don't feel like it.

If the problem seems to be mental, check out Chapter 17 for tricks you can try to get your two fish to like each other. Unfortunately, there are no fish psychologists to help you along, so if these tricks don't work you may as well forget it.

Understanding Breeding Types

Fish reproduce in one of two basic ways: Either they bear live young (livebearers), or they lay eggs (egglayers). Each type of breeder is unique, and has special requirements.

Livebearers

Livebearers give birth to free-swimming young that are fully formed and resemble tiny adults. A female livebearer is internally fertilized (all use this method) by her partner and carries the fry internally for about a month *(gestation period)* before birthing them. Immediately after entering this world, the young fry swim and search for food.

All live-bearing fish are either *ovoviviparous,* (the female produces eggs that contain yolk to feed the embryo) or *viviparous* (the young are nourished by the mother's circulatory system). Ovoviviparous females tend to lose their brood to miscarriage problems more often than viviparous ones.

How do I tell them apart?

A few well-known examples of livebearers include guppies, swordtails, mollies, and platys. Most livebearers are brightly colored and make great community fish. It is easy to determine the sex of most livebearers because the female is usually larger and more full-bodied than the male. Most males have a rod-like organ (developed from the anal fin) called a *gonopodium.* This unique organ is used to internally fertilize a female. After a single fertilization, a female can produce multiple *broods* (batches of fry) month after month without a male being present.

Fish in drag

In some species of livebearers, females can develop secondary male sexual characteristics. Where there are not enough males present to ensure survival of the species, the female's anal fin may change into a gonopodium.

The egglayers

Egglayers lay eggs (which usually range in size from 1.4 to 3 millimeters) that eventually hatch into newborn fry. The fry of egglayers are not as hardy and fully formed as those produced by livebearers. The babies of egglayers take much more time to mature. Popular egglayers include angelfish, cichlids, goldfish, and bettas.

When breeding egglayers, be aware of the following dangers to eggs:

- The eggs in your breeding tank can be seriously damaged by lack of oxygen. Without oxygen, their normal rate of cell division decreases. But you don't want heavy turbulence in the tank either. Hook up a small air-stone or bubble disk (which splits the air into smaller bubbles) to a gang value (which splits up an air supply to supply several pieces of equipment) so that you can adjust the oxygen flow. This provides beneficial aeration for the eggs without creating a hurricane that may blow the eggs into the next county.

- Eggs can also be damaged if the mother lacks the essential vitamins needed to help them grow correctly. Diseased females can produce bad eggs. If the eggs from an unhealthy mother hatch, the young are usually defective. Make sure that your spawning female is in good health before you attempt to breed her.

- Intense lighting can also damage fish eggs. Minimize lighting in your breeding tank.

Getting a free baby-sitter

One fascinating egglaying strategy is that of the cuckoo catfish _(Synodontis petricola),_ which lays its eggs in cichlid territory so that their eggs are cared for by mouthbrooders — fish that gestate eggs in their mouth. The cuckoo catfish often eats the eggs of the cichlids it has chosen for parenting, and then cleverly put its own eggs in their place.

Bubblenest builders

Bubblenest builders lay and incubate their eggs in a nest of bubbles that usually floats at the surface, or is attached to plants. Bettas and gouramis are the most famous of these bubblenest builders. A male betta builds a floating nest that he carefully constructs from mucus-coated air bubbles he blows out of his mouth. Males often use plant debris as a "glue" to help keep the bubbles together. In some species, the entire nest has a foamy appearance.

Nests are built in different shapes and sizes, depending on the individual male. Some males complete a nest in a few hours, while others take their time and end up working several days to accomplish the same task. If excess circulation or other factors damage the nest, the male constantly repairs it as needed. Often males build more than one nest to impress a female and entice her into breeding.

Egg scatterers

Egg scatterers must hide their eggs because they do not take care of them after birth. These species scatter their eggs around decorations, rocks, plants, and gravel. During courtship of these species, the male actively chases his mate and fertilizes her eggs as they fall freely into the water. They lay large numbers of eggs at one time, ensuring that some survive by sheer numbers alone. A few common examples of egg scatterers are danios, barbs, rasboras, and tetras.

Substrate spawners

Substrate spawners lay their eggs in such a manner that the eggs attach to one particular area of rocks, driftwood, plants, or substrate. The male of the species fertilizes the eggs while the female lays them. Common examples of substrate spawners include some cichlids, catfish, and killifish.

Mouthbrooders have all the fun

Mouthbrooders are unique, because they incubate their eggs in their mouth until it is time for them to hatch. As the eggs are laid, the male fertilizes them. The parents (either the male or female) gather them up in their mouths for protection and incubation. Popular examples of mouthbrooders include some labyrinth fish and cichlids.

Saving Everyone from Everyone Else

After spawning is complete, there may be a few problems between Mom and Dad; Mom and the kids; or Dad and the kids. (Hey, sounds like my family!) It is crucial that you keep an eye on everyone after breeding — This is when the third world war may break out among aggressive species. Let me put it this way: Your fish can suddenly develop a bad attitude. If fish had nuclear weapons after spawning, we would all be vaporized.

Saving Mom and Dad (from Mom and Dad)

Just because your fish had a great night out on the town doesn't mean that they like each other now. In fact, there's a really good chance that they want to tear each other limb from limb (or fin from fin). No one seems to know why they get like that. Perhaps they're just really tired after spawning or are suffering from *PASS* (post aquatic spawning syndrome). Whatever the reason, many fish have to be separated after they spawn.

If you have a pretty decent-sized fish room, you can move the female to her own holding tank (this can be as small as 4 gallons depending on the size of the fish), and then move the male to his own quarters. It is not a good idea to move spawners back to a main aquarium with other fish. The male may still be aggressive because his hormones are as high as a kite on a windy day. He may look for his next victim in your community or species tank. The female may be torn up or worn out, and you should allow her to rest in a tank of her own for at least 48 hours in order to recover properly.

The *slime coat* (coating on the body that helps to protect the fish from disease) on a mating pair can be easily damaged during breeding. After you move the male and female to their own quarters for recuperation add a little Stress Coat to the water to guard against bacterial infections.

Saving the fry and eggs from Mom and Dad

Many fish (such as cichlids) normally make good parents and perform tasks such as caring for their brood and defending their nesting spot. However, should this pair suddenly be upset by outsiders, they can turn from Ward and June Cleaver into Bonnie and Clyde in a heartbeat. Unfortunately, the young fry or eggs suffer most from their parents' newfound wrath.

One way to avoid this problem with aggressive species is to use a large tank equipped with many hiding places. Try to keep their breeding tank in a quiet, low traffic area so that the fish aren't irritated by people walking by and making a lot of noise. You can also use *spawning grates* (a plastic sheet with holes that allows the eggs to fall though) for protection.

Livebearers (such as guppies) often eat their young. To prevent this, you can purchase a *breeding trap* to separate the young after birth (see Figure 18-1). Breeding traps come in a couple of different designs. A *net trap,* shown in Figure 18-2, is a simple rectangular device that floats in your aquarium (kind of a net shaped like a box). You put the female inside the net, so that her young are protected from other fish in a community tank. Unfortunately, the net trap does not protect the young from their Mom. The advantage of the net breeder is that the net allows free water flow from the aquarium.

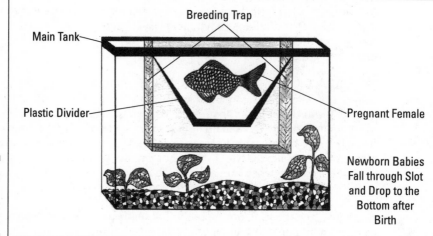

Breeding Trap

Main Tank

Plastic Divider

Pregnant Female

Newborn Babies Fall through Slot and Drop to the Bottom after Birth

Figure 18-1:
Using a breeding trap.

You can also put the expectant mother in a plastic *breeding tank* and float it in your larger aquarium until the mother gives birth. One added advantage of this type of breeder is that after the fry are born they drop through a small slit and are separated from their mother as well as their future tankmates. Unfortunately, the plastic breeder does not allow water flow to keep the interior clean, and can foul rather quickly if the birth is delayed.

Most breeding traps are too small to accommodate a pregnant female for any length of time. While under restraint for long periods, she may struggle to escape, and damage herself or her unborn fry. Pregnant females should only be placed in breeding traps when they are ready to deliver.

Figure 18-2:
A net trap.

Saving the fry from each other

Fry eventually reach a stage where they are sexually mature. If you have a bunch of juveniles in a growout tank, you should separate the males from the females as soon as you can determine their genders. If you don't, you may end up with a lot of unwanted spawning that interferes with your breeding plan. As the fry grow, you need to start culling.

A problem with growing fry is that the larger ones (the males usually grow quicker) start eating the smaller ones after a short period of time. This is a very common occurrence, even if the youngsters are fed properly.

Raising the Fry

After the fry are born and the parents have been moved to a resting tank, you can begin feeding the babies. The fry (depending on the species) are usually very small and should be fed liquid foods or infusoria cultures through an eyedropper. Microworms are another good food choice.

Brine shrimp rule

After a few weeks, you can begin feeding the fry baby brine shrimp — live foods help them gain maximum growth. Brine shrimp is a great choice because of the relatively low odds of introducing disease into the tank.

Give them a real home

Be sure to feed your newborn fry several times a day to ensure maximum growth. Baby foods tend to foul water quickly, so you need to change the water frequently in order to keep their tank clean. Raising your newborns in a well-planted aquarium allows them to mature at a more normal rate than in a bare tank with no decorations.

Check each species specifications before removing the parents! Some fry, such as discus, depend on their parent's slime coat for nourishment, and may not survive if their parents are removed from the tank.

Picking new stock

When selecting future breeding stock, choose the most colorful, vigorous fish in the group. You don't want to rely upon chance sexual encounters, or you may never be able to develop the strain you're seeking.

Understanding Genetics

A while back, a bored young monk named Gregor Mendel did a few experiments with peas in a quiet monastery garden. He *selectively bred* pea plants for certain characteristics and kept track of those characteristics. He was surprised to see *traits* (physical signs) not seen in either parent plant appear in their offspring. Everyone thought he was weird, but he learned a lot of cool stuff — such as, what you see is not necessarily what you get. *Selective breeding* allows you to choose fish that have the characteristics you're searching for and to breed them until that characteristic remains stable from generation to generation. And, like Mendel, you may end up with a few surprises to boot.

Choosing the best

To breed selectively, you need to choose a male that possesses characteristics you want to develop into a *pure strain* so that generation after generation of fish display the same certain colors, fin types, and whatever other factors you isolate. Selecting a good female may be a little more difficult, because they usually do not carry as much color as the males. Just try to pick a full-bodied female in good health.

Obtaining variation the good way

Few strains produce identical fish from generation to generation. If they do, it can take a very long time to reach that point. Because genetics are so varied, it is possible that you may end up with a brand new characteristic (not seen in the parents) within a few years. This occurs because of *recessive genes* (not shown in the physical makeup) which make an appearance periodically.

Obtaining variation the bad way

Another way you can obtain variation is when a *mutation* occurs. A mutation is a more radical change from one generation to the next, and does not occur in increments. The main disadvantage of a mutation is that many mutants are often sterile or, if they're fertile, they may carry deformed genes that are not passed along to future generations. The odds of carrying a mutation long enough to make it pure are staggering to say the least.

Acquiring a pure strain through inbreeding

The breeding process used to produce a pure strain of fish is known as inbreeding. After the first brood is born and raised, pick a healthy male and breed him back to his mother. From the next generation, select the best quality grandson (who displays the characteristics you want) and breed him with his grandmother. Keep repeating this process for successive generations. This helps solidify the characteristics you want.

As each new brood is born, check for males born with unique characteristics that you want to continue on with. If the females that you started with die, select a healthy daughter and continue on. This method of inbreeding is more effective than *line breeding*, which involves mating half-brothers and sisters.

Choosing the Right Species for You

It's best to start out with a few of the easier-to-breed species so that you can learn the ropes before plunging into difficult waters. The following examples give you basic information on a few species that are relatively easy to breed so that you can get started on this fascinating adventure without encountering a lot of difficult problems.

Guppy (Poecilia reticulata)

The guppy is probably the easiest aquarium fish to breed. Guppies would breed in a puddle of water if given half a chance. You can combine several males with a few females in a species tank, and within a year you will have to purchase a new aquarium to house all your new fish. Guppies readily breed in a community aquarium, species tank, or spawning tank. Males have a gonopodium and are more brightly colored than the larger-bodied females. The young fry are born fully formed and ready to eat. Standard water temperature for breeding is 74–78 degrees F; dH 12; pH 7.

Convict cichlid

Breeding convicts is very easy. Because breeding convicts can be very aggressive toward their tankmates, put the convicts in their own spawning tank with a few plants and rocks, or a flowerpot turned on its side. The female of the species is larger and shows much more color than the male. She also exhibits black and red bars during the breeding cycle. Water temperature for breeding is 69–79 degrees F; dH 8; pH 7.2.

Convict spawning occurs very rapidly. They lay their eggs in a rock cave or in a flowerpot. Both parents help take good care of the young — unless they begin to quarrel. If the parents fight, remove the losing partner. The young eat readily, and flee to the parents when they feel threatened.

Angelfish (Pterophyllum scalare)

Angelfish breed steadily when you provide the proper conditions. Angle a piece of slate, 2 to 3 inches wide, against the glass of the tank for your angelfish to lay their eggs on. The spawning pair clean off the slate before using it. When the housework is done, the female lays her eggs on the slate, which the male then fertilizes. Angelfish often pair up, so the easiest way to start matching them with a spawning partner is to pay attention to who hangs out with whom. Male angelfish have a bump (common among cichlids) on the front of their heads. The genital papilla is round in the female, and pointed in the male.

After the eggs are fertilized, both parents use their fins to gently fan them with water, and remove any infertile or damaged eggs during the process. The eggs hatch within 48 hours, and the fry absorb their yolk sacs before searching for food. Some angelfish are carnivorous and eat their own eggs. (Angelfish also help their young emerge from the eggs by removing the case, so make sure you know what you're seeing before you do anything about it.) If the angelfish are eating their eggs, remove the piece of slate with the eggs on it, and place it in another tank with an airstone for circulation. Water temperature for breeding is 75–78 degrees F; dH 7–16; pH 6.7–7.5.

Part VI
Fun Stuff

The 5th Wave   By Rich Tennant

Kyle spent many happy hours admiring his handcrafted fish/reef/flooded basement aquarium

In this part . . .

1f taking pictures of your fish, keeping logs of their growth, and showing 'em off at fish shows isn't fun, than I don't know what is. The next few chapters have all the details.

Chapter 19

Recording Data and Photography Methods

*O*ne great way to enhance your fishkeeping hobby is by taking pictures of your prize aquatic pets. Photos are a good tool for learning more about your fish and their natural social interactions. Photography is also a fun way to enhance your social standing by impressing your friends with your great pictures. The equipment you need for fish photography is inexpensive and can be easily obtained.

Keeping a Log Book

Keeping track of your fish's individual health, breeding schedule, and food preferences can be quite a difficult job, especially if you have a large variety of species, or your bedroom alone has more aquariums and aquatic pets than the National Aquarium in Baltimore.

One good way to keep tabs on your aquarium fish is to use a log book. A complete record of each fish in your aquarium provides you with the opportunity to monitor your pet's history, social habits, growth, water conditions, and spawning successes.

If you keep track of each new acquisition as you purchase it, you gain a better understanding of each species' needs, which can be beneficial in decisions regarding purchases of future tankmates. For example, the "calm" oversized molly you bought a couple of months ago has cleverly turned your community tank into a World Wrestling Federation battle royal, and you noted its bizarre behavior carefully on your written log. On your next trip to the fish shop, this individual fish's rap sheet will remind you to run at warp speed past the giant molly section toward calmer waters.

Beginning a log is kind of like starting a diary (except that you don't have to make up a bunch of junk). Keep a separate sheet for each fish. I suggest encasing each sheet in a plastic slip-folder and placing the individual sheets in a three-ring binder to protect the logs and impress your friends. To get you off on the right foot, the following list details the information I record:

✔ Date and place of purchase

✔ Common and scientific names

✔ Sex, size, and color

✔ Preferred temperature, pH and dH levels, and salinity and lighting requirements

✔ Type of feeder and preferred diet

✔ Environmental distribution (for example, freshwater found in Guatemala and Mexico)

✔ Social behavior (whether it gets along with other species or needs its own tank) and what type of tankmates it tolerates

✔ Spawning date and number of fry

✔ A disease record that includes the type of disease, the date contracted, the treatment, and how long the treatment took to work

✔ Date and cause of death

✔ Any personal comments

Photographing Your Fish

Okay, just admit it, buried deep within your creative depths is a shutterbug itching to get the old, dusty, 35-millimeter (mm) camera out of the upstairs attic and snap a few quick photos. Or maybe you're just an enthusiastic hobbyist like myself, continually searching for new and exciting ways to enhance your aquarium-keeping records and show off at the next block party.

Many hobbyists try their hands at selective breeding at one time or another. Have you finally succeeded in breeding the perfectly colored platy, and now feel an overwhelming need to capture and preserve that beauty? Fish photography may be the perfect adventure and challenge for you.

There are a variety of reasons for photographing fish: You may have a desire to capture the beauty of your aquarium to show these aquatic treasures to your family, friends, and colleagues. Nothing compares to the pride you feel when others openly admire your aquatic creativity.

Another good reason to consider fish photography is that you can turn good-quality fish photos into extra spending money if you catch the right scene, interaction, or pose on film. Many aquarium magazines purchase photos to use in their articles. (Magazine publishers can be tightwads, though, so don't quit your day job!)

All types of fish photos are an important resource for freshwater and marine historical preservation. In today's world where once-abundant species are slipping into extinction at an alarming rate, photographs may become the only true but sad reminder to future generations that a particular species of fish once existed, and is now extinct due to human carelessness.

Get to know the personalities and habits of the fish you're taking pictures of, and make sure the fish are healthy and happy before starting your photo shoot. After all is said and done, just remember the most important rule of fish photography: Have fun!

The camera

Almost any camera works well for fish photography. However, a single-lens reflex (SLR) camera has several options that other cameras lack.

- ✔ The picture you see through the camera lens on an SLR is basically the image that you see in the finished and developed photo.

- ✔ You can equip an SLR with auxiliary wide angle, telephoto, and zoom lenses.

- ✔ SLRs are capable of taking synchronized electronic flash pictures, which can help you capture the action on fast moving pets.

- ✔ You can purchase a wide variety of cool attachments to help you deal with difficult shots.

- ✔ A 35mm SLR makes you look like a pro if you get a cool camera strap and have a bunch of accessories crammed into a stylish bag.

Start with a camera equipped with automatic exposure so you don't miss shots fumbling with the light meter. Some cameras are so complex that by the time you set up everything for your shot, your fishy subject has spawned several times and is about to collect Social Security. (If someone is watching as you take photos, simply wipe imaginary sweat off your forehead, fiddle with all the camera buttons and look relieved when the shot is over.)

Another good reason to begin with an SLR is that you can start with a 35mm camera body and a standard 50mm lens, and then gradually add to the unit as your interests and experience expand. Inexpensive instamatic cameras usually have a fixed lens, and the quality of the picture compared to that of an SLR is the difference between a Rembrant and my son's attempt at finger-painting his bedroom walls.

Mount your camera on a sturdy tripod to help eliminate blurred pictures caused by camera shake. If you don't have a tripod, support your camera on a table or another firm surface.

The film

The simple fact is, if you want good-quality photos, you must purchase the highest quality film on the market. Cutting costs with inexpensive or low-grade films costs you much more in the long run than if you had just spent a few extra pennies on a better quality roll. Ask any professional photographer, and she'll tell you the same thing. When you are first starting out, you can save money by purchasing rolls of film with fewer exposures (12 instead of 36 exposures).

Always choose the slowest film possible to avoid the grainy pictures produced by faster films. A slow, fine-grained film such as ASA 100 produces higher quality images that can also be enlarged with better results than a faster film such as ASA 400, which often makes your pictures look as if they were taken during a desert windstorm. Increase the lighting before you attempt to increase film speed. Begin with an ASA 100 film and work from there.

Make sure to have plenty of extra film on hand, because it may take several rolls to get the one perfect shot you're seeking. After you achieve lighting proficiency and mastery of the camera and lenses, consider using slide film, which gives you the ultimate in color saturation and picture quality.

Remember not to overlook black-and-white film, which can be a simple yet exciting medium that adds artistic impact to shots of rugged fish such as a convict cichlid, or shows the delicate hues and fin details of a veiltail angel. Black-and-white photography can be an art form in itself, and you can get even more creative with it if you decide to develop your own film in a darkroom.

Lenses

A standard 50mm lens works on fish longer than 5 inches. But, when working with smaller fish, use a zoom, telephoto, or macro lens to help eliminate background material. A macro lens is designed for taking close-ups and offers a 1:1 ratio, which results in a life-sized subject in the finished photo. A 105mm macro lens works great for small fish such as a goby. Macro filters result in decreased sharpness and depth of field.

A zoom lens allows you to change the focal length of your lens to capture different sizes of fish (and spy on your neighbors after the photo session). A 100 to 200mm zoom lens is a good lens to use for most smaller fish.

Telephoto lenses enlarge images that are far away, and provide you with the freedom to work at a distance from the aquarium. Taking photos from a healthy distance helps avoid the possibility of your fish going into cardiac arrest from fright during photo sessions.

The three disadvantages of telephoto and zoom lenses are as follows:

✔ Camera shake due to the larger size and heavier weight of the lens

✔ A shallower depth of field (zone of sharp focus), which tends to blur out any background

✔ A slight loss of quality in the finished prints

Take time to experiment with different lenses to become aware of the advantages and disadvantages of each type. Look through photo magazines and books to gain new ideas on the various uses of each lens length. Talk to other photographers about their experiences using different lenses. To maintain your professional shutterbug image, nod your head frequently and pretend their advice is something you already knew.

Lighting techniques that really work

The main light on an aquarium usually does not provide sufficient lighting to take good photos. If your tank has fluorescent lamps, you may end up with a green cast on your finished pictures; if you use tungsten lamps, an orange cast may appear. You're much better off using electronic flash or strobe units that provide proper lighting and freeze motion.

Ideally, you place your photography tank (which I explain further on in this chapter) in natural sunlight, which far exceeds artificial lighting in terms of color, shadow, and mood. The disadvantage of natural lighting is that the direct sunlight can quickly heat up the water in a small tank to lethal levels and turn your fish into a broiled sidedish if they are not wearing 300 SPF sunblock. Take great care to ensure that the water remains cool until you're ready to start the photography session. A large, thick towel to cover the entire tank and block out the heavy sunlight is a great tool to have handy.

Another factor to take into consideration is that the sunlight two hours after sunrise and two hours before sunset is generally discolored and should be avoided. Photos taken in sunlight during these times tend to have a yellowish cast unless you use special filters. It is much better to take photos in natural sunlight during the late morning or early afternoon hours when the sun is at its highest point in the sky.

In recent years, large flood lights have become quite popular in fish photography. Caution is advised when using these lights as they have the potential to quickly heat water. Always check the heat intensity of these floodlights before using them.

If you're using one strobe light, direct it at the tank from a 45-degree angle near the top of the aquarium. If you use two strobe lights, place them at the same angle on opposite sides of the tank.

The 45-degree angle offers these advantages:

- ✔ Shadows appear below the fish and give your photos a natural look. These shadows also possess a softer tone than those in photos using straight-on lighting, and are more appealing to the eye.

- ✔ You get no flash reflection off the glass, which could ruin an otherwise good shot. Another method to avoid excess reflection is to wrap a black-cardboard tube around the lens on your camera. This tube is known as a mask. (Make sure you use that term around other photographers so that you look like a pro.)

Strobe lights generally have a flash duration of one-fifteen-hundredth of a second and are very effective in stopping action if you are photographing a fast-swimming fish in a large tank that isn't equipped with *restraining glass*. A restraining glass is an inserted piece of glass that is used in small photo tanks (usually 2 to 5 gallons) to gently pin the fish against the aquarium glass so that it will not move while its picture is being taken. These lights are usually powered either by electricity or rechargeable-cadmium batteries.

If the subject of your photo session is a very dark fish, move the lighting closer to the tank to compensate. On the other hand, if the fish is white or of a very light complexion, move the lighting back from the subject.

If your pictures are too dark or too light, try adjusting the lighting before you start messing around with any settings on your lens. For optimal results, take a series of pictures as you slowly adjust your lighting from near to far. You'll be rewarded with at least one picture with the best lighting possible on your roll of film. A series of photos can be valuable to your future shots, too. You can sit down and review different lighting angles and distances to see what worked.

Red-eye (also known as the vampire syndrome) is the common name for reflections caused by lighting placed very close to the subject. You can avoid this by working with the light adjustments I mention in the previous paragraph.

Another option is to aim your flash or strobes into a mirror or white card suspended above the tank. The light reflects off the mirror or card and bounces back onto the subject, creating a softer look. This method is popular for delicate-looking species, such as angelfish and other long-finned tropicals. Make sure that the mirror and cards you use are clean and free of streaks.

If you're a fairly serious photographer, you can purchase a photographic umbrella to reflect light. The manager of your local photo shop can make sure you get the proper piece of equipment for the job. Remember that a bounced flash loses up to half of its original intensity, so adjust your calculated exposure accordingly.

Focus: Making sure you can distinguish the angel in the coral

The focus of a camera is determined by the *aperture,* or opening, of the lens, which decreases as the size of the image increases. The aperture itself is a hole in the lens which regulates the amount of light striking the film. The aperture is adjusted by a diaphragm inside of the lens and is calculated in *f stops* on a ring that fits on the outside of the lens. The higher the aperture (small f stop number), the smaller the depth of field, or zone of focus.

To get a large amount of the background in focus, you need a larger f stop — or more light. The lens manufacturer usually supplies a table to help you determine the aperture you need for the magnification you want.

If your calculations point to an f stop of 11, take one photo at f 8, one at f 11, and another at f 16. This *bracketing* technique reduces your margin of error, insures a useable shot, and keeps you from having to take out a second mortgage to pay for film. Keep a log of each exposure and ask the developing lab to number your pictures so that you can gain a better understanding of how each aperture affects your shot.

Larger lens openings (f 2, f 1.4) have a narrower *depth of field* (how much area behind or in front of the subject will be in focus), which means you have to focus more carefully. Smaller lens openings (f 16, f 22) have a larger plane of sharpness and require less focusing to get the correct image. Depth of field increases with distance. The farther your camera is from your subject, the greater the depth of field. Macro photos (extreme close ups of small objects) have little depth of field because the lens is so close to the subject.

If all else fails, you can always have a photo studio *crop* your picture, which entails having a professional cut out parts of the picture that don't appeal to you. What's left is usually the shot that you were trying to get in the first place.

Composition: Getting a fish to actually show up in the photo

You need to organize all the visual elements into a balanced and appealing scene. All photos require a center of interest (the most important image in the picture).

Obviously, most of the fish that you take pictures of are of some interest, but other subjects in the aquarium can be accented by your aquatic pets. For example, a piece of driftwood with an unusual shape, or a brightly colored castle can provide a center of interest that you can highlight by capturing a small school of fish swimming nearby.

Using the rule of thirds

One general rule of composition that always produces a pleasing balance is to place the subject at the point in the frame where imaginary lines dividing the entire scene into thirds, horizontally and vertically, meet, as shown in Figure 19-1. This simple but effective placement of subjects, known as the *rule of thirds,* gives you excellent results. If there are other lines in the picture (such as a flowing river), try to arrange their colors, contrast, or lines in such a way that they lead the viewer's eye toward the main subject.

Following composition's rule of thirds gives you excellent results. The rule of thirds tells you to place the subject of the picture at a point in the frame where imaginary lines dividing the entire scene into thirds, horizontally and vertically, meet. Try to arrange lines and colors in the picture so that they lead the viewer's eye toward the main subject.

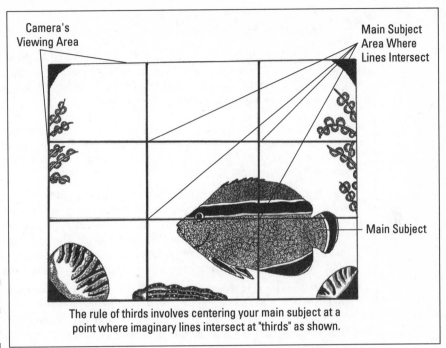

Figure 19-1:
The rule of
thirds.

Camera's
Viewing Area

Main Subject
Area Where
Lines Intersect

Main Subject

The rule of thirds involves centering your main subject at a
point where imaginary lines intersect at "thirds" as shown.

Panning the scene

To obtain unique photos that stand out from the rest, try taking pictures of
interesting moments, such as mating rituals or feeding sessions. Or experiment with specialized effects such as *panning* — following a fish with the
camera as it swims: You continue moving the camera as you depress the
shutter. The effect is a blurred afterimage that can be quite interesting. To get
the most realistic photo, keep the camera on the same horizontal plane as
the fish. (If you suddenly look down and can see the back of your knees, you
probably panned too far and should seek medical attention immediately.)

Setting up for close-ups

For good close-ups, make sure that your subject fills at least 75 percent of the
frame — this keeps the background from overrunning the shot. Focus on the
best aspects of the fish (a piranha's teeth, for example).

The photography tank

Fish can be a difficult subject to catch on film, so you need to do everything possible to improve your odds of getting quality photos. If you plan to photograph your fish in your main tank, you must take a few important factors into consideration to insure good quality photographs.

- Avoid reflected light by making sure that the aquarium's water is as clear as possible. Any debris or suspended particles (your toddler's uneaten lima beans from dinner) may reflect light and produce spots in your finished photos.

  It's a good idea to add extra mechanical filtration to the tank a few days before you take the pictures. Another effective process is to filter all the main tank water through standard floss (the same type you put in many filters and can be bought at your local pet store). The only drawback to this procedure is that it is quite time-consuming and can take anywhere from two days to five years, depending on the size of your tank.

- Clean the tank itself, the substrate, and the decorations. Remove all unsightly algae from the glass of the aquarium, otherwise your photos may end up resembling a bad still-life of chunky pea soup. Clean all plastic plants, rocks, and other artificial decorations before your photo session begins.

  Allow enough time for the mechanical filtration unit to capture any debris set loose during cleaning. The gravel in the tank should be vacuumed prior to shooting — a photographic lens does not miss nearly as much intricate detail as the human eye does.

- Check the aquarium glass or acrylic surface for scratches. The surface must be scratch-free in order for you to obtain the best photos. Several commercial scratch removal kits on the market remove imperfections from acrylic walls.

- If you're using overhead or hood lighting in the photography session, make sure that the cover glass is clean so that it allows maximum light to enter. It is mandatory that the outer glass covering each light remains translucent and clean.

Shut off all tank lights at least thirty minutes before you clean for safety purposes. (Photo lighting can be very hot and can cause serious burns if touched or electrocution if accidentally knocked into the tank while cleaning.)

Building your own photography tank

One of the easiest and most practical methods to insure great photos of your fish is to construct a miniature aquarium to use exclusively for photo sessions. This technique was founded by Dr. Herbert Axelrod and is an important part of the famous Axelrod technique of photographing fish.

A photography tank is much smaller than any standard aquarium and offers several unique advantages over a larger tank:

✔ Keeping the water in a mini-tank clean and clear for your pictures is easy in a small tank.

✔ Arranging plants, rocks, and other decorations is simple.

Building a photography tank is something even a beginning hobbyist can do — it doesn't require much time, knowledge, or lessons from Bob Vila to complete a simple tank 7 inches high by 7 inches long and 2 inches wide. You can build tanks of other sizes to accommodate the size of the fish you're photographing and the materials at hand. The glass you use to construct your mini-tank should be thinner than standard aquarium glass.

The four sides and the bottom glass of the new tank can be easily positioned using clamps and then siliconed with aquarium sealer or cement to obtain a small rectangle. No frame or supports are really necessary if the glass you used in construction is thin. The newly siliconed sides should be allowed to dry for 48 hours before water is added (unless you plan on checking out your new galoshes) or the tank is moved. This will ensure that the seal is tight and waterproof. A sixth piece of glass should be cut to size so that it fits into the tank like a partition.

Clamp (with any size standard padded C clamps) the four sides and the bottom glass in position. Join all pieces using silicon aquarium sealer or cement (which can be purchased at an aquarium store and needs no special equipment to apply). Cut a sixth piece of glass so that it fits into the tank like a partition. The safest way to do this is to go to a glass cutter and have it done for you, because glass cutting can be very dangerous.

The Axelrod technique involves using a small photo tank with an interior restraining glass embedded in fine sand and angled from the bottom front to the back top of the tank. The angled glass restricts fish movement when the restraining glass is leaned forward.

Gently place the fish you're photographing between the front glass on the photo tank and the restraining glass — which works like a cover slip on a microscope slide. (If your fish's eyes start popping out like Marty Feldman's, you might want to back off on the pressure a little bit.) Another advantage to this restraining technique is that you, the photographer, have the freedom to place the fish in creative arrangements that aren't possible in a larger tank. This glass restricts movement of faster swimming fish as well.

Using different backgrounds (The Cayman Islands sound good!)

Because flying off to the Cayman Islands or Cancun every time you feel the urge to photograph fish is not financially practical, you can use simple non-distracting backgrounds to allow the natural attributes and colors of your fish to capture center stage. Many materials found around the home — a towel, solid-color wrapping paper, thick construction paper — make excellent backdrops.

When choosing a background, take into consideration the color of your subject. A darker background is appropriate for a light-colored fish, such as a glass catfish. On the other hand, you're better off using a light background for a dark-colored fish, such as a tiger oscar.

Try to avoid cluttering the tank or the glass with too many objects (three plastic divers, a shipwreck, and Donald Duck on a life raft is too many) — they may take away from the natural beauty of your fishy subject.

Keep all decorations, such as gravel, plants, and rocks to a minimum, especially in a smaller photo tank. But these decisions are a matter of personal preference, and ultimately rest with the individual photographer. Some of the best fish photos come about as a result of the trial-and-error method of artistic arrangement.

The darkroom

Learning the art of developing black-and-white photos in a darkroom provides you with a good opportunity to display not only your fish photos, but your creativity as well. You can sandwich negatives to create double images, and enhance or darken certain areas of the photo to suit your needs. Manipulating photos in the darkroom helps you cover up any embarrassing mistakes before your friends see them. After learning a few tricks, you can even add a cool-looking fish to your aquarium photo just in case all of your aquatic pets resemble a piranha with a hangover.

Do not overlook the beauty and creativity of black-and-white film, which presents a style and mood that cannot be found in color photos. I've spent years developing black-and-white photos and have obtained many interesting effects.

If you're not familiar with darkroom techniques, your local college or photography shop can probably provide you with a course in developing film. It's worth your time and effort to check out this exciting aspect of photography.

Storing and displaying your fish photos

Store your favorite photos in plastic sheeting and alphabetize them by the fish's common name so that your visitors can enjoy them. Another option is to create an interesting slideshow using background music to set the mood you want to present. (If your photos are not top of the line, simply zip through the slideshow at the rate of about 10 slides per second, and then quickly steer your friends toward the free munchies on the kitchen table.)

Chapter 20

Fish Shows

*E*ntering a local or national fish show can be a great way for you to expand your fishkeeping hobby; win a bunch of cool prizes such as trophies, ribbons, equipment, and money; display your aquarium-keeping and breeding skills; and impress your family and friends at the same time.

Besides, fish shows offer quite a few other personal attractions worth checking out as well. For example, you often find people dressed up as fish, aquariums, and equipment at these shows because they are either promoting a product or attempting to get a little extra mileage out of their leftover costumes from the previous Halloween. Either way, a full-grown adult trying to win a 5-pound bag of gravel by walking around with a glass fish bowl on his head can be a real scream.

Many other cool things go on at fish shows — like door prizes and special drawings. Just by showing up, you may have a chance to win neat fishkeeping supplies, such as heaters and filters. You also find many experts in the aquarium field waiting to answer any questions you may have concerning your hobby. These pros can be representatives of manufacturing companies, or hobbyists who have become experts in their individual field, such as Jack Watley.

If you finally decide to involve yourself in a little bit of friendly competition, your aquarium-keeping skills will steadily improve. After all, to display only top quality fish at every competition, you need to do lots of research on nutrition, water conditions, and other factors that influence proper growth, good coloring, and vibrant health. (Hey, another good reason to buy this book!)

Only through research and improving your aquarium-keeping skills can you consistently produce high-quality show fish. Everyone can get lucky once in a while and purchase a guppy for a couple of bucks at a local fish store and have it grow into championship material. But this is the exception rather than the rule. So you need to do your homework.

Why Fish Shows Are Good for Your Fish

Participating in fish shows keeps your aquatic pets from becoming totally bored with their lives. (If you had nothing to do but swim back and forth in your bathtub all day, you'd probably be looking for a way out, too.) Fish are a lot like humans in that they need a little mental stimulation every once in a while.

In the wild, competing for food, avoiding larger predators that want to have them over for lunch (literally), and other factors such as unpredictable weather keep a fish's senses alert and stimulate it into constant action. After sitting in a home aquarium for month after month, most fish appreciate a change of pace, even if it means being carted off to a weird place where strange-looking people with large, distorted faces walk by and stare into the tank.

Getting to Know the Shows

The great majority of aquatic competitions are organized by aquarium societies. These aquatic societies can be international in scope, as is the International Betta Congress (IBC), or local groups in large towns and cities. The following is a list of the types of shows you're likely to encounter.

Small shows

Small shows (also known as bowl shows) are usually sponsored by local clubs and generally include all different classes of fish such as goldfish, cichlids, and tetras. Bowl shows are set up for only a few hours so that their paid members can exhibit their favorite wet pets. These shows are usually not open to the general public. So, to enter the competition, you must become a member of the society.

Regional shows

Aquarium societies often enter larger fish shows that cover a broad geographic area within a marked region that can include several states. In this type of competition, different societies compete against each other to see who is really the top dog (or in this case, the top piranha). A regional show forces you to become a team player, so make sure you have several good excuses ready, just in case your entry doesn't place very well.

Open shows

An open show is similar to a regional show, except that anyone can enter the competition — you don't have to belong to a particular aquarium society. These shows are cool because if you don't win, you can sneak out the back door without having to answer to anyone else. If you lose, you can still receive a lot of sympathy by simply going back home and sadly informing your family members that you had a flat tire on the way to the show and missed the entire competition.

Exhibitions

One of the largest shows you can enter is known as an exhibition, or aquatic convention. These types of shows are generally put together by tropical fish magazines and international societies. Exhibitions are massive affairs, generally held in huge auditoriums and fancy hotels. Many aquarium manufacturers are usually present to demonstrate their newest line of tanks, food, chemicals, and equipment to people they consider prospective buyers. (If you really don't want to spend the entire day listening to sales pitch after sales pitch, just wear old clothes and look poor.)

Understanding Classes

You need to learn a little bit about how fish shows operate so that you know what to expect when you enter your very first serious competition. Despite the fact that fish shows have more rules than cribbage or basketball, you can still go to a competition, have a great time, and pick up some important aquarium-keeping skills.

To make sure that the competition between individual fish is fair, you have to enter your contestant in a specific class. Classes are usually grouped by similar species. For example, if you have an oscar *(Astronotus ocellatus)*, you don't want to place it in a livebearer class, normally intended for guppies

(*Lebistes reticulatus*) and mollies (*Mollienesia sphenops*). Your fish would be instantly disqualified simply because it was in the wrong class. Trying to convince a judge that your 11-inch oscar is really a champion guppy that has eaten too much usually goes over like a lead balloon.

Classes can also be divided into smaller sub-categories. For example, a guppy class may be divided into fantails, lyretails, and spadetails. So, before you enter your fish in any competition, check with the show's sponsors to make sure that you are placing it in the correct category. It would be a shame if your potential best of show was disqualified from the competition just because you mistakenly placed it in the wrong class.

Getting Your Fish in Shape

At competitions, you want your fish to make the best overall impression it possibly can. If your entry bolts for the corner of the tank when the judge comes up for her first look, your entry probably won't receive high marks because the judge didn't have the opportunity to look it over properly.

A good show fish swims upright and smiles

A good show fish isn't shy around strangers and doesn't panic every time someone walks by its tank. There probably will be many visitors — competitors and other hobbyists — sneaking over to take a quick peak at your entry before the judging begins. Make sure to pick up the thumb tacks you *accidentally* dropped in front of your fish's tank before the first judge arrives. You don't want a bunch of people hanging around your tank and spooking your fish while it is trying to remain calm after being transported from its home to the show.

If your fish happens to be shy, it most likely will be digging an escape tunnel by the time the judge gets around to looking in the tank. So a little training is in order. There is really no big difference between fish and other domesticated pets as far as training is concerned. Conditioning works well for your aquatic pets, just as it does for your four-legged friends. To keep your show fish from being easily frightened by the presence of strangers, you need to create conditions at home similar to those found in competition.

Placing your show fish's holding tank in a high traffic area gets your entry used to people passing back and forth. How your fish reacts to people socially is known as *deportment*. Ideally, your fish should act naturally, be active and alert, and show no fear after being trained for a short period of time. Another trick that you can use at home is to periodically shine a light into the water so that your fish is prepared for sudden illumination — just in case a judge uses a flashlight during observation.

A bad show fish swims upside down and looks bummed out

A poor show fish exhibits unusual behaviors such as hanging out in areas of the tank that it normally wouldn't. For example, if your cory *(Corydoras)* normally lives on the bottom level of the tank but is trying to fly 2 inches above the water level, a judge probably will mark it down for its odd behavior. If your fish is floating upside down, or looking like it is ready to pass on to the great fish bowl in the sky, then you need to reevaluate your strategies and goals for raising top-quality fish.

Your entry should always be in top physical form. In order to achieve this goal, you need to start with a good specimen and then make sure it receives proper nutrition by feeding it a varied diet consisting of commercially pre-manufactured flakes and different types of live food. The water conditions your show fish is raised in should always be optimal, with good filtration and the proper water chemistry for the species.

The holding tank

When you spend a great deal of time, effort, and expense raising a show-quality fish, you want to make sure that it does not encounter any physical problems prior to a competition. For example, if you were a professional model, you probably would not begin taking karate or boxing lessons a week before a photo shoot — the results could be disastrous.

A small holding tank is a great (and inexpensive) way to keep your show fish healthy and free from physical harm in the month or two preceding its competition. A holding tank negates the possibility of other fish damaging your prize entry's fins or scales by not allowing physical contact, which in turn prevents untimely fighting or breeding.

Your holding tank should be free from large decorations (such as sharp rocks) with the potential to damage your show fish. A few floating plants and a couple of rooted specimens give your entry the security it needs to remain stress-free. A smaller tank also allows you to carefully monitor your fish's progress, and makes cleaning and frequent water changes a snap.

The smaller environment of a holding tank allows you to check for any disease that may manifest during this waiting period. Physical ailments can be treated quickly and easily in the confides of a smaller tank. Solitary confinement also keeps your entry stress-free and calm until it's time to enter competition and really show off. Being alone in a semi-bare tank prepares your pet for the same conditions it faces during an exhibition. Besides, holding tanks look cool and make your friends and family think you're a real pro.

Exhibiting Your Fish Properly

After you find and train your show fish, you need to have the guidelines for exhibiting them properly. The tips following can help your fish put its best fin forward.

- ✔ Study the rules before you fill out an entry form so that you have a good idea of the requirements for the individual competitions.

- ✔ Fill out all your paperwork properly and legibly, and submit it on time.

- ✔ Get your show fish to the competition with plenty of time to spare. This gives your entry an opportunity to calm down and regain any color it lost. (Fish lose color when they're distressed, and transporting them is stressful for them.) Adding a couple pinches of salt to the water can help your fish regain some of its color.

Water conditions

Bring water with you so that your fish can remain in familiar conditions during the competition. Water supplies provided at the show may be very different from those at your home. Discontinue feeding your fish the night before the competition to avoid water fouling (remember, it's good for fish to fast one day a week), and change the water frequently to keep your show tank looking crystal clear. If possible, use water that is a couple degrees warmer than what your fish is accustomed to — this generally helps fish show better. Make sure to provide an airstone, if possible, to keep the water well-oxygenated.

Tank considerations

It is important to place your show fish in a tank that correctly matches its size. For example, a single guppy in a 10-gallon tank is dwarfed by the sheer water volume and tends to look rather minuscule. It's better to show this type of fish in a 5-gallon container. On the other hand, an 8-inch plecostomus (plex) doesn't look very good in a 2-gallon container. It doesn't have the room to display all its fins, or the other attributes that may make it a winner. Let me put it this way: If you have to use a shoehorn to cram your entry into its show tank, then the aquarium is probably too small.

To set up an exhibition tank properly, you need to read the competition's rules. For example, some categories and competitions allow gravel and decorations, while others do not. If you use gravel, make sure it complements the fish you're showing. If you have a dark-colored fish, a lighter gravel shows off its colors much more naturally than a darker-toned substrate. However, make sure that you use the same color gravel you choose for the show in the fish's home tank for at least two weeks before a competition so that it feels safe and secure with that color.

Here are more tips for competitors:

✔ If the competition allows tank backgrounds, choose a solid-colored sheet over one with a pattern that takes away from the natural beauty of your show fish.

✔ When using plants for decorations, in such categories as community or species tanks, always use fauna native to the region of the fish you're showing. Take my word for it, judges _do_ know the difference. A natural set up always scores higher points than one that is a mishmash of plants from completely different geographic regions.

✔ The tank or container you use to display your entry should be immaculate. The glass walls should be clean inside and out. Vacuum any dirt or debris off the bottom of the tank right before the competition begins. (Or avoid this problem by bringing extra water with you.)

✔ Make sure that your show tank is well covered because you do not want your fish jumping out during all the excitement, and a lid also prevents other people's hands and foreign objects from getting into the water.

After you get everything set up, step back for a moment and take a good look at the overall picture. Does the entire tank look clean and well kept? Is the water crystal clear? Are the decorations in the tank placed so that your fish has the best chance to show itself in front of the judge? Does the tank look natural? Does your fish look calm and happy? Does your entry seem to be adjusting to its surroundings well? If you can answer yes to all these questions, then your fish is ready for competition.

Judging Your Fish: Another Point of View

In most competitions, judging guidelines are very strict. Usually, contestants are not allowed to be present when the judging takes place. So, if you want to do a little brown-nosing, do it before the competition starts. Simply walk up to each judge, smile, and compliment them on how much they look like Jacques Cousteau.

Each class usually has its own judge. The judge is supposed to mark your entry on its own merit, not compare it to the other fish in the competition. But judges are human, and an outstanding fish sitting in the next tank over may have a slight bearing on the outcome of your own entry's marks.

After all fish are judged, the "best of show" is awarded to the highest quality entry of all the classes combined. This decision is usually reached by a group conference — the individual judges all get together to vote for what they consider to be the best overall fish at the show. An important thing to remember is that the marks that your fish receives generally are from a single judge's point of view. So try to resist the temptation to turn the competition into a free-for-all while you verbally tear every judge limb from limb because of what you consider to be serious oversights and bad vision.

To keep judging from becoming too personal, aquarium societies devised a set of standards that each individual fish in a competition can be judged against. The fish that comes closest to matching a set standard in each category is usually determined the winner. This policy keeps the fish from being judged on personal preference only. Judges come from a wide range of backgrounds and aquarium-keeping skills. Most are experienced hobbyists or dealers who complete special training at schools that teach them how to judge fish shows efficiently.

Each competition's evaluation system varies slightly, but most show fish are judged on a point system. A certain number of points are allotted for different physical traits, such as size and color. The fish with the most total points after the judging is complete is considered the winner. In the event of a tie, the fish are judged again, or a decision is made by all the judges together. Judges disagree quite a bit, so don't hold your breath waiting for a unanimous decision, or you may end up passing out from lack of oxygen.

Size and body weight

One of the main physical traits that consistently inspires judges to give a fish high marks is its overall size. Judges generally look for a fish that has reached its full stage of adulthood and is the maximum size for that particular species. (No big deal, my teenage boys accomplished that physical feat last year.) In other words, the bigger the better. So an oscar, which should be 10 or 11 inches long, probably won't win if it resembles a minnow with anorexia. Only if you are able to raise a fish to achieve its full physical potential can a judge feel that you are a responsible hobbyist.

Your fish's body is judged on several different criteria.

✔ To begin with, your entry should have all of its body parts intact.

✔ Your fish should not have any unusual growths, such as humps on the head (except in the case of some cichlids, where a hump is consider normal in the males of the species) or large bends in the back, which is considered a sign of old age in most aquatic species.

✔ The body of a good-quality show fish is free from deformities and is in correct proportions for its species. (If you plan to enter a goldfish resembling a blown-out flat tire, you may as well check out of the motel before the competition begins and quickly head back home so that you can save your entry money for other important things such as pizza delivery.)

Color and fins

A fish's body color is produced by pigmentation and reflected light. In the wild, fish use these colors for defensive and mating purposes. In competition, fish must meet the coloration standards expected of an aquarium-bred species. Especially in show species such as the discus (which is bred artificially to produce amazing colors like tangerine and numerous cobalt variations), color can be a major factor in determining points.

Fish have the ability to darken and lighten their colors or change them completely, depending on their surroundings and the time of day. Moods such as fright, stress, and excitement, and other factors, such as illness, can change a fish's color quickly. Take all these variables into consideration while monitoring your candidate's color. (If your fish glows in the dark like a radiation dial, then it probably has sufficient color to sweep any competition.)

The color on your entry should be evenly disbursed, and it should not look faded or patchy. The color itself should be very dense, not superficial, and your fish should not look as if it's been run through a couple of chlorine cycles in your washer. The area where two colors meet should be distinct and well-defined, not blurred or run together so that the fish resembles a tie-dyed shirt.

Recently, a few unscrupulous breeders started using enhancing devices to increase the coloration of their fish. As far as hobbyists are concerned, this practice is immoral. The artificial color fades in time, and generally doesn't look natural at all. An artificially colored fish is similar to a studio's colorized version of an old movie. If you saw Humphrey Bogart running around in a shocking pink hat and purple trousers, you'd know that *Casblanca* was colorized. The same type of color errors show up on your fish and are noticed immediately by the judges when you use color-intensifying foods (spirulina) or hormones to artificially enhance your fish's appearance.

Fins are judged very strictly in a competition. Your entry should have all the fins standard for its species. If your fish should have one dorsal fin, one anal fin, two pectoral fins, one caudal fin, and two pelvic fins — that's a total of seven fins. Some species of fish have an extra adipose fin. If your fish falls into this category, make sure it has one. If it doesn't, don't enter it. If your fish is missing its tail or dorsal fin, wait until the next competition, because this physical problem doesn't go over very well with judges.

All the fins on your entry should be in good condition. Make sure there are no frayed or ragged fins to detract from your fish's natural beauty. The fins should be erect and of good color, not clamped or folded. To keep a show fish's fins in top-quality condition, keep it by itself prior to the competition so that more aggressive fish don't get a chance to tear or damage its fins.

Other causes of poor quality fins include inadequate water conditions, netting, genetic problems, and breeding spats. Make sure that the water conditions in your show fish's tank always remain optimal so that the fish doesn't contract a fungal disease that can easily damage its fins. To avoid having your entry's fins destroyed by netting, always use a plastic bag or cup to capture your fish.

Genetic problems are permanent, and the only thing you can do when you come across a deformity is to weed out that particular fish and eliminate it from your list of candidates for fish show competitions. Often, certain species of fish damage their pectoral fins when they fan eggs during breeding. For that very reason, it is best not to breed your show fish before competition.

Fins are no different from any other physical attribute and are judged against an accepted norm. Many species of betta *(Betta splendens)* are bred for long-flowing fins, and judges expect fin lengths and sizes in the proper proportion to the fish's body size. All fins should have a symmetrical (even) look pleasing to the judge's eye. If one pectoral fin is quite a bit shorter than the other, your entry probably will lose some points for this deformity right off the bat.

It is so important to check out the requirements and rules of every competition carefully ahead of time so that you know exactly what the judges are looking for. Talk to hobbyists who have entered competitions in the classes you're interested in. You can pick up a lot of interesting ideas and learn a few good tips by talking to seasoned pros who have already battled the "ins and outs" of many fish competitions.

Overall condition

Many physical factors can have a bearing on your entry's final point score. Judges look for an overall picture of perfection — a combination of many individual physical traits. Even minor blemishes or irregularities can lose points for your entry.

The scales on your fish's body should be intact and in excellent condition. In many species, scales form standard patterns. This must always be taken into consideration. Scales should lie flat against the body, have a proper mucus coating, and not protrude at odd angles. Gill covers should be straight and preferably be red in color, which is an indication of good health.

Your entry's eyes must be clear and bright, and not clouded over or protruding abnormally from the sockets. (If your fish looks like it has a hangover, pack up and go home.) Your fish should be completely free from disease because any signs of parasites, fungus, or other illness is just cause for an immediate mark down on the judge's score sheet.

Transporting Fish to and from a Show

Transportation to and from a show is an important aspect of your fish's overall health. You want to avoid stressing out or physically damaging your entry on the way to the show so that it has the best chance of remaining happy and healthy and can display its beautiful physical attributes to the best of its ability.

The first thing to do when considering transportation is to look at the distance between your home and the show area. You need to give yourself plenty of time so that you don't have to rush to the show and hastily try to set up your entry tank at the last minute. Always allow plenty of time in case something should go wrong. Any unforeseen delay can become disastrous if you're forced to rush your entry in right before the judging begins.

Drive your route to the competition ahead of time so that you know exactly how long it takes and what the road conditions are like. If the roads are rough, plan on adding a little more cushioning to your packing box. Check the predicted weather for the day of the competition, so that you're prepared in the event of heavy rain, extreme heat, frigid cold, or snow. These factors are especially crucial on longer trips.

It really doesn't matter if you plan to show one fish or several fish as far as transportation containers are concerned. You should always transport your fish in a proper carrying case or tank to make sure that their journey is as comfortable as humanly possible.

A good transportation tank can be a small plastic or acrylic aquarium that is insulated by a Styrofoam container. Or you can use a 5-gallon bucket with a tight fitting lid.

Place your transportation tank in something that will insulate it and absorb shocks while you're carrying it in your car. A homemade wooden case that you place in the back seat or hatchback of your vehicle works well. Try to avoid carrying your fish in the trunk or other uninsulated areas that can quickly overheat or chill the water during the trip.

Cover your containers with dark cloth to help calm your entry during transportation. You should always use a battery-operated air pump to keep the water aerated.

Part VII
The Part of Tens

The 5th Wave   By Rich Tennant

"It's that weird Ahab friend of yours. He probably wants to come in and stare at the Albino tigers again for about 9 hours."

In this part . . .

Every *...For Dummies* book ends with top-ten lists, and this one is no exception. You may think that this part is just filler material, but we actually provide useful information, all at no extra charge.

Chapter 21

Ten Cool Aquarium Gadgets (For Work and Play)

•••

Aquarium Claws (Those Handy Picker-Upper Doodads)

An aquarium claw is really not as menacing as its name might imply. This little plastic claw is a very handy tool for use in the home aquarium. The claw makes moving tank decorations as simple as spending mega bucks at the fish store. A button located on the end of the handle closes the claw around an object as you depress it. After moving the item, simply release the button to release the grip.

The claw can also be used to safely feed strips of meat and fish to carnivorous species. (Don't try this with a piranha or large shark unless you want your new aquarium claw whittled into a giant toothpick.) The long handle on this device allows you to reach almost any area of a standard aquarium without getting your hands wet.

Other good uses for this tool include planting, removing unwanted objects from the tank (the cat), and removing of dead fish. At an average total cost of about five dollars, you really can't go wrong with this marvelous little gadget.

Awesome Algae Scrapers That Are Fun to Use

One simple way to remove excess algae (the green alien-looking glop that is blocking the view) from the aquarium glass is to use an algae scraper. There are several types to choose from, including a long stick with attached scrub pad that you simply slide up and down the interior glass, one that comes with a two-way magnet system so you slide your end up and down the exterior glass, and a "glove type" that fits over your entire hand.

Although algae can be beneficial as a natural food source, an overgrowth can quickly turn your crystal-clear water into mushy-pea soup. Allowing a small amount of green algae to remain on rocks and decorations can be beneficial, but a tank that is excessively overrun with "the green terror" is unsightly at best.

Nets Are Us! (Why Owning One Net Won't Cut It)

As you have already noticed, fish come in a wide variety of different shapes and sizes (see Figure 21-1). Therefore, aquarium manufacturers were kind enough to create nets to match the individual physical characteristics of whatever uncooperative aquatic prey you happen to be chasing around the tank.

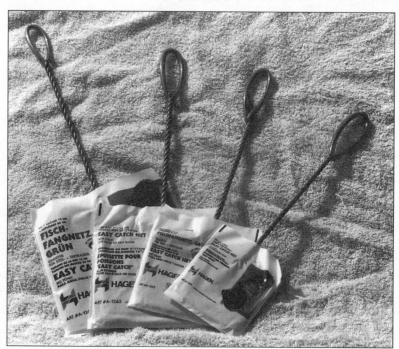

Figure 21-1: Nets!

If you buy one of those complete aquarium kits in a box, it probably comes with a net. After enjoying your aquarium for a few months, you will begin to get the idea that one net just isn't going to cut it. Owning one net would be kind of like a fisherman who expects to catch everything from a three-inch blue gill to a 10-foot shark with one size line.

Nets are one of the most inexpensive items that you can buy for your hobby, and they have the advantage of being very compact and easy to store. While shopping for nets, make sure to purchase one with fine mesh for catching fry, add a selection of small to large nets for different size fish, and finally, include a few specially constructed nets for barbed and razor-toothed fish.

A Tool Box for Storing Stuff You Don't Want to Lose

If you're like me, your fish supplies are probably pretty well spread out along the entire length of the house, garage, and backyard. When your spouse or kids start complaining because they found fish food stored in the flour bin, extra rocks and gravel in the Christmas fruit bowl, and airline tubing in their underwear drawers, then it is probably time to purchase a storage box.

A plastic tool container or tackle box (see Figure 21-2) works wonders for keeping excess aquarium equipment, fish food, test kits, and other supplies all in one neat little place. And you can carry it from tank to tank if you happen to have more than one aquarium. I prefer to buy boxes that have removable trays on top. These trays can hold small items like thermometers, airstones, and medications while the bulkier items are stored underneath.

Extra Tubing for Emergencies

As standard airline tubing ages, it may become brittle and split or leak. You should periodically replace the tubing that is attached to your equipment (unless you want a free water fountain to suddenly spring up in your living room).

Tubing is inexpensive and can be purchased in short rolls or by the foot. Whenever I find myself purchasing supplies, I always pick up a little extra airline tubing because it never hurts to have it lying around. Tubing can also double as a mini siphon in case of emergencies.

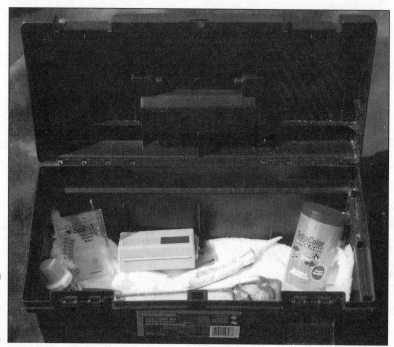

Figure 21-2:
A handy
tool box.

Aquarium Sealer (Flood Insurance)

If you live in a desert and you wake up one morning and find the floor of your home looking like the aftermath of Hurricane Andrew, then chances are, one of your aquariums may be leaking. No hobbyist should be without a tube of aquarium-safe silicone sealer in case this catastrophe strikes. Besides, aquarium sealer is cool and squishy and can be fun to play with.

Unfortunately, in order to repair a leak, you must first drain and dry the tank to allow the sealer to set properly. But in the long run, it is also better to spend a couple of dollars on a tube of sealer instead of several hundred dollars on a new tank. Once in a while, sealer will fail due to age, weather conditions, and high or uneven water pressure. So make sure that you are always prepared. (Or buy extra flood insurance.)

Gang Valves to Hookup a Bunch of Neat Junk

Despite the fact that as caring hobbyists we always strive to create a "natural environment" for our aquatic pets, we all fall prey at one time or another to the uncontrollable urge to buy those cool-looking plastic aquarium toys that do all sorts of wild and wonderful things.

As we move into our second childhood, the colorful bubbling divers, scuba diving cartoon characters, and sunken treasure ships that bob up and down become just too inviting to pass by. These toys are lots of fun to watch and will impress your friends as well.

In order to hook up all this cool junk, you need a few gang valves. A gang valve works like a splitter. It redirects one main air supply into several outlets all at once. The flow of air to each outlet can be individually controlled by built-in valves. With this neat device, you can hook up many cool aquarium toys that will keep your kids (and yourself) preoccupied for several hours at a time.

Buckets to Slosh Around In

Just as buckets have a variety of uses around the home, they can also be beneficial tools to the fishkeeping hobbyist as well. Small plastic buckets can be used to carry hoses and other equipment, transport water, move gravel, and temporarily hold fish. Besides, when everything in your aquarium has suddenly jumped out of whack, simply fill two buckets with cold water and stand in them. This procedure lowers your blood pressure every time!

Multi-Outlet Plugs

The average tank has one heater plug, one or two light plugs, one to three air pump plugs, powerfilter or powerhead plugs, and more. As you can see, an electrical setup can quickly outnumber your available wall plugs. A good multi-outlet plug or bar with a built-in circuit breaker can take care of this problem.

Razor Blades (The Miracle Cleaner)

After algae and water minerals have remained on aquarium glass for any length of time, they can be very difficult to remove and can make your tank look like an encrusted beach pier. A dirty peace of glass spoils the appearance of your aquarium and blocks out beneficial light that your fish and plants need to remain healthy and happy.

You can purchase single-edged razor blades with a safety handle at your local hardware store. This instrument will quickly remove buildups on glass and equipment faces. As with any other sharp object, extreme caution is advised.

Chapter 22

Ten Ways to Kill Your Fish without Even Trying

• •

*B*efore I go into discussing the ways that you can kill your fish, I want to mention one thing to avoid if you want to keep your fish reasonably happy: Pressing your face into a distorted jumble against the aquarium glass in the morning to get a better look at your swordtail's mating habits can also frighten the fish into thinking that Frankenstein has taken over your lease. Overkill is never good in any situation. Give your fish a little privacy once in a while, and they will be much happier and healthier.

Go Away on Vacation and Forget Them

Okay, on your last day at Disneyland, you call your boss and sadly inform him that all of the airplanes in California have broken down, and you are being forced to stay for an extra week. No problem. But what about your fish?

While on vacation, make sure you have a reliable friend who can continue to care for your pets just in case you are gone longer than originally planned. Another option is to purchase tablets or automatic feeders from your local fish dealer, which dispense food to your fish while you are gone. Always leave enough food to cover a time period that is longer than your intended stay.

Playing Doctor without a License

I once had an aunt who had a pill to cure every real or imaginary ailment known to man. The inside of her purse resembled a large pharmacy.

Many new hobbyists tend to overmedicate their tanks at the very first sign of disease. This is a pattern that we all learned during childhood. If we thought chicken soup would help cure our fish, we would probably dump that into the tank as well.

But a large number of diseases can be taken care of through natural methods such as frequent water changes. Avoid the temptation to pour medicine after medicine into your tank in hopes you will find the right cure. Seek the advice of an advanced hobbyist or tropical fish merchant who can help you pinpoint your problem. If medication is necessary, always follow the manufacturer's instructions to the letter.

Your Cat's Sushi Bar

Have you ever wondered why many cat foods are shaped like fish? Yep, you're right. In your cat's tiny and distorted little brain, your new aquarium will be considered a free sushi bar. If your tank is not covered properly, your cat will sneak in for a quick snack as you are left to wonder why his regular food is collecting dust in the bowl.

Take my word for it: No amount of pleading or yelling will keep your cat from this habit if it decides that fresh fish is its favorite food. Make sure that the hood you buy for your new aquarium fits properly and snugly. If you happen to own a particularly strong or fat cat, weigh the hood down with books or some other heavy objects.

Seven-Course Meals

Many different varieties of fish food are on the market. A good combination of flake, frozen, and live food help to promote good health in your wet pets. However, you need to realize that a fish's stomach is no larger than its eye, and overfeeding will rapidly foul the tank and eventually lead to disease or death.

Fish do not require seven-course meals to survive. If your fish are beginning to resemble the Pillsbury dough boy and are constantly getting stuck between two rocks, then it's time to cut down on the chow.

Mixing Apples and Oranges

While browsing through the local fish shop, you find yourself suddenly becoming attached to a large cichlid who looks as if it has been feeding on "instant grow" flakes for a decade or two. You automatically figure that this toughie will provide leadership skills for your unmotivated guppies. Within an hour of adding your new leader to the tank, you are surprised to find that all of your guppies have vanished.

Mixing apples and oranges may be great for a summer fruit salad, but it does-n't work in the home aquarium. Check with your local dealer if you are unsure about the compatibility of any species.

Adding Too Many Fish (The Shoehorn Syndrome)

It is really tempting to add just one more fish to your home aquarium. All fish-keepers fall prey to this "shoehorn syndrome" at one time or another. If the fish in your aquarium resemble a bunch of college kids in a phone booth-packing competition, then you have probably overstepped the capacity rule. Remember, overcrowding can be deadly.

Not Doing Your Homework

If you want to learn more about any subject, you need to do a little research. Skilled fishkeepers do their homework before setting up a new type of system, and they investigate specific habitat requirements prior to purchas-ing unknown species of fish. (Hey, isn't that one of the reasons that you bought this cool book?)

The Internet, a local library, and tropical fish magazines can provide you with a lot of good information that will keep you informed.

The Neighbor's Nasty Kid

A nasty neighbor kid can be every fishkeeper's nightmare. This is the same kid who always shows up at dinnertime, mows down your freshly planted petunias, and in later years, escorts your only daughter to the senior prom.

A home aquarium is often a prime target for the neighbor's nasty kid who will drop all sorts of interesting objects into the tank, such as your cat, coins, sticks, and peanut butter sandwiches. These offerings will not be appreciated by your fish and can prove to be lethal as well. It is always best to prohibit strange children from touching your aquariums.

Hypochondriac Hobbyists (The Love/Kill Relationship)

It does not take long for a new hobbyist to get emotionally attached to their fish. The more we bond with them, the more we tend to overpamper them. Checking in on your fish every 30 minutes, constantly fiddling around with the equipment, and rearranging the decorations in order to achieve the perfect environment just isn't good for the fish.

Buying Used or Inexpensive Equipment

Always check out used equipment before purchasing it if possible. When buying new stuff from a local dealer, make sure to purchase the best equipment that your budget (and your spouse!) will allow. Cheaply made or worn-out equipment will inevitably lead to disaster down the road.

And be wary of old aquarium stuff at the neighbor's garage sale. Don't get me wrong, I have purchased some good aquarium equipment at garage sales, but as the old saying goes, you get what you pay for.

Chapter 23

Nine Horrible Fish That You Never Want to Own

Several varieties of fish in this world are just not suitable for the beginning hobbyist. Many of these fish are either too large or too dangerous for the standard home aquarium. And some species may have difficult water or dietary needs that can be better taken care of by an experienced hobbyist. The following list contains ten fish that I personally believe that novice aquarium keepers should avoid purchasing until they have sharpened their fishkeeping skills.

Piranha (Loseafingerfish)

Freshwater piranhas *(Serrasalmus)* are an interesting species of fish that are native to the Amazon region. Most piranhas reach a total length of 9 to 14 inches (oh joy), and they will feed on anything that swims, lies on the bottom, floats, moves, or is dead.

Generally, piranhas are dull in color and spend most of their time lurking behind rocks and plants. If you are one of those rare optimists who is expecting a pet piranha to be user-friendly like Microsoft Windows, don't hold your breath. Many hobbyists have bought this particular fish as a novelty item and have ended up seriously regretting it.

There have been a few rare cases when large fish of a different species have successfully coinhabited a tank with a piranha, but these unrealistic situations are few and far between. To make matters worse, piranhas produce a lot of protein waste, so a superb filtration system is essential to their survival.

Piranhas are illegal to own, sell, or buy in many states, and they can become extremely dangerous and violent if they happen to become agitated. I once owned a piranha that would continually slam itself against the glass every time someone walked near its tank. No matter how much cover it was given, the piranha (his name was Loco) would end up blowing a gasket when it caught sight of any human form.

Piranhas really have no place in the beginner's aquarium, so do yourself a favor and don't bother adding them to your aquatic shopping list.

Gar (Loseahandfish)

The gar *(Lepisosteus osseus)* is a cigar-shaped freshwater fish that can be occasionally found for sale in a few aquarium shops. Gars are armored with thick scales and ready for battle most of the time.

A gar spends most of its day and part of the evening cruising near the top of the tank in search of food. When live food is offered, the gar proceeds to destroy anything and everything in sight (including any other tank inhabitants that happen to get into its way.)

Gars can easily grow to over 1.5 feet in length in the home aquarium, and they will abuse almost any other fish that they can catch. They really belong in lakes and not in the beginning hobbyist's aquarium.

Sharks (Loseyourarmfish)

Sharks have never ceased to amaze me. These diverse marine animals are undoubtedly nature's first creation as far as physical form (all cartilage and no bone) and adaptation are concerned. These beautiful animals have remained virtually unchanged for over 300 million years and are the perfect eating machines. (Hey, just like my two teenagers!)

In order to keep these marvelous fish healthy and happy, you need to possess a few things: high-quality equipment (lots of money), an extremely large tank the size of your living room (lots of money), and, you guessed it, lots of money.

Only smaller species of sharks (bamboo and cat) are generally found in the aquarium marketplace. However, there are a few unscrupulous dealers who still offer larger species such as the blacktip and leopard sharks to uninformed buyers who really have no idea what they are getting themselves into until it's too late.

Sharks require near perfect water conditions in order to remain healthy. When keeping sharks, there is little room for error. Live food is the main staple of this animal's diet, and getting them to feed can be quite difficult. Sharks (despite their high resilience to disease) often arrive in poor health from the stress of rough and inadequate shipping procedures. Later, after being placed in the hobbyist's tank, a shark may refuse to eat entirely. The unsuspecting hobbyist is left to watch this new acquisition die slowly from stress-induced starvation.

Sharks are a beautiful sight to behold, but these aquatic marvels are better left in the hands of expert hobbyists and the pros at public aquariums who can handle their special needs.

Pacu (Mutatedmonstrosityfish)

A large relative of the piranha is the freshwater pacu (*Piaractus brachypomus*), which can grow to lengths of over 3 feet and may look like it weighs as much as your refrigerator. The juvenile form of the pacu (three inches) is usually sold to the novice hobbyists by fish dealers. After a year has passed, this same fish is usually on its way to being adamantly refused by the local zoo, which has already received several hundred pacu donations by other disgruntled hobbyists.

Pacus are generally vegetarians by nature, but they have been known to eat almost any food that is offered to them in the home aquarium. These monster-sized fish have inefficient digestive systems and in turn produce a very high amount of waste products that can rapidly foul the water in any home aquarium that is not set up with a super filtration system.

Despite the fact that they are one of the more peaceful relatives in their entire family, pacus are still easily alarmed and tend to panic quickly. I once witnessed a large, agitated pacu completely shatter an entire glass wall on its aquarium after it dashed full speed along the length of the tank in search of cover.

Unless you have large facilities in which to house a pacu, you are definitely better off looking for a smaller species that are easier to manage.

Channelcat (Wontevenfitinthepondfish)

Sometimes aquarists decide that it would be all right to save a few bucks by adding wild-river and lake fish to their freshwater aquariums. For example, Uncle Billy-Bob catches a river catfish that appears to be in good health and is only about 5 or 6 inches long. You graciously volunteer to take the catfish off of his hands and subsequently add it to your tank.

The hidden danger in obtaining channelcats or any other wild livestock is that these fish carry diseases that can quickly spread to your aquarium's other inhabitants. And these hidden diseases may not even manifest themselves during the quarantine process.

Another hazard of adding channelcats and other such animals is that you never really know what their adult size may end up being. I once went scuba diving in a lake and saw a catfish that was nearly 4 feet long and probably weighed 150 pounds.

Unless you relish borrowing your neighbor's truck in order to haul a monster back to the lake, then I would not even consider accepting fish from Uncle Billy-Bob every time he gets the urge to go toss his lure into the local mud hole. It is safer to stick with purchasing fish from a local dealer who can supply you with good-quality stock.

Granny's Inherited Cichlid (Bitterattitudeforlifefish)

It is true that the cichlid family has been popular with hobbyists for many years. Cichlids really are wonderful and fun fish to own, and they come in a wide variety of shapes, sizes, and colors to match almost any hobbyist's individual taste.

But cichlids do have their drawbacks in the attitude department. Many cichlids are similar in temperament to the town bully and often prey on other fishes in their tank. This predation tends to intensify as these fish grow older and larger. Territoriality is a way of life for cichlids, and not a single inch of an aquarium will be overlooked as they painstakingly mark out their habitat.

If your grandma happens to call you up on the phone one afternoon to inform you that she is leaving her 10-year-old cichlid to you in her will, my advice is to leave town without a forwarding address as soon as humanly possible. Chances are, Granny has been overfeeding and pampering her fish since the day she originally obtained it. The last thing that this monstrous fish will want to look at is the face of an unfamiliar new owner (you).

Granny's prize cichlid will turn your hair grey in two months, dine on the peaceful fish in your home tank, and wreak aquatic havoc until you are ready to call an exterminator.

So if you find yourself hopelessly stuck with your grandmother's aging and bitter fish, nicely suggest to her that a zoo would be better equipped for the job of handling her wet pet.

Octopus (Whyohwhydidibuythisfish)

The marine octopus *(Octopus vulgaris)* is not really a fish at all; it is an invertebrate. This highly intelligent animal can be found in temperate and topical seas worldwide. In the wild, the octopus spends most of its time hiding among rocky crevices and preying on crustaceans and fish. (So guess what's on its dinner menu in your home aquarium!)

An octopus is a beautiful animal indeed, but there are many drawbacks to owning one of these sensitive and interesting invertebrates. To begin with, there is no hole in an aquarium hood that an octopus cannot manage to squeeze through. This aquatic contortionist can pull more vanishing acts than David Copperfield. It has been proven through scientific research that a 10-inch octopus can fit through a hole less than an inch in diameter. Preventing this animal from escaping can be a full-time job.

Another problem with owning an octopus is their short life span. An octopus will not generally live longer than six months to a year in your tank. Depending upon your point of view, this can be a mixed blessing, as these animals can reach lengths of over 10 feet in the wild!

If you do happen to acquire a female and she lays eggs, then you are in for a double heartache right off the bat. After an octopus lays eggs, the female dies. And as of this writing, I know of no single instance where a hobbyist has successfully raised a large number of babies to maturity.

There is another risk that is worth noting. An octopus can expel an "ink" when frightened or threatened, and this material can harm delicate invertebrates. Many times during shipment, an octopus expels its own ink in its small compartment, and as a result, it can be in poor health upon arrival.

Scorpionfish (Whydidmyotherfishdisappearfish)

The marine scorpionfish *(Scorpaenidae)* is a hardy predator that is armed with several venomous spines that can be very dangerous to the hobbyist if it is not handled properly. (This fish's name should tell you something.) Generally, this species can be kept with larger fishes, but it must also be continually well fed with live fish, shrimp, and tubifex worms. If not, you may soon find out that the other fish in your tank have disappeared faster than your tax refund.

A scorpionfish has one mission in life: eating. Normally, the scorpionfish lies beneath a rock and silently waits for its next meal to crawl, swim, or float by. A hungry member of this species may even consider your wiggling fingers as a main course.

Great care is needed when rearranging the decorations or cleaning the tank if you own a scorpionfish. You might end up playing pincushion to this potentially dangerous fish. Scorpionfish are for the experts, in my opinion, and not for beginners at all. Just trust me on this one and save yourself a whole lot of grief.

Groupers (Thisgotasbigasmystationwagonfish)

Purchasing a marine grouper *(Cephalopholis urodelus)* is a lot like buying your very first puppy. In the beginning, you proudly bring this cute little animal home and are instantly attracted to its playful antics and personality. But it is important to remember that this animal will eventually grow up.

About the time that your grouper has attained the same length as the family station wagon, you will probably be working on your second mortgage in order to pay your aquatic food bill. A grouper will sadly beg for food after it has finished polishing off the other fish in your aquarium.

Chapter 24
Ten Scientific Fish Laws

The Fish Law of Thermodynamics

The fish law of thermodynamics states that all heat in a house will flow directly into your aquarium at all times. Window light will be absorbed by your overheating tank immediately so that the remaining sections of your house will convince the local astronomer that there is a black hole in the neighborhood.

To take care of this problem, you need to make sure that your aquarium is placed in an area that has plenty of air movement and a consistent room temperature. Check to make sure your heater is functioning properly, and do not set your aquarium up near doors or windows.

The Fish Law of Metamorphosis

The fish law of metamorphosis states that any fish in your tank, when given the right opportunity, will be able to instantly morph into any shape necessary to escape from the aquarium. My own fish have morphed into the shape of a French fry in order to squeeze through an unattended airline hole.

The second part of this law states that after escape, this same fish will morph into either a carpet dust ball or a kitty snack. To fix this problem, make sure that all holes in the top of the tank lid are completely covered.

The Fish Law of Motion

The fish law of motion states that any sluggish or ill-looking fish will instantly be able to dash madly at twice the speed of light when a net is inserted into the aquarium. The fish will always move directly at right angles to the net's strategic placement — a manuever which will leave you with wet clothes, a lot of frustration, and a torn-up tank.

To avoid this problem, try adding a little food to coax your fish up to the top of the tank when you need to catch one. Gently lift out large aquarium decorations, such as rocks, before you attempt to capture your fish. This will provide you with more space and maneuverability.

The Fish Law of Anti-Matter

The fish law of anti-matter states that fish are the only animals on earth that are capable of destroying their own body matter after death so that they can never be found. On a good day, Sherlock Holmes would not be able to find a dead guppy in a 1-gallon bowl because of this law.

It is important to have good filtration in your tank because of this unusual problem. If a dead fish cannot be located, then a buildup of waste will occur and cause water fouling and disease.

The Fish Law of Nutrition

The fish law of nutrition states that your fish will consider all food that is offered as unfit for consumption, and they will eat only after the feeder has left the room. The second part of this law states that any uneaten food will fall directly into an area that cannot be seen by the human eye. Because of this problem, it is important to feed your fish small meals several times per day, instead of dumping half a can of flake food into the tank while you are still half-asleep.

The Fish Law of Company

The fish law of company states that all aquarium fish will lethargically lurk in a corner or disappear behind decorations at the exact moment when your company arrives to see them. The fish will return to their normal activity level after dark.

If you want to successfully show your fish to your company, arrange to have your friends come over at a time when you would normally give your fish a treat. This will allow your friends to get a glimpse of your prize pets.

The Fish Law of Potential Energy

The fish law of potential energy states that a fish's energy can be stored indefinitely and will only be released when the aquarium hood is opened and a direct escape route is in sight. To avoid this problem, make sure that your aquarium hood fits securely.

The Fish Law of Psychic Felines

The fish law of psychic felines states that any cat within a hundred miles of your aquarium will be able to zero in on and physically engulf any fish that has jumped from your tank — before you can cross the room to save it. A fish out of water is fair game, so make sure to keep a distrustful eye on any other pets that are living in the same household or neighborhood.

The Fish Law of Aggression

The fish law of aggression states that any two fish will show aggression toward each other without just cause at any given moment of time. For this reason, it is vital that you keep track of your fish's social habits to make sure that a minor scuffle does not end up turning into a major war.

The Fish Law of Time

The fish law of time states that a fish will be prone to contract an illness the day before your vacation starts, or at the beginning of a holiday weekend when all of the pets shops are closed. That is why it is important to have extra medication on hand for such emergencies. Training a friend, neighbor, or relative in the basics of fish disease and treatment will come in handy if you happen to be on vacation when disaster strikes.

Chapter 25

Ten Aquatic New Year's Resolutions

. . . .

When January 1 rolls around, you will be once again forced into the mind-boggling task of making up those dreaded New Year's resolutions.

On December 31, announce to all of your family, friends, neighbors, and coworkers that you have made several aquatic resolutions that will improve your fish's lifestyle. When your associates start to bet against you like last year, simple tell them that you will take cash, check, or money orders.

I (state your name out loud) promise to do the following in the new year:

Feed the Fish

I promise to feed my fish properly and on a regular basis so that when they turn sideways I will still be able to see them. When my fish run out of food, I promise not to toss anymore leftover onion rings into the tank as I am strolling out to catch the movie of the week. I also promise to throw away all extra cans of sticky-flake food that have been sitting in the attic since World War I. I promise to feed three light meals a day.

Clean the Tank

I promise to clean my tank regularly so that my fish stop running into the tank walls and decorations. I also promise to clean the tank properly with water changes and an aquarium vacuum instead of just removing my children's floating Cheerios periodically. I promise to clean the aquarium at least once a month.

Reduce Celibacy

I promise to buy my 10 male swordtails a female. I promise to provide my fish with a little stimulation by keeping an equal number of males and females in the tank (with standard exceptions, such as the betta).

Remove Algae

I promise to faithfully remove excess algae from the aquarium glass so that my tank will no longer resemble the loaf of bread that has been laying under my son or daughter's bed for three months. If the algae is more than three inches thick, I promise to remove any floating chunks. I promise to do this at least once a week.

Change the Filter Pads

I promise to replace my clogged filter pads so that the tank water will stop overflowing onto the floor. After changing the pads, I will remember to refill the dog's water bowl as well. I promise to change or rinse the pads every month.

Turn on the Lights

I promise to turn on my aquarium lights daily so that my fish can rest assured that power hasn't gone out. I also promise to slowly increase the room lights before switching the tank light on so that I won't be forced to give my lionfish CPR.

Use My Test Kits

I promise to brush the dust off of my test kits and use them before the chemicals turn into something that resembles pottery clay. I will regularly test my water for excessive levels of nitrates and ammonia. I also promise to keep an eye on the pH and carry these tests out faithfully at least once a week.

Pay Attention to My Fish

I promise to spend more quality time with my fish so that they will stop snuggling up to the bubbling plastic diver who is wielding a knife. I also promise to wiggle my fingers near the glass and tell my kids to stop sticking their plastic shark into the water. I will acknowledge my fish's presence at least twice a day.

Change the Airstones

I promise to change the aquarium's airstones when they become clogged so that my fish don't begin to think that they are living in a stagnant rice paddy. I will check the airstones daily.

Redecorate the Tank

I promise to rearrange the tank decorations at least twice a year and add a few new plants now and then. Then maybe my fish won't look bored and will stop spitting gravel at me when I pass by their tank.

Chapter 26

More Than Ten Resources

Ten Great Web Sites

Hanging out on the Internet can be a lot of fun as long as it is practiced with moderation. (When you start naming your kids after cool Web sites and turning your head sideways to smile at people, it may be time to unplug the machine.) If you are an Internet addict like I am, you may want to take advantage of the time you have surfing the Web to gain a little information on your tropical fishkeeping hobby.

If you are new to computers, you might want to grab the latest edition of *The Internet For Dummies,* 6th Edition or *America Online For Dummies* (both published by the fine folks at IDG Books) and begin the adventure from there.

- ✔ **The Krib** (www.cco.caltech.edu/~aquaria/Krib): A really cool site that offers many photos, discussions, and personal e-mail posting on aquarium-related subjects. The graphics on these pages are neat as well.

- ✔ **The Aquatic Book Shop** (www.seahorses.com): This is a really radical site that offers new and used books, magazines, and videos for beginner- to advanced-level aquarium hobbyists. This site is similar to browsing through one of those neat old book stores that smell musty.

- ✔ **The Info Service** (info-s.com/fish.html): Okay, I have to admit its name isn't too exciting, but its Web page is outstanding! This site offers a huge variety of links to aquarium businesses, fish societies, and breeding information.

- ✔ **Page O'Links-Aquaria** (www.kkreate.com/aqlinks.htm): This is another Web site that offers a bunch of aquarium links.

- ✔ **Tropical Fish and Aquarium Home Page for Montreal** (www.total.net/~scz/tropical.html): A neat place to buy fish and visit Canadian-tropical-fish-related subjects.

- ✔ **Tropical Fish** (home.earthlink.net/~squint2/ti01000.html): A lot of beautiful photos and good basic information on diet, habitat, and breeding requirements for several different types of tropical fish families can be found on this site.

✔ **Master Index of Freshwater Fishes** (www.geocities.com/heartland/7130): This master index of freshwater fish contains over 20,000 references to aquarium books and magazines. This site also features fish and plants of the week, articles, classifieds, events calendars, and more.

✔ **Badmans Tropical Fish** (www.geocities.com/Heartland/Plains/8115): This site is geared to the beginner and features descriptions of six commonly kept fish families and informative links. These pages also offer information on products, the low-down on mail-order companies, and a complete glossary of aquarium-related terms.

✔ **Fish Link Central** (www.fishlinkcentral.com): On this Web page, you can find the largest collection of links plus information on fish, plants, public aquariums, and clubs.

✔ **Aquarium Global Resource** (www.digiserve.com/global): This site provides information on corals, fish, invertebrates, live rock, and plants. It's very well put together.

Aquarium Magazines

Aquarium magazines are accessible resources for the beginning hobbyist to gain useful information on aquarium fish, systems, and new equipment.

To get you started, I am providing a list of popular fishkeeping magazines along with their contact information.

Tropical Fish Hobbyist

TFH
One TFH Plaza
Neptune City, NJ 07753
Phone: 908-988-8400

Freshwater and Marine Aquarium

FAMA
P.O. Box 487
Sierra Madre, CA 91024
Phone: 818-355-1467
Web: www.animalnetwork.com/fish/index.htm

Practical Fishkeeping

Motorsport
RR1 Box 200 D
Jonesburg, MO 63351
Phone: 314-488-3113

Marine Fish Monthly

Publishing Concepts Corporation
3243 Highway 61
East Luttrell, TN 37779
Phone: 800-937-3963

Aquarium Fish Magazine

P.O. Box 6040
Mission Viejo, CA 92690
Phone: 800-365-4421
Web: www.aquariumfish.com

Aquarium Societies

Aquarium societies can be great places to hang out, believe it or not. Many of these organizations print their own newsletters, which help keep their members informed on current fishkeeping events and environmental issues.

Fish auctions, equipment and livestock sales, lectures (on fish, not manners), and conventions are only a part of the smorgasbord that these organizations have to offer their members.

You will always find at least one person in an aquarium society who shares a similar interest in a particular system or species that you do. The following list gives you a starting point from which to contact a society near your home area.

Alabama

Mobile Aquarium Society
11450 Boe Road
Grand Bay, AL 36541

Alaska

Juneau Aquarium Society
3051 Glacier Dr.
Juneau, AK 99801

Arizona

Dry Wash Aquarium Society
8245 N. 27th Ave. #1115
Phoenix, AZ 85051

Arkansas

Marine World
209 Lakeshore Dr.
Hot Springs, AR 71913

California

California Organization of Aquatic Show Tropicals
13581 Arizona St. #2
Westminster, CA 92683

Colorado

Colorado Aquarium Society
P.O. Box 1253
Arvada, CO 80005

Connecticut

Norwalk Aquarium Society
Nature Center
10 Woodside Lane
Westport, CT 06880

Delaware

Diamond State Aquarium Society
5420 Valley Green Dr. Apt. C-2
Wilmington, DE 19808

Florida

Central Florida Aquarium Society
1017 Alpug Ave.
Oviedo, FL 32765

Hawaii

Honolulu Aquarium Society
3024 Puhala Rise
Honolulu, HI 96822

Idaho

Idaho Water Garden Society
10023 W. Ripley St.
Boise, ID 83704

Illinois

Central Illinois Aquarist
P.O. Box 225
Pekin, IL 61555

Indiana

Indianapolis Aquarium Society
6246 N. Rural
Indianapolis, IN 46220

Iowa

Eastern Iowa Aquarium Society
P.O. Box 2327
Cedar Rapids, IA 52406

Kansas

Air Capitol Aquarium Society
P.O. Box 3235
Wichita, KS 67201

Kentucky

Marine Aquarium Society of North America
1426 Hidden River Road
Horse Cave, KY 42749

Louisiana

Baton Rouge Aquarium Society
5218 Sleepy Hollow Road
Baton Rouge, LA 70817

Maine

Maine State Aquarium Society
P.O. Box 487
North Berwick, ME 03906

Maryland

Baltimore/Washington Area Aquaria Society
3915 Blackburn Lane #42
Burtonsville, MD 20866

Massachusetts

Worcester Massachusetts Aquarium Society
P.O. Box 972
Worcester, MA 01613

Michigan

Greater Detroit Aquarium Society
P.O. Box C
Royal Oak, MI 48068

Minnesota

Minnesota Aquarium Society
P.O. Box 130483
Roseville, MN 55113

Mississippi

Norfield Aquariums
3017 Hwy. 51 SE
Bogue Chitto, MS 39629

Missouri

Heart of America Aquarium Society
6712 Linden Road
Kansas City, MO 64112

Nevada

Las Vegas Marine Society
3001 Cabana Dr. #283 Box 51
Las Vegas, NV 89122

Washington

South Sound Aquarium Society
948 Summit Lakeshore Road NW
Olympia, WA 98502

West Virginia

West Virginia Koi and Water Garden Club
6631 Roosevelt Ave.
Charleston, WV 25304

Wisconsin

Central Wisconsin Aquarium Association
5339 Highway 54
East Plover, WI 54467

Canada

Montreal Aquarium Association
P.O. Box 653, Station B
Montreal Quebec, Canada H3B 3K3

England

Association of Aquarist
610 Abby Road, Popley 4
Basingstoke, Hants RG24 9ET, United Kingdom

Mexico

Association Nacional Acuarofila Mexicana, AC
APDO Postal 73-112
Santa Cruz Atoyac, Mexico DF 03310

Tank Figures and Facts

• •

My math teacher once told me that I looked exactly like a zombie from a B horror movie when mathematical equations and formulas were presented to me in test form. Lets be honest: Numbers can be more boring than your neighbor talking about his last round of golf. But the fact remains, that numbers are important in the aquarium hobby. Numbers tell you how big your tank is, how much it weighs, and how many fish you can safely put into it during one shopping spree.

So in order to preserve you mental health, I have included a few tables to help you get a better idea of just how much room your aquarium really has.

Common Table of Tank Measurements

You want to make sure that when you set up your mega-aquarium that it does not end up in the apartment downstairs. Don't laugh because this has actually happened on numerous occasions! If you live in an upstairs apartment, you probably don't want to place a 200-gallon tank directly over the downstairs resident's bedroom. Homes with older floors my have weak spots that cannot be seen. Always use common sense when choosing an aquarium size to match the home you live in.

In order to give you a better idea of what an aquarium weighs when it is full of water, and also empty, the following table has been provided for you. All weights in the table are accurate to within a few pounds, depending on what equipment you use, the amount of gravel in the tank, and other factors such as the weight of decorations.

Tank Measurements

Tank Size	Outside Dimensions (inches)	Weight Full	Weight Empty
10 gallon	20 ¼ x 10 ½ x 12 ⁹⁄₁₆	111 pounds	11 pounds
10 gallon long	24 ¼ x 8 ½ x 12 ⅝	116 pounds	16 pounds
15 gallon	24 ¼ x 12 ½ x 12 ¾	170 pounds	21 pounds
15 gallon high	20 ¼ x 10 ½ x 18 ¾	170 pounds	22 pounds
20 high	24 ¼ x 12 ½ x 16 ¾	225 pounds	25 pounds
20 long	30 ¼ x 12 ½ x 22 ¾	225 pounds	25 pounds
29 gallon	30 ¼ x 12 ½ x 18 ¾	330 pounds	40 pounds
30 gallon	36 ¼ x 12 ⅝ x 16 ¾	343 pounds	43 pounds
30 high	24 ¼ x 12 ½ x 24 ¾	340 pounds	41 pounds
38 gallon	36 ¼ x 12 ⅝ x 19 ¾	427 pounds	47 pounds
40 gallon breeder	36 ³⁄₁₆ x 18 ¼ x 16 ¹⁵⁄₁₆	458 pounds	58 pounds
40 gallon long	48 ¼ x 12 ¾ x 16 ⅞	455 pounds	55 pounds
45 gallon	36 ¼ x 12 ⅝ x 23 ¾	515 pounds	66 pounds
45 gallon long	48 ¼ x 12 ¾ x 23 ¾	510 pounds	60 pounds
50 gallon	36 ⅞ x 19 x 19 ⅝	600 pounds	100 pounds
55 gallon	48 ¼ x 12 ¾ x 21	625 pounds	78 pounds
60 gallon	48 ⅜ x 12 ⅞ x 23 ⅞	710 pounds	111 pounds
65 gallon	36 ⅞ x 19 x 24 ⅝	775 pounds	126 pounds
75 gallon	48 ½ x 18 ½ x 21 ⅜	850 pounds	140 pounds
90 gallon	48 ½ x 18 ½ x 25 ⅜	1,050 pounds	160 pounds
110 gallon high	48 ⅞ x 19 x 30 ¾	1,320 pounds	198 pounds
120 gallon high	48 ½ x 24 ¼ x 25 ½	1,400 pounds	215 pounds
150 gallon	72 ½ x 18 ½ x 28 ½	1,800 pounds	338 pounds
180 gallon	72 ½ x 24 ½ x 25 ⅝	2,100 pounds	368 pounds

Conversions (And Other Useful Data)

If you were bad in high school math like the rest of us and spent most of your time sleeping near the window in the back of the classroom, then you might find these simple tables quite helpful. (Saves on the calculator batteries too.)

Many tropical fish magazines and books use different types of systems to get their mathematical points across. One publication may choose to use the metric system, while another will crank out figures that would give even Albert Einstein an embolism. The following tables will allow you to sort through the numbers game to come up with information that you can actually understand and use to your best advantage.

1000 cubic centimeters = 1 liter

1 liter of water = 1 kilogram in weight

1 cubic foot of water = 6.23 imperial gallons

1 imperial gallon of water = 10 pounds in weight

1 U.S. gallon = .8 imperial gallons

1 imperial gallon = 4.55 liters

Hardness

     1 English degree of hardness = 14.3 ppm of calcium carbonate

     1 French degree of hardness = 10.0 ppm of calcium carbonate

     1 American degree of hardness = 17.1 ppm of calcium carbonate

     1 German degree of hardness = 17.9 ppm of calcium oxide

One liter = 0.26 gallons

One gallon = 3.78 liters

1 inch = 2.54 centimeters

One foot = 30 centimeters

One yard = 36 inches

One meter = 39.4 inches

Once ounce = 29 grams

To convert centimeters to inches, multiply by 0.40

To convert inches to centimeters, multiply by 2.54

To convert kilograms to pounds, multiply by 2.2

To convert pounds to kilograms, multiply by 0.453

Temperature

$$\text{Celsius} = (\text{Fahrenheit} - 32) \times 5/9$$
$$\text{Fahrenheit} = (\text{Celsius} \times 9/5) + 32$$

Volume = Length × Width × Height

Aquarium Weight

1. **Determine capacity.**

   Capacity in gallons = (Length × Width × Height [in inches]) divided by 232.

2. **Use capacity to determine weight.**

   One gallon of fresh water at 4 degrees Celsius = 8.57 pounds of weight.

What's in Sea Water

Understanding the contents of marine water allows you to become a better reef keeper, and it will impress all of your friends.

If you find yourself at a fish show and want to get one up on the local fish nerd with the dolphin tie, just start spurting out these facts and figures at a rapid rate and people will instantly consider you a pro.

Elements Found in Sea Water	
Element	*Parts per Million*
Oxygen	857,000
Hydrogen	108,000
Chlorine	19,000
Sodium	10,500

Element	Parts per Million
Magnesium	1,350
Sulfur	885
Calcium	400
Potassium	380
Bromide	65
Carbon	28
Strontium	13
Boron	4.6
Silicon	3
Fluorine	1.4
Nitrogen	0.5
Lithium	0.18
Rubidium	0.12
Phosphorus	0.07
Iodine	0.06
Barium	0.03
Aluminum	0.01
Iron	0.01
Molybdenum	0.01
Zinc	0.01
Nickel	0.005
Arsenic	0.003
Copper	0.003
Tin	0.003
Uranium	0.003
Manganese	0.002

(continued)

Elements Found in Sea Water *(continued)*	
Element	**Parts per Million**
Manganese	0.002
Vanadium	0.002
Caesium	0.0005
Silver	0.0004
Yttrium	0.0003
Cobalt	0.00027
Selenium	0.00009
Thorium	0.00005
Lead	0.00003
Gold	0.00001
Lanthanum	0.00001
Mercury	0.00003

Tank Capacity Chart

It is very important to remember that fish need space in order to be healthy. (Think about it, would you want to live in an elevator with 10 other people?) A crowded tank that has exceeded its stocking limits leads to poor water conditions that can adversely effect your fish's health. Overcrowded tanks are low in oxygen levels and pollute quickly — much more than the filter medium or biological bacteria can handle efficiently.

The following chart gives you an idea of how many fish can safely be put into a tank with given dimensions. This system allows you to figure capacity even for tanks that are not on the list and can also help you to understand how this formula (oh no, there's that word again!) works.

The first column is simply the length of the tank multiplied times the width of the tank. This can be measured with a yardstick or measuring tape. If you have neither, just snag mom's measuring tape from her sewing box while she is busy in the kitchen on your next visit, or borrow one from your neighbor's tool box while he is under the car changing his oil.

The second column simply tells you the total surface area of what you measured. The third and fourth columns give you the total length of fish *in inches* that can be safely put in that size tank, depending on whether they are freshwater or marine fish. Remember that the total length of the fish is measured from the snout to the beginning of the tail fin.

Smaller tanks (under 36 inches in length) are not recommended for salt water, except when being used as a hospital tank.

How Many Fish Can Fit in Your Tank

Tank Length x Width	Surface Area	Freshwater Fish (inches)	Marine Fish (inches)
20 x 10	200	16	4
24 x 12	288	24	6
30 x 12	360	30	7
36 x 12	432	36	9
48 x 12	576	48	12
48 x 18	864	72	18
72 x 18	1296	108	27
72 x 24	1728	144	36

Index

FOR DUMMIES®

The easy way to get more done and have more fun

PERSONAL FINANCE

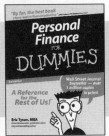

0-7645-5231-7

0-7645-2431-3

0-7645-5331-3

Also available:

Estate Planning For Dummies
(0-7645-5501-4)
401(k)s For Dummies
(0-7645-5468-9)
Frugal Living For Dummies
(0-7645-5403-4)
Microsoft Money "X" For Dummies
(0-7645-1689-2)
Mutual Funds For Dummies
(0-7645-5329-1)

Personal Bankruptcy For Dummies
(0-7645-5498-0)
Quicken "X" For Dummies
(0-7645-1666-3)
Stock Investing For Dummies
(0-7645-5411-5)
Taxes For Dummies 2003
(0-7645-5475-1)

BUSINESS & CAREERS

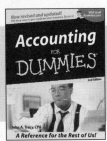

0-7645-5314-3

0-7645-5307-0

0-7645-5471-9

Also available:

Business Plans Kit For Dummies
(0-7645-5365-8)
Consulting For Dummies
(0-7645-5034-9)
Cool Careers For Dummies
(0-7645-5345-3)
Human Resources Kit For Dummies
(0-7645-5131-0)
Managing For Dummies
(1-5688-4858-7)

QuickBooks All-in-One Desk Reference For Dummies
(0-7645-1963-8)
Selling For Dummies
(0-7645-5363-1)
Small Business Kit For Dummies
(0-7645-5093-4)
Starting an eBay Business For Dummies
(0-7645-1547-0)

HEALTH, SPORTS & FITNESS

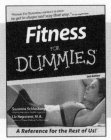

0-7645-5167-1

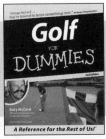

0-7645-5146-9

0-7645-5154-X

Also available:

Controlling Cholesterol For Dummies
(0-7645-5440-9)
Dieting For Dummies
(0-7645-5126-4)
High Blood Pressure For Dummies
(0-7645-5424-7)
Martial Arts For Dummies
(0-7645-5358-5)
Menopause For Dummies
(0-7645-5458-1)

Nutrition For Dummies
(0-7645-5180-9)
Power Yoga For Dummies
(0-7645-5342-9)
Thyroid For Dummies
(0-7645-5385-2)
Weight Training For Dummies
(0-7645-5168-X)
Yoga For Dummies
(0-7645-5117-5)

Available wherever books are sold.
Go to www.dummies.com or call 1-877-762-2974 to order direct.

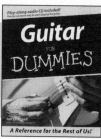

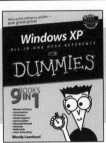

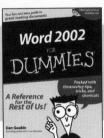

FOR DUMMIES®

Helping you expand your horizons and realize your potential

INTERNET

The Internet FOR DUMMIES
0-7645-0894-6

The Internet ALL-IN-ONE DESK REFERENCE FOR DUMMIES
0-7645-1659-0

eBay FOR DUMMIES
0-7645-1642-6

Also available:

America Online 7.0 For Dummies
(0-7645-1624-8)

Genealogy Online For Dummies
(0-7645-0807-5)

The Internet All-in-One Desk Reference For Dummies
(0-7645-1659-0)

Internet Explorer 6 For Dummies
(0-7645-1344-3)

The Internet For Dummies Quick Reference
(0-7645-1645-0)

Internet Privacy For Dummies
(0-7645-0846-6)

Researching Online For Dummies
(0-7645-0546-7)

Starting an Online Business For Dummies
(0-7645-1655-8)

DIGITAL MEDIA

Digital Photography FOR DUMMIES
0-7645-1664-7

Photoshop Elements 2 FOR DUMMIES
0-7645-1675-2

Digital Video FOR DUMMIES
0-7645-0806-7

Also available:

CD and DVD Recording For Dummies
(0-7645-1627-2)

Digital Photography All-in-One Desk Reference For Dummies
(0-7645-1800-3)

Digital Photography For Dummies Quick Reference
(0-7645-0750-8)

Home Recording for Musicians For Dummies
(0-7645-1634-5)

MP3 For Dummies
(0-7645-0858-X)

Paint Shop Pro "X" For Dummies
(0-7645-2440-2)

Photo Retouching & Restoration For Dummies
(0-7645-1662-0)

Scanners For Dummies
(0-7645-0783-4)

GRAPHICS

PowerPoint 2002 FOR DUMMIES
0-7645-0817-2

Photoshop 7 FOR DUMMIES
0-7645-1651-5

Macromedia Flash MX FOR DUMMIES
0-7645-0895-4

Also available:

Adobe Acrobat 5 PDF For Dummies
(0-7645-1652-3)

Fireworks 4 For Dummies
(0-7645-0804-0)

Illustrator 10 For Dummies
(0-7645-3636-2)

QuarkXPress 5 For Dummies
(0-7645-0643-9)

Visio 2000 For Dummies
(0-7645-0635-8)

FOR DUMMIES®

The advice and explanations you need to succeed

SELF-HELP, SPIRITUALITY & RELIGION

0-7645-5302-X

0-7645-5418-2

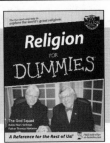

0-7645-5264-3

Also available:

The Bible For Dummies
(0-7645-5296-1)

Buddhism For Dummies
(0-7645-5359-3)

Christian Prayer For Dummies
(0-7645-5500-6)

Dating For Dummies
(0-7645-5072-1)

Judaism For Dummies
(0-7645-5299-6)

Potty Training For Dummies
(0-7645-5417-4)

Pregnancy For Dummies
(0-7645-5074-8)

Rekindling Romance For Dummies
(0-7645-5303-8)

Spirituality For Dummies
(0-7645-5298-8)

Weddings For Dummies
(0-7645-5055-1)

PETS

0-7645-5255-4

0-7645-5286-4

0-7645-5275-9

Also available:

Labrador Retrievers For Dummies
(0-7645-5281-3)

Aquariums For Dummies
(0-7645-5156-6)

Birds For Dummies
(0-7645-5139-6)

Dogs For Dummies
(0-7645-5274-0)

Ferrets For Dummies
(0-7645-5259-7)

German Shepherds For Dummies
(0-7645-5280-5)

Golden Retrievers For Dummies
(0-7645-5267-8)

Horses For Dummies
(0-7645-5138-8)

Jack Russell Terriers For Dummies
(0-7645-5268-6)

Puppies Raising & Training Diary For Dummies
(0-7645-0876-8)

EDUCATION & TEST PREPARATION

0-7645-5194-9

0-7645-5325-9

0-7645-5210-4

Also available:

Chemistry For Dummies
(0-7645-5430-1)

English Grammar For Dummies
(0-7645-5322-4)

French For Dummies
(0-7645-5193-0)

The GMAT For Dummies
(0-7645-5251-1)

Inglés Para Dummies
(0-7645-5427-1)

Italian For Dummies
(0-7645-5196-5)

Research Papers For Dummies
(0-7645-5426-3)

The SAT I For Dummies
(0-7645-5472-7)

U.S. History For Dummies
(0-7645-5249-X)

World History For Dummies
(0-7645-5242-2)

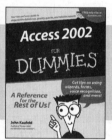